SHAW 19

SHAW

The Annual of Bernard Shaw Studies

Volume Nineteen

Fred D. Crawford   John R. Pfeiffer
General Editor   *Bibliographer*

SHAW

AND

HISTORY

Edited by

Gale K. Larson

The Pennsylvania State University Press
University Park, Pennsylvania

Quotations from published Bernard Shaw writings are utilized in this volume with the permission of the Estate of Bernard Shaw. Shaw's hitherto unpublished writings © 1999 The Trustees of the British Museum, The Governors and Guardians of the National Gallery of Ireland, and the Royal Academy of Dramatic Art.

ISBN 0-271-01918-2 ISSN 0741-5842

It is the policy of The Pennsylvania State University Press to use acid-free paper for the first printing of all clothbound books. Publications on uncoated stock satisfy the minimum requirements of American National Standard for Information Sci-ences—Permanence of Paper for Printed Library Materials. ANSI Z39.48–1992.

Note to contributors and subscribers. *SHAW*'s perspective is Bernard Shaw and his milieu—its personalities, works, relevance to his age and ours. As "his life, work, and friends"—the subtitle to a biography of G.B.S.—indicates, it is impossible to study the life, thought, and work of a major literary figure in a vacuum. Issues and people, economics, politics, religion, theater and literature and journalism—the entirety of the two half-centuries the life of G.B.S. spanned was his assumed prov-ince. *SHAW*, published annually, welcomes articles that either explicitly or implicitly add to or alter our understanding of Shaw and his milieu. Address all manuscript contributions (in 3 copies) to Fred D. Crawford, Department of English, Central Michigan University, Mt. Pleasant, MI 48859. Subscription correspondence should be addressed to *SHAW*, Penn State University Press, Suite C, 820 North University Drive, University Park, PA 16802. Unsolicited manuscripts are welcomed but will be returned only if return postage is provided. In matters of style *SHAW* recommends the *MLA Style Sheet* and advises referring to recent volumes of the *SHAW*.

Shaw 19
Is Dedicated to the Memory of
Fred Dean Crawford
1947–1999
Editor, **Shaw**
1989–1999

"Life levels all men: death reveals the eminent."
—G. Bernard Shaw

Fred Crawford died of a heart attack on Monday, January 4, 1999, the very day he said that the manuscript and proofs of **SHAW 19** would be at Penn State Press. His 27 December 1998 letter to me ended with these words: "Well, this has been fun. You are an easy man to work with!" Believe me, it cuts both ways.

Fred's death comes as a shock to all who knew him, especially those of us who have had the privilege of working closely with him as the General Editor of **SHAW: The Annual of Bernard Shaw Studies.** He edited **SHAW 9** in 1989, co-edited **SHAW 10** with Stanley Weintraub, and thereafter served as its General Editor. Through his attentive care, he continued the journal's fine reputation for outstanding Shaw scholarship. His enthusiasm for, knowledge of, and commitment to things Shavian have benefited us all, and for this we will be forever grateful.

To his family, colleagues, and friends, we extend our sympathies. He will be missed, but he will be remembered uniquely by those who knew him.

—Gale K. Larson

CONTENTS

NOTICES

38th Annual Shaw Festival, Niagara-on-the-Lake
9 April–28 November 1999

The 1999 season of the Shaw Festival (Artistic Director, Christopher Newton) will feature three plays by Bernard Shaw: *Heartbreak House* (25 May to 31 October, directed by Tadeusz Bradecki); *Getting Married* (29 May to 26 September, directed by Jim Mezon); and *Village Wooing* (3 July to 19 September, lunchtime theatre production). The 1999 playbill also includes *You Can't Take It With You* (George S. Kaufman and Moss Hart), *Easy Virtue* (Noël Coward), *All My Sons* (Arthur Miller), *The Madras House* (Harley Granville Barker), *S. S. Tenacity* (Charles Vildrac), *Uncle Vanya* (Anton Checkhov), *A Foggy Day* (George and Ira Gershwin), *Rebecca* (Daphne du Maurier), and *Waterloo* (Arthur Conan Doyle).

For further information, write to Shaw Festival, Post Office Box 774, Niagara-on-the-Lake, Ontario, Canada L0S 1J0; or call 1-905-468-2153 (toll free: 1-800-511-SHAW [7429]).

18th Annual Milwaukee Chamber Theatre Shaw Festival
14–30 April 2000

The Milwaukee Chamber Theatre Shaw Festival (Artistic Director, Montgomery Davis) will feature performances of Shaw's *Pygmalion* and Shakespeare's *The Winter's Tale*.

For ticket information, write to Milwaukee Chamber Theatre, Broadway Theatre Centre, 158 N. Broadway, Milwaukee, WI 53202; or call (414) 276-8842.

Gale K. Larson

GENERAL INTRODUCTION:
SHAW AND HISTORY

[to Fred, whose patience is endless!]

Anyone familiar with the breadth of Shaw's work can be only impressed with the extent to which he incorporated his own historical research into that work. His dramatic output demonstrates how well-read he was in history, especially his readings of the historical writers of the nineteenth century. For example, in writing *Caesar and Cleopatra* in 1898, he prepared himself well in historical and biographical background reading, even though he flippantly claimed in an interview published in the 30 April 1898 issue of *The Academy*, entitled, "Mr. Shaw's Future: A Conversation," that he had not read "a bit" on Caesar since to do so would only result in a repetition of the same old lies about him. Moreover, as he claimed, he knew "human nature," and "given Caesar, and a certain set of circumstances, I know what would happen, and when I have finished the play you will find I have written history."[1] The "real Caesar," says Shaw, was beyond Shakespeare, "Who knew human weakness so well, [but] never knew human strength of the Caesarian type," and thus "it cost Shakespear no pang to write Caesar down for the merely technical purpose of writing Brutus up."[2] Caesar, for Shaw, was the symbol of greatness, and with passionate fervor he took the torch from Goethe, who had referred to Caesar's assassination as "the greatest crime in history" but who did not write a play dramatizing that belief, so the field, says Shaw, was left open to him, and he took the challenge to set the historical record right.[3] He read widely before he put pen to paper. We know that he came under the influence of Theodor Mommsen's five volumes of *The History of Rome* (William P. Dickson's translation, 1908), especially volume five that deals with Caesar, his life, achievements, and personality. He was familiar with Plutarch's *Lives*,

Shakespeare's source, with James Froude's biography, *Caesar: A Sketch* (1898), and was equally familiar with Ward-Fowler's biography, *Julius Caesar and the Foundation of the Roman Imperial System* (1899). He was acquainted with Suetonius's account, in French, of *The Twelve Caesars*. He read Egyptian history and perhaps took much of his characterization of Cleopatra from J. P. Mahaffy's *The Empire of the Ptolemies* (1895).[4]

This rather quick sketch of Shaw's familiarity with historical sources relative to his writing of *Caesar and Cleopatra*, now all documented, clearly demonstrates his real method, first, of familiarizing himself with various historical materials; second, of privileging those materials that were more closely allied to his own views; and, finally, of rearranging history for the stage so that the selection and organization of that material would be determined by Shaw's unique perception and interpretation of history and stage exigencies. Shaw's view of history is that of an artist who readily recognizes that the truth of history has more to do with perspective and interpretation than with the so-called "facts" of history alone. How one interprets those "facts" is what constitutes history writ large. As J. L. Wisenthal rightly states in *Shaw's Sense of History*, "Shaw regards ideas rather than events as the essence of history, and his dramatic practice reflects this attitude."[5] In the case of Caesar, for example, Shaw recognized that history divides itself into various epochs and that those epochs often define the assessment of historical figures in a way that can be radically at variance with previous assessments. Each age in assessing and reinterpreting history has its own "Zeitgeist." In the nineteenth century, hero worship and Carlyle were synonymous, the works of Nietzsche were very much in vogue, and reassessments of great men of history were prolific. Shaw was a part of that tradition and came under its influence. Whenever Shaw's interest took him to a particular historical figure for dramatic purposes, he followed the same procedure: he read widely in the field, became aware of the many conflicting views, chose to dramatize his unique Shavian view, and, when finished, argued vigorously for the accuracy of his dramatic depiction of history. This approach to playwriting is apparent not only in *Caesar and Cleopatra*, but also in *Saint Joan* and in *"In Good King Charles's Golden Days"* as well.

This special volume of *SHAW*, devoted to Shaw and History, treats history rather broadly. History within a Shavian context can be seen in this volume as a reflection of the unique productions of Shaw's plays and their respective stage histories; it can be a reflection of Shaw's use of an historical figure for dramatic purposes; it can be a reflection of Shaw's use of settings and movements that inform the intellectual and social nuances of the plays; and it can be a reflection of Shaw's views and use of historical materials to express his ideas within a dramatic structure.

Instead of trying to find clever intersections of these historical reflections among the various articles in this volume, I have decided to fall back upon the most common form of organization—a rigid chronological placement.

At the beginning of Chapter VII of *Cashel Byron's Profession* (1882), Shaw's narrator makes reference to the arrival of an African king in London who stirred little out of doors except to visit the Woolwich Arsenal and to attend an "assault-at-arms," an "exhibition of swordsmanship, military drill, gymnastics. . . ."[6] Stanley Weintraub identifies the king as the Zulu warrior Cetewayo and gives an account of the short, tragic history of his rule in Zululand, his forced trip to England, his meeting with Queen Victoria, and his eventual alienation from power back home. Cetewayo's trip inspired Shaw to portray him in his novel and later to put him into the novel's adaption to play form as *The Admirable Bashville.* Weintraub points out that Cetewayo was the first historical figure within contemporary times to appear in Shaw's works.

John Allett, examining the historical background of prostitution in the nineteenth century, explores the liberal, socialist, and radical feminist views of prostitution of the period and demonstrates how those political views are developed within the unfolding of the action of *Mrs Warren's Profession.* The liberal notion of the connection between prostitution and economics, made abundantly clear in the first confrontation scene between Vivie and her mother, Mrs. Warren, gives way to the socialists' concept of prostitution as a more pervasive societal exploitation of male/female relationships, exemplified in Crofts's long speech to Vivie in Act III. Those views are expanded to incorporate a radical feminists' perception of prostitution as just another illustration of men's pervasive and persistent desire to dominate women. This latter view emerges in the final confrontation between Mrs. Warren and Vivie.

Sidney Albert, after reviewing the literature of the Utopian movements at the turn of the century, focuses on the ideal communities of various industrialists, including those of Krupp at Essen, Cadbury at Bournville, and Lever at Port Sunlight, to determine whether Shaw came under their influence when rendering his locale of Perivale St. Andrews. Albert revisits the works of such Shavian critics on the subject as Stanley Weintraub and Maurice Valency regarding the Krupp association for the purpose of pointing out many dissimilarities, especially regarding members of the Krupp family as analogues of Undershaft and Barbara. He carefully examines the Garden City movement, Shaw's personal involvement in it, and the extent to which that movement influenced his concept of Perivale St. Andrews. Since the movement itself was pervasive, it is, argues Albert, quite possible that Shaw was not narrowly confined to a single industrial experiment of establishing utopianlike communities, but was aware of the general milieu of such communities. Thus his Perivale St. Andrews is perhaps a distillation of multiple experiments. His answers to his early questions as to whether

Perivale St. Andrews is a Garden City and whether the play, *Major Barbara*, preaches the gospel of the Garden City movement are well qualified and insightfully presented.

In association with a production of *The Dark Lady of the Sonnets* in 1910, Shaw prepared an interview for W. R. Titterton regarding Frank Harris, the editor of the *Saturday Review* and a dabbler in Shakespearean criticism. In that interview, Shaw reveals that the theory that Mary Fitton was Shakespeare's Dark Lady of the Sonnets was first propounded by Thomas Tyler, a fellow researcher in the British Library. Shaw goes on to explain his own relationship with Harris and then specifically answers the question whether he had stolen Harris's concept of Shakespeare. The play in question was produced by Harley Granville Barker with costumes and set design by Charles Ricketts.

David Gunby examines the rocky road to the first-night performance of *O'Flaherty, V.C.*, the Shaw playlet written to boost a flagging Irish recruitment campaign and to aid the financially strained Abbey Theatre. Gunby's intent in this article is to set the historical record straight as to where, when, and by whom this first production of the play was performed.

Wendi Chen goes back in time to the first production of a Shaw play in China, *Mrs Warren's Profession* in 1921, to demonstrate Shaw's influence in shaping the history of the modern Chinese drama. *Mrs Warren's Profession* was translated in 1919 into Mandarin Chinese and, a little more than a year later, had its first performance in China. Chen asks whether the play had something to say to a China in the throes of social and cultural change. Her answer argues that the 1921 production was part of a larger movement in China to save the "Civilized New Drama," which had been in decline since 1915. The production was an unfortunate fiasco, mostly because of the gap between Chinese and Western theater and the inability of the Chinese actors, all members of the Beijing Opera, to adapt readily to Western style of naturalistic acting. Moreover, as Chen points out, there was precious little understanding of the play's content to sustain audience interest. In spite of the play's failure, it was a major event in the history of "The New Drama" in China.

Rodelle Weintraub, who has interpreted the significance of "dreams" as a frame in *Misalliance* and again in *Arms and the Man*, does the same with *Too True to Be Good* (1932), the difference being that in *Too True*, the manifest play is itself the dream. Using the dream as a vehicle to interpret the various themes of the play, Weintraub uses the typical Oedipal conflict in which the daughter seeks independence from her mother, and the other characters, some evoking the likes of Lawrence of Arabia and Winston Churchill, are seen as captives of the nightmarish times of World War I. All this adds up to a need for a society to come out of its dream, to make the repressed horrors of war conscious realities so that the waking world can indeed achieve the reversal of the play's title.

Michael O'Hara, focusing on the five productions of *Androcles and the Lion* in America during the late 1930s, argues that Shaw has manipulated an historical narrative of the past to point up its relevance in the present and its continuity across time and geography. O'Hara's article treats America's Federal Theatre Project's five productions of the play, three by Black/Negro companies and two by white companies, in five different cities: Atlanta, Seattle, Los Angeles, Denver, and New York. The first two productions of the play by the Negro cast were without overt racial overtones; however, the third production, in New York City, was billed as an illustration of the oppression not only of religious minorities but also of the Negro race. Also incorporated into the production were uses of political symbols, some removed before production, to suggest Hitler and Nazi Germany. The two white companies performed Androcles in Atlanta and Denver. Absent from the Atlanta production were the overt references to Nazi Germany, but the text was greatly modified, presumably to accommodate the religious conservatism of the region. References to "God" were increased, and references to loss or doubts of faith were deleted, thus pretty much sabotaging Shaw's satire on religious fervor. The Denver production was the most manipulated of the five: Caesar was made to resemble Hitler, and the swastika on the door to the Coliseum was unmistakable. The play was geared to deliver a message of political and religious repression. O'Hara's demonstration of these contemporary manipulations of *Androcles* in order to leave off explaining the past in the interest of aiding the audience to grapple with the present would be applauded by Shaw. In "Better Than Shakespear?" Shaw writes, "the playgoer may reasonably ask to have historical events and persons presented to him in the light of his own time . . ." (p. xxxiv).

In my article on *"In Good King Charles's Golden Days"*, I reveal Shaw's paradoxical approach to history, one that is both fanciful and factual simultaneously, in order for the playwright to achieve a "fresh and interesting" understanding of the "real Charles." While the approach is purely Shavian and thus easily dismissable by historians generally, I undercut that potential judgment by demonstrating not only Shaw's acquaintance with various historical and biographical sources of Charles and his times, but also that those views influenced Shaw's characterization and thus gave him tremendous confidence in claiming that his dramatic imagination had indeed captured the "real Charles." Imagination and historical research balance each other in Shaw's need "to invent Charles all over again," that is, to do justice to Charles by setting the historical record right.

Shaw had written to Gabriel Pascal in 1939 while the latter was filming *Major Barbara* and had mentioned the Ballycorus smelting works and its

surroundings as well as the campanile, or Folly, at Faringdon as suggestive
of Perivale St. Andrews in *Major Barbara.* Sidney Albert narrates his personal attempt, while on a visit there in 1982, to identify those sites that
loomed as possible scenic sources for Shaw's Perivale St. Andrews. His narrative fills in the historical background of Ballycorus, the Irish setting, and
the Folly, the alternative English setting, and argues convincingly that such
places may indeed have been what Shaw had visualized for his final scene
of *Major Barbara,* for the Ballycorus reference in the play script and the
reference to the Folly at Faringdon in the printed film script. Weintraub's
treatment of Shaw's use of a contemporary historical figure in his work and
Albert's study of the Ballycorus and the Folly at Faringdon as scenic sources
provide the reader with two historical perspectives that greatly enhance,
enrich, and illuminate their respective Shavian texts.

This volume of *SHAW* with its historical theme explores a particular side
of Shavian scholarship that has been far too often neglected. "We can
never get enough of Shaw as an historian," says Harry G. Jacobs in an
unsigned article in the *Brooklyn Daily Eagle* of 27 September 1919. He adds
that Shaw's "dramatizations of history after the idea of Irving's Knicker-
bocker are the best in print or on the stage. . . . We must have perspective,
and Shaw is one of the few men who can give it to us."[7] How true!

Notes

1. Bernard Shaw, "Mr. Shaw's Future: A Conversation," *The Academy* 53 (30 April 1898) :
476.

2. Bernard Shaw, "Better Than Shakespear?" Preface to *Three Plays for Puritans* (London:
Constable, 1931), p. xxxix.

3. Bernard Shaw, "Letter to the Editor," *The Times* (London), 31 December 1945, p. 5.

4. See Louis Crompton, *Shaw the Dramatist* (Lincoln: University of Nebraska Press, 1969),
pp. 66–67. Shaw had answered Gilbert Murray's charge that he had "overdone Cleopatra's
ferocity" by pointing out the hereditarily fratricidal side of her nature. Professor Crompton
attributes Shaw's view of Cleopatra's ferocious character to his reading of the Irish historian
John Pentland Mahaffy.

5. J. L. Wisenthal, *Shaw's Sense of History* (Oxford: Oxford University Press, 1988), p. 48.

6. Bernard Shaw, *Cashel Byron's Profession* (London: Constable, 1932), p. 105.

7. "SHAW COMES BACK WITH PLAYS—NEW POETRY—PUBLISHER'S VIEW: Shaw's
Latest Plays Libel English in War, But Have Typical Fun," *Brooklyn Daily Eagle* (New York), 27
September 1919, p. 9. This article was brought to my attention by Dan H. Laurence, who also
identified the unsigned author as Harry G. Jacobs.

Stanley Weintraub

CETEWAYO: SHAW'S FIRST HERO FROM HISTORY

Zululand, the region to the north of Durban and to the east of Johannesburg, hardly seems like Bernard Shaw country, and it is not, although G.B.S. did write his *Black Girl* novella in southernmost South Africa in 1932. In his earliest writing days, when his travels were limited by lack of means to London and environs, he merely moved his Zulu chieftain to England, where, indeed, he had briefly and incongruously turned up in 1882.

In the later 1870s, disputes along the boundary between the Boers in the Transvaal and the Zulus in what is now Natal threatened what tenuous peace there was east of the Drakensberg Mountains. The tribal king was Cetewayo, then forty-seven, who had earlier overthrown his brother, Umbulayo, in a bloody civil war over which should be heir apparent. The British were troublemakers themselves, exercising more and more authority north of the Cape. Cetewayo had been crowned in 1873, an event presided over by the watchful Sir Theophilus Shepstone, British secretary for Native Affairs in Southern Africa, who spoke Zulu and Xhosa and was known to Africans as *Sometsu*, or Mighty Hunter. It was the occasion for extracting assurances from the newly crowned king that indiscriminate shedding of blood would cease, that no one would be condemned without a fair trial for a capital crime, that there would be a right of appeal, and that the death penalty would not be exacted for minor offenses. For Shepstone, the son of a Wesleyan missionary, the goal was, in effect, a Methodist Africa—under British suzerainty.[1]

Cetewayo's failure to keep such Westernized stipulations would become an excuse for a British invasion of Zululand six years later.[2] In the interim, he remained popular among most of his quarter-million people. The scattered kraals in which the Zulu people lived were reasonably orderly and, by African standards, prosperous. Each Black dweller on communal Zulu lands had several cattle and several wives, and, Sir Theophilus notwithstanding, adultery and some other civil crimes remained punishable by death. As high priest as well as king of his people, Cetewayo presided over a belief system in which evil spirits that could not be propitiated by magic had to be exorcised by the death of the victim they possessed, and his witchdoctors often managed to "smell out" evil in persons who had more cattle than their jealous neighbors did. The Zulu army, Cetewayo's other power base, created as a professional force by his late uncle, Shaka, was built upon draftees by age group, who lived celibate in military kraals and could marry only with the king's permission, usually not granted until the warrior was forty, or had killed an enemy in battle ("the washing of the spears"), when by custom he could request any unmarried Zulu woman. Wealth remained measured in women and cattle. War offered almost the only chance to gain honor, women, and cattle. Soldiers without such rewards for service chafed at postponements of their manhood.

Polyglot British and Boer settlements, relentlessly encroaching upon Zulu lands, would furnish Cetewayo both opportunity and motive to halt the occupation. Seeing himself as the Queen's proconsul everywhere in southern Africa, Shepstone considered it necessary to move in the other direction—to force the Zulus, for the sake of order and progress, "to submit to the rule of civilisation." He worried about "a kind of common desire in the Native mind . . . to try and overcome the white intruders," language that hid nothing in euphemisms. The possibility of acquiring firearms from free-lance dealers lifted Black hopes of reversing land confiscations and made colonial politicians nervous. Shepstone, who had become sixty in 1877, was reluctant to retire before accomplishing his personal mission. A paternalist and imperialist "improver," he viewed the seemingly idle life of the native as a handicap to achieving Christian acculturation. The African had to be persuaded to work for Europeans and for wages rather than to eke out an existence in backward traditional villages.

Attempting to federate colonies under the Union Jack—Shepstone included by legal sleight-of-hand Boer-settled Transvaal, which had a vocal British minority—he pushed both the Zulus and the Voortrekkers into taking up arms. Cetewayo attempted to avoid outright war in order to keep the British from seizing an excuse to obliterate the tribal system, but disorders on the undefined frontiers emboldened the new high commissioner, Sir Bartle Frere, operating from Government House in Cape Town, to employ the Raj formula. (He had served in India.) What he described as a "rising of Kaffirdom against white civilisation" demonstrated to his satisfaction the need for a White federal state. Shepstone had long deplored the "terrible incubus of the Zulu Royal family," and Frere needed little urging to mount a campaign. He delayed reporting to London the findings of a Natal boundary commission that might have prejudiced an attack on what he called Cetewayo's "man-slaying human military machine," and on 11 January 1879 began to move against the Zulus.

Cetewayo had thirty thousand warriors but few firearms. For a while, mass attacks with spears held off the redcoats, costing the British heavily at Isandhlwana, where there was a gallant but vain attempt to save the regimental colors. Imperial troops were temporarily embarrassed, but as the Zulu king put it, he was in the situation of "a man warding off a falling tree." Reinforcements arrived for the Great White Queen's army, and Cetewayo's royal kraal at Ulindi fell on 4 July 1879. Sir Garnet Wolseley, the British commander, imposed a settlement dismembering the Zulu nation into thirteen "kinglets," each with its own splinter chieftain, several of them both cousins and rivals (one a half-brother) to Cetewayo, whose Usuthu tribe lost most of its lands and cattle. Young Henry Rider Haggard (who would write *King Solomon's Mines*), although then Shepstone's secretary, privately called the dictated peace an "abomination and a disgrace to England."

Greed among the Zulu factions inevitably led to cattle-raiding and bloodshed, and insistent calls for the return of Cetewayo, who had been captured at Ulindi and exiled with a few retainers to the Cape. By April 1882 the British resident official in Zululand, Melmoth Osborn, admitted to London that the disorders were such that he could travel only "a mile or two" from his headquarters: "I have no authority." From Cape Town came a pathetic plea from Cetewayo himself, "I do not know what we have done, and I pray the Queen to let me go back . . . for though a man be allowed to breathe, he is not really alive if he is cut off from his wives and children."

Lacking realistic alternatives, the imperial authorities looked to Cetewayo, who had been a model prisoner. "All the Zulus wish him back," Osborn appealed desperately if untruthfully. Obviously none of the surviving puppet chieftains wanted a restoration, but in London the prime minister, W. E. Gladstone, who hated all colonial entanglements, a definition in which he included Ireland, wrote hopefully, "If it should appear that the mass of the people in Zululand are for Cetshwayo, . . . so far from regarding him as the enemy of England . . . I should regard the proof of that fact with great pleasure . . . and that would be the sentiment of my colleagues."

Shaw had begun his fourth novel, *Cashel Byron's Profession*,[3] that April, as talk of Cetewayo's possible restoration reached the English press. Inspired in part by enthusiasm for boxing, which had gone from reading, as a boy, such sporting magazines as *Bell's Life* to sparring with his poetasting friend Pakenham Beatty and even to entering amateur competitions as a light heavyweight, Shaw had begun the saga of a prize fighter. Cashel Byron is a young gentleman, unruly son of a Shakespearean actress, who runs away from school at seventeen, ships out to Australia as a cabin boy, and learns there how to make a living at pugilism. Seven years later he returns to

Fig. 1.   Viewed by the British public as half king and half
savage, Cetewayo was caricatured as combining both guises
in a *Punch* cartoon published as his arrival in London was
anticipated.

England to compete in the prize ring, where he quickly gains a reputation
in his brutal, and still-illegal, profession. Training in a corner of a country
estate where his manager, who has accompanied him from Australia, has
rented a cottage, he encounters its owner, Lydia Carew, a beautiful blue-
stocking millionairess. However attracted they are to each other, social prej-
udice against his retrograde occupation keeps her from encouraging his
attentions.

Escorted by Henrique Shepstone, eldest son of Sir Theophilus (and his
deputy), and three tribal chiefs, Cetewayo, his name variously spelled in
the London press, arrived in London in July 1882 as Shaw was halfway
through his novel and seeking a strategy to maintain Miss Carew's reluctant
fascination with Byron. *Punch*[4] had even published a cartoon in advance of
the king's arrival depicting him, dockside, about to embark for England,
amid packing cases and black attendants. Prophetically, Cetewayo was at-
tired in incongruous top hat, gold-braided military tunic, tribal skirt, and
bare feet, and carried an umbrella sword-tipped at its base. "CETEWAYO'S
COMING!" read the caption. "WHAT'LL THEY DO WITH HIM?"

"Society," Shaw began chapter 7,

> was much occupied . . . with the upshot of an historical event of a
> common kind. England, a few years before, had stolen a kingdom
> from a considerable people in Africa, and seized the person of its
> king. The conquest proved useless, troublesome, and expensive;
> and after repeated attempts to settle the country on impracticable
> plans suggested to the Colonial Office by a popular historian who
> had made a trip to Africa, and by generals who were tired of the
> primitive remedy of killing the natives, it appeared that the best
> course was to release the captive king and get rid of the unprofitable
> booty by restoring it to him. In order, however, that the impression
> made on him by England's shortsighted disregard of her neigh-
> bour's landmark abroad might be counteracted by a glimpse of the
> vastness of her armaments and wealth at home, it was thought advis-
> able to take him first to London, and shew him the wonders of the
> town.

The king's freedom from Western ways, Shaw went on, puzzled him as to
why a private person "could own a portion of the earth" and make others
pay for permission to use it or live on it, and why others toiled incessantly
to create wealth for others, leaving neither laborers nor the class that dissi-
pated the wealth any the happier for it. Even worse,

> He was seized with strange fears, first for his health, for it seemed to
> him that the air of London, filthy with smoke, engendered puniness
> and dishonesty in those that breathed it; and eventually for his life
> when he learned that kings in Europe were sometimes shot at by
> passers-by, there being hardly a monarch there who had not been
> so imperilled more than once; that the queen of England, though
> accounted the safest of all, was accustomed to this variety of pistol
> practice; and that the autocrat of an empire huge beyond all other
> European countries, whose father [Czar Alexander II] had been
> torn asunder in the streets of his capital [in 1881], lived surrounded
> by soldiers. . . . Under these circumstances, the African King was
> with difficulty induced to stir out of doors. . . .

Cetewayo had in reality arrived in England dressed in as much civilized
garb as he could successfully manage and was squired about London in
morning coat, topper, and bare feet. His appearance, and his many wives
left behind in Zululand, both noted in the press, inspired a music-hall song
performed as he went about:

> White young dandies, get away, O!
>   You are now 'neath beauty's ban;
> Clear the field for Cetewayo,
>   He alone's the ladies' man.[5]

To British officials he spoke of his anticipated new role, the best he could hope for, as a "child" in the service of his "mother," Queen Victoria. At the Colonial Office he nevertheless protested the planned land "Reserve" to be carved out of Zululand as a sanctuary for tribes claiming to be threatened by the restoration of the Usuthu, but he knew that resistance was futile and that the best he could compromise for would be a rump state. Visiting Mr. Gladstone, who only noted in his diary, "Interview with Cetewayo at noon for half an hour. I was much interested and pleased," the king was shown as part of his tour of Number 10 Downing Street a portrait of the Radical politician John Bright, described by the prime minister as "our Great Orator." Demurring, Cetewayo insisted that the authentic "Great Orator" was standing at his side. Diplomatic despite his bared toes, and with no more English than Shaw would give him in his novel, Cetewayo was even more winning at Marlborough House, the London residence of the often-absent Prince of Wales. "After he had been made known to the young princes and princesses," Gladstone's private secretary, Edward Hamilton, noted in his diary, "he asked where was the Princess of Wales. He declined to believe that the lovely young woman he saw before him was the mother of such tall children.[6]

When Shaw reached chapter 9 he set the scene for a grand Roman-style exhibition that the fictional Cetewayo would attend, in which Cashel would spar with the chief contender for the championship, the ruffianly giant Billy Paradise. Only one fight had been lost by the burly Paradise, Cashel's trainer, Bob Mellish, warns. "Shepstone, clever as he is, only won a fight from him by claiming a foul." Reading the papers, Shaw had found the name, awarding the Shepstone family its only entry in literature. The real Shepstone, meanwhile, guided the Zulu king on a visit to Victoria at her home on the Isle of Wight, Osborne House, across the Solent from Portsmouth and Southampton. "Our Portsmouth correspondent telegraphed last night," *The Times* reported. "Cetewayo and his two native generals of division left Victoria station by special train for an audience with the Queen. . . . It must . . . be said of Cetewayo that he has a wonderful command of countenance, and that his equanimity is of the highest character. Nothing appeared to surprise him. The gaping, struggling crowd, the capacious harbour, the gigantic men-of-war, and the other sights of the port never disturbed his imperturbable gravity." Although a lunch would be set out for Cetewayo's party, and it was indeed assumed that the Queen would preside, she limited her brief audience to small talk. ("Will not the Queen spoil our 'fat friend'. . . ?" Lord Kimberley, the colonial secretary, wondered to Gladstone.)

Cetewayo was, Victoria wrote in her journal, "a very fine man, in his native costume, or rather no costume. He is tall, immensely broad, and stout, with a good-humoured countenance, and an intelligent face. Unfortunately he appeared in a hideous black frock coat and trousers, but still wearing the ring round his head, denoting that he was a married man.[7] His companions were very black, but quite different to the ordinary negro. I said, through Mr. Shepstone, that I was glad to see him here, and that I recognised in him a great warrior, who had fought against us, but rejoiced we were now friends. He answered much the same, gesticulating a good deal as he spoke, mentioned having seen my picture, and said he was glad to see me in person. I asked about his voyage, and what he had seen." When she mentioned her three daughters in England the chieftain tried out an English response, which seemed to be "Ah!"

After further commonplaces "the interview terminated. Both in coming in, and going out, they gave me the royal Zulu salute, saying something altogether, and raising their right hands above their heads." (The tribal salute was "Bayete!") Cetewayo walked about on the terrace to take in the view high above Cowes and the Solent, and indoors again was served lunch with his party. From the Colonnade, Victoria watched them leave. "As they drove away. Cetewayo caught sight of me, and got up in the carriage, and remained standing till they were out of sight."[8]

Afterwards the London correspondent of the *Manchester Guardian* asked Cetewayo his opinion of the Queen. "She is born to rule men," he said; "she is like me. We are both rulers. She was very kind to me and I will always think of her."

Despite gifts of hunting dogs and horses, the visits of Temperance League ladies who exhorted him to eschew beer, and tours of places thought likely to impress him, Cetewayo was bored and eager to take up his restored, if reduced, throne. To further keep him busy he was extended the hospitality of the huge Crystal Palace, since 1853 removed from Hyde Park to Sydenham, south of the Thames. His appearance was advertised by the management for the thirty thousand shilling-visitors that day along with the Company Band and the Electric Exhibition. The great organ pounded as he paced, unhappily nursing an English cold, and at twilight the nightly fireworks exhibition, for all he knew, was put on specially for him. Fictionally exploiting the Colonial Office's being at wit's end to devise entertainments to keep the king in good humor until his departure, Shaw devised the Cashel-Paradise spar as part of a military and athletic tournament at the Agricultural Hall in Islington, a real-life venue built in 1862 for cattle shows and used also for horse shows, military exhibitions, and evening entertainments. There Lydia, persuaded to attend by her cousin Lucian, a

Fig. 2.   A medallion cartoon by "Face" in *Punch,* 26 August
1882, showing an idealized Victoria formally restoring Cetewayo
to his throne.

minor diplomat, sees across the arena "a gaudy dais, on which a powerfully-
built black gentleman sat in a raised chair, his majestic impassivity contrasting with the overt astonishment with which a row of savagely ugly attendant
chiefs grinned and gaped on either side of him."

In the main event, despite employing every ring illegality for which he
has opportunity, Paradise is badly beaten. But Cashel, first pleased by his
victory, turns pale and ashamed when he notices Lydia unexpectedly in the
audience. "He seemed in a hurry to retire. But he was intercepted by an
officer in uniform, accompanied by a black chief, who came to conduct
him to the dais and present him to the African King: an honour which he
was not permitted to decline."

Through an interpreter, the king explained "that he had been unspeak-
ably gratified by what he had just witnessed; expressed great surprise that
Cashel, notwithstanding his prowess, was neither in the army nor in parliament; and finally offered to provide him with three handsome wives if he
would come out to Africa in his suite. Cashel was much embarrassed; but
he came off with credit, thanks to the interpreter, who was accustomed to
invent appropriate speeches for the king on public occasions, and was kind

Fig. 3.   Cetewayo's problems in regaining his throne caused concerns in London that he might return to plead for government help. Here he is imagined returning to the house he used in Melbury Road, Holland Park, provided for his entourage by the Colonial Office.

enough to invent equally appropriate ones for Cashel on this." On the king's authentic departure *Punch*[9] closed its "Adieu to Cetewayo" with lines that Shaw either echoed or paralleled earlier in his episode:

> *Good-bye, Great CETEWAYO! I think you'll understand*
> *That what is right in London may be wrong in Zululand!*

Cetewayo, the first major figure out of contemporary history to appear in Shaw's pages, would reappear in one of his plays, but nothing beyond the visit to England would supplement the scenario. Given Shaw's propensity for mixed dramatic modes, the king would be more seriously drawn, yet also more comic. As for Cetewayo himself, nothing even remotely comic would happen to him thereafter. In January 1883 he was returned on board the *H.M.S. Briton* to his shrunken kingdom only to find civil war brewing. "I did not land in a dry place," he said ruefully. "I landed in

[January 13, 1883.]   PUNCH, OR THE LONDON CHARIVARI.   15

"I HOPE I DON'T INTRUDE!"

Fig. 4. *Punch* pictures Cetewayo's less-than-welcome
return to Zululand, where rivals had already carved up his
kingdom. John Dunn (above, right) was a Scot who had
adopted Zulu nationality and had once been right-hand-
man to Cetewayo.

mud." His situation was precarious. He was no one's chief, rather "an ant
in a pond of water." He had to flee for his life into the Nkandla forests,
where he was injured when his small force was attacked by rebels who rejected him as an English puppet. He was forced, for his own safety, to go
"into Mr. Osborn's armpit" and accept British protection. In Eshowe, in
the "Reserve" he had resisted, he died early in 1884, officially of a heart
attack. Laughter greeted the announcement of his death during one of the
less proud sittings of the House of Commons.

The agents of empire who in the name of the Great White Queen had
reduced Cetewayo from warrior chieftain in a relatively stable agrarian
kingdom would have years of instability and disorder as Cetewayo's legacy.
Although Shaw would make only stylistic changes in his episodes involving
Cetewayo when he had the novel reissued in 1889 and again in 1901, in
the 1901 edition he included as an appendix a dramatic adaptation, *The
Admirable Bashville*.[10]

Veteran prize fighters had begun seeking opportunities out of the squared circle to exploit their fading celebrity onstage as Cashel Byron. In December 1900 an unauthorized play version opened in New York at the Herald Square Theatre. (In 1909 the famed James J. Corbett would play Cashel.) In the next month—Shaw claimed it took only a week—to protect his copyright, he dashed off a comedy in mock-Elizabethan blank verse, which he claimed was easy to write. Possibly because of the contemporaneity of the events in 1882, Shaw had not named the Zulu king. Since that reason had vanished into history, he was less reticent in 1901.

Cetewayo remained as unidentified in the play's title as, now, was Cashel Byron himself. Featured instead as part of Shaw's extended joke was Lydia Carew's lovesick butler, Bashville, who in the novel has a brief spar with Cashel. (James Barrie in 1902 would echo Shaw's title in his own comedy about an ambitious butler, *The Admirable Crichton*.) Cetewayo, however, is featured in Act II, Scene 2, and Shaw recalled thirty years later in a new preface to the play that "James Hearn's lamentation over the tragedy of Cetewayo"—Hearn played the king—"came off, not as a mockery, but as genuine tragedy, which indeed it also is."[11] The costly Boer War had been in embarrassing progress when Shaw wrote the play and had ended only on 31 May 1902, barely a year before the first professional production on 7 June 1903.

The episode of the forced visit of the captured Zulu king to encourage his appreciation of the benefits of British civilization would have an ironic subtext in the early years of the new century that Shaw had no need to explicate, although he inserted late in the play a wry dig at jingoism that may have been overly subtle then as now. "The moral position of the Boers and the British," he had already written to a Fabian friend, "is precisely identical in every respect; that is, it does not exist. Two dogs are fighting for a bone thrown before them by Mrs Nature. . . ."[12]

In *The Admirable Bashville*, the second scene of Act II is set, as in the novel, in the Agricultural Hall, where Cetewayo asks Lucian about the spectators, "Are these anaemic dogs the English people?" He pours out more scorn about a civilization that requires "a pall of smoke" across the sky for its well-being, but Lucian Webber, who is the Government's representative at the exhibition, explains,

> You cannot understand
> The greatness of this people, Cetewayo.
> You are a savage, reasoning like a child.
> Each pallid English face conceals a brain
> Whose powers are proven in the works of Newton
> And in the plays of the immortal Shakespear.
> There is not one of all the thousands here
> But, if you placed him naked in the desert,

> Would presently construct a steam engine,
> And lay a cable t' th' Antipodes.

Cetewayo sees through the brag to the down-side of alleged progress:

> Men become civilized through twin deseases,
> Terror and Greed to wit: these two conjoined
> Become the grisly parents of Invention.
> Why does the trembling white [man] with frantic toil
> Of hand and brain produce the magic gun
> That slays a mile off, whilst the manly Zulu
> Dares look his foe i' the face; fights foot to foot;
> Lives in the present; drains the Here and Now;
> Makes life a long reality, and death
> A moment only; whilst your Englishman
> Glares on his burning candle's winding-sheets,
> Counting the steps of his approaching doom,
> And in the murky corners ever sees
> Two horrid shadows, Death and Poverty. . . .

Further, he sees technology as wresting from "wearied Nature" such secrets as will rocket the brave Black "explosively from off the globe," while the "white-livered slaves" of "Dead and Dread" are enabled to overrun the earth. Still, he reminds Lucian,

> Thou sayest thou hast two white-faced ones who dare
> Fight without guns, and spearless, to the death.
> Let them be brought.

But Lucian cautions the king that English warriors of the ring "fight not to death" under the civilized rules of the sport:

> Half of their persons shall not be attacked;
> Nor shall they suffer blows when they fall down,
> Nor stroke of foot at any time. And, further,
> That frequent opportunities of rest
> With succor and refreshment be secured them.

Cetewayo scoffs at codified gentlemanly limits on courage. The land of the Zulus would scorn such "Personified Pusillanimity." But Lucian retorts that only a "rude savage" of "untutored mind" can doubt "That Brave and English mean the self-same thing," and the king taunts,

> Well, well, produce these heroes. I surmise
> They will be carried by their nurses, lest
> Some barking dog or bumbling bee should scare them.

William Paradise enters, "hateful" in appearance to the ladylike Lydia, and the godlike Cashel follows. Cetewayo asks the "sons of the white queen" in turn to identify themselves. Paradise calls himself "a bloke" who makes his honest living by his fists, and the king is pleased:

> Six wives and thirty oxen shalt thou have
> If on the sand thou leave thy foeman dead.

Unimpressed, Cashel challenges Cetewayo

> To name the bone, or limb, or special place
> Where you would have me hit him with this fist.

"Thou has a noble brow," the king warns, but he fears that Paradise, a Goliath, is likely to "disfigure it."

They spar violently, and an uppercut followed by a hook causes Paradise to topple on his face and remain "quite silly." While Cashel explains to Cetewayo scientifically what blows were landed, the prescribed ten seconds pass. "I might safely finish him," says Cashel, but he does not, out of respect for "your most gracious majesty's desire" to see more "of the science of self-defence." But Paradise refuses to be finished according to the rules, and tears off his gloves, complaining,

> How can a bloke do hisself proper justice
> With pillows on his fists?

"Unfair!" the crowd shouts. "The rules!" Cetewayo, however, is caught up in Paradise's willingness to rise from the floor to fight:

> The joy of battle surges boiling up
> And bids me join the mellay. Isandhlana
> And Victory!

Cetewayo's chiefs join in and fall upon the bystanders, recalling with their king the great victory of 22 January 1879 over the British encamped on the plain at the base of Isandhlwana Mountain when 20,000 Zulu warriors shouting "Usuthu! Usuthu!" and carrying only shields and assegais advanced against rifle fire and wiped out the 2nd Warwickshire Regiment and its native adjuncts. Of the European soldiers encamped there only

20   STANLEY WEINTRAUB

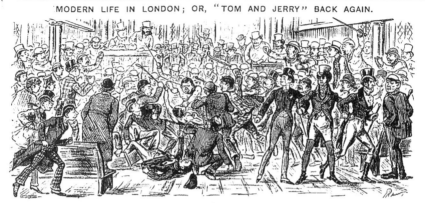

APRIL 22, 1882.]   .   PUNCH, OR THE LONDON CHARIVARI.   185

MODERN LIFE IN LONDON; OR, "TOM AND JERRY" BACK AGAIN.

TOM, JERRY, AND YOUNG LOGIC, AT A GLOVE FIGHT.

Fig. 5. The "Glove Fight" cartoon, published while Shaw was writing *Cashel Byron*, may have inspired his altercation between fans of Cashel and Paradise.

fifty-five escaped Zulu spears. Six months later, at Ulundi, a second invasion succeeded in overwhelming Cetewayo's kraal; but now, in the shouting and the chaos in the Agricultural Hall, his cohorts recall only the victory:

> THE CHIEFS. Victory and Isandhlana!
> *[They run amok. General panic and stampede.*
> *The ring is swept away.]*

Cashel drags Lydia out of harm's way, and in the confusion Lucian calls for the police.

Strikingly, the 22 April 1882 issue of *Punch*, as Shaw was beginning his novel, included a cartoon with a text entitled "MODERN LIFE IN LONDON; OR, 'TOM AND JERRY' BACK AGAIN." It was the second part of a satirical feature that would run through the year, this episode picturing two gloved pugilists going at each other in a crowded indoors setting, while rowdy spectators ranging from toffs in checked trousers to monocled gentlemen in formal morning attire intrude enthusiastically into the glove fight on the sides of their heroes. Could Shaw have remembered it, or returned to it?

In the play, the police arrive, and a mock-heroic parody of the attempted rescue of the colors at Isandhlana[13] ensues:

> A POLICEMAN. Give us a lead, sir. Save the English flag.
> Africa tramples on it.

CASHEL. Africa!
Not all the continents whose mighty shoulders
The dancing diamonds of the seas bedeck
Shall trample on the blue with spots of white. . . . [*He charges the Zulus.*]
LYDIA. . . . See: the king is down;
The tallest chief is up, heels over head,
Tossed corklike oer my Cashel's sinewy back;
And his lieutenant all deflated gasps
For breath upon the sand. The others fly.
In vain: his fist oer magic distances
Like a chameleon's tongue shoots to its mark;
And the last African upon his knees
Sues piteously for quarter. . . .
CETEWAYO[*trying to rise*] Have I been struck by lightning?

The symbolic victory becomes, however absurdly here, an English one. Cashel is victorious but injured—not by the Zulus, but by his white rival—in his throwback crudity now, with a war ongoing with the Afrikaners, perhaps a Boer symbol. When Lydia sees the blood and discovers that Paradise has taken a bite out of her lover's flesh, she swoons in Cashel's arms. Cetewayo vanishes from the play. "The Queen's peace" prevails.

Ironically, Shaw was finishing *The Admirable Bashville* as the old queen lay dying at Osborne. Two days before her burial at Windsor on 4 February 1901, he posted the completed script to Grant Richards, then his publisher. Almost forgotten in the chaos of African history since, Cetewayo lives on in Shaw's farce and the novel from which he drew it.

Notes

1. Rupert Furneaux, *The Zulu War* (London: Weidenfeld & Nicolson, 1963), pp. 13–16.

2. Further background on Zulu history unless otherwise cited is from D. M. Schreuder, *The Struggle for South Africa, 1877–1895* (Cambridge: Cambridge University Press, 1980), pp. 14–82. Quotations attributed to Cetewayo himself, unless cited from other sources, are also from Schreuder.

3. The text of Shaw's novel is from its first appearance, in serial form, in *To-Day*, April 1885–March 1886, as reprinted from the magazine plates by Modern Press, London, also in 1886, with misprints corrected. Later editions of the novel made further minor stylistic changes but no substantial revisions. A new edition of the Modern Press text, noting all the textual alterations, was published, ed. Stanley Weintraub (Carbondale: Southern Illinois University Press), in 1968.

4. *Punch*, 8 July 1882, p. 3.

5. Quoted by James [Jan] Morris in *Heaven's Command. An Imperial Progress* (New York: Knopf, 1979), pp. 438–39.

6. H. G. C. Matthew, ed., *The Gladstone Diaries* (London: Oxford University Press, 1990), 10: 310; and D. W. R. Bahlman, ed., *The Diary of Sir Edward Hamilton* (Oxford: Oxford University Press, 1972), 1: 370. The entries are for 9 August and 19 August 1882.

7. The Zulu head-ring, or *isi-coco*, was the most coveted distinction for a Zulu male, as it symbolized permission to marry. See E. A. Ritter, *Shaka Zulu: The Rise of the Zulu Empire* (New York: Putnam, 1957), p. 396.

8. Christopher Hibbert, ed., *Queen Victoria in Her Letters and Journals* (London: John Murray, 1984), entry for 14 August 1882, pp. 275–76. *Punch* depicted Cetewayo in one of its satirical "Prize Medals" (26 August 1882) being re-crowned by Victoria to "celebrate the promised Restoration."

9. *Punch*, 2 September 1882, p. 105.

10. *The Admirable Bashville*, text from Bernard Shaw, *Collected Plays with Their Prefaces* (London: Max Reinhardt, 1971), 2: 432–78.

11. Shaw discusses Hearn as Cetewayo in a 1941 addition to the *Bashville* preface, reprinted in Shaw, *Selected Short Plays* (New York: Penguin, 1987), p. 5.

12. Shaw's letter on the equivocal "moral position" of both British and Boers is to George Samuel, quoted in Michael Holroyd, *Bernard Shaw. The Pursuit of Power* (New York: Random House, 1989), p. 42.

13. I owe this suggestion to South African scholar Leon H. Hugo.

John Allett

MRS WARREN'S PROFESSION AND THE POLITICS OF PROSTITUTION

> With Mrs. Warren these girls feel, "Why waste your life working
> for a few shillings a week in a scullery eighteen hours a day?"
> —Emma Goldman, 1917[1]

Although the word is never explicitly mentioned in the play, the fact that
Mrs. Warren's profession is prostitution is no secret. Indeed, the Lord
Chamberlain's Office felt fit to ban the play partly because of this unsavory
even if unstated fact. Nor has the point been lost on commentators that
Shaw, as a socialist, uses the profession of prostitution to indict capitalism.
Charles Carpenter, in his study *Bernard Shaw and the Art of Destroying Ideals*,
for example, comments that prostitution in *Mrs Warren's Profession* "represents an ultimate example . . . of the bartering of human lives and destinies
that the capitalist ethic condones."[2] Nevertheless, what is missing from
these commentaries is an appreciation that Shaw's play actually explores
several distinct positions on prostitution. The issue of prostitution was and
is of interest not only to socialists but also to liberals and radical feminists,
and, remarkably, Shaw's play manages to incorporate the key positions of
each. Moreover, he did this in such a way that it is possible to see a progressive yet complicating development in the play's unfolding.

Prostitution was not made illegal in England until 1839,[3] and even then
it continued to have some public sympathy. This was especially the case
among the lower classes who had yet to be afforded the luxury of finger-
pointing "the fallen woman" as the "living violation of bourgeois notions
of female sexual propriety."[4]

In 1857, official estimates put the number of prostitutes in London at
8,600 (out of a population of two million). Unofficial figures, however,

such as those produced by Henry Mayhew in his study *London's Labour and the London Poor* (1851–62) and William Acton's *Prostitution, Considered in its Moral, Social, and Sanitary Aspects in London and other Large Cities* (1857), suggested that 80,000 was a more accurate figure.[5]

Only in the early 1860s, when it was determined that Britain's military strength was at risk because of the spread of sexually transmitted diseases among the troops, was a concerted effort made to control street prostitution. Under a series of Contagious Diseases Acts, 1864–69—which were applied with even greater severity in the British colonies[6]—any woman suspected of prostitution and who plied her trade in certain designated garrison towns and sea ports could be forcibly taken to a hospital for medical examination and treatment. Refusal to comply could result in imprisonment. More often, it resulted in police harassment.

For some, like Josephine Butler and Harriet Martineau, such legislation was outrageous because it seemed both to sanction prostitution, provided it was officially regulated, and simultaneously to victimize the prostitute, while excusing her (male) clients. The lesson of ancient Rome was frequently recalled, where prostitutes were "compelled to register . . . and declare that they intended to make [prostitution] the calling of their lives, [thus] closing all doors against the reformation of such women."[7] The Contagious Diseases Acts were viewed as a similar kind of duplicitous entrapment. For others, the legislation smacked too much of "big" government, especially as each succeeding Act extended the area of regulation. In particular, it was objected that although "the law is ostensibly framed for a certain class of women . . . in order to reach these, all women residing within the districts where it is in force are brought under the provisions of the Acts."[8] For still others, the legislation had simply proven ineffectual in controlling sexual disease. As August Bebel pointedly commented, "The surveillance and control exercised by the officers of the state do not touch the men, as they ought to do as a matter of course, if the sanitary superintendence were to have any *raison d'être* and any chance of success, even if we leave the equality of the sexes before the law in the interest of ordinary justice out of the question. . . . England affords a striking proof of the uselessness of this medical police control."[9] And Shaw himself, when writing the 1902 Preface to *Mrs Warren's Profession*, chose to highlight the double standard inherent in the legislation as a central failing. He found unacceptable the lingering judgment of "the medical gentleman who would compulsorily examine and register Mrs Warren, whilst leaving Mrs Warren's patrons, especially her military patrons, free to destroy her health and anybody else's without fear of reprisals."[10]

Thus it was for a variety of reasons that the Contagious Diseases Acts were finally repealed in 1886.

Josephine Butler was also a keen activist in exposing the Continental traffic in teenage prostitution that was taking place mainly between England and Brussels and Vienna, where brothels had been made legal in the 1870s. One of Butler's main allies in this endeavour was W. T. Stead, the editor of the *Pall Mall Gazette*. Stead (abetted by Bramwell Booth, the son of Salvation Army founder William Booth, and Rebecca Jarrett, who was herself a prostitute before becoming a Salvation Army convert)[11], arranged to procure a thirteen-year-old girl, Eliza Armstrong, from her mother, ostensibly for the purpose of reselling her abroad as a prostitute. This trade cost Stead a few pounds only. (Eliza was in fact kept safe in France for a short time and then returned to her parents). Eliza's age is significant because at the time this was the legal age of consent in England, while on the Continent it was twenty-one years of age. Butler and Stead were determined to get this age limit raised, believing that the difference in the age of consent between England and the Continent was an important inducement to trade in young English women. In this one regard they were quickly successful. Under new legislation the legal age of consent was set at sixteen years. The government had not been unaware of the "traffic" in women that had been taking place, but had seen fit, based on the reports of its own investigators, largely to discount claims that these young women were innocent of any knowledge as to their fate, or entirely unwilling. As one investigator reported to Parliament, prostitution was simply "an accepted fact of lower-class life, a sort of family tradition handed down from mother to daughter."[12] Stead was able to bring fresh focus and urgency to this issue, however, by concentrating on one (oversimplified) remedial action: raising the age of consent.[13]

The "White Slave Traffic" scandal sold out the *Gazette* for weeks, the interest in the story being prolonged by the fact that Stead and Jarrett, despite precautions, were successfully prosecuted for abduction. Stead's series of articles, "The Maiden Tribute of Babylon," first appeared on 6 July 1885. Bernard Shaw had started contributing book reviews to the *Gazette* in May of that year. He took a keen interest in Stead's campaign, and even though he soon came to regret Stead's sensationalist approach to the issue, he nevertheless gave Stead his support, writing him that he would be "quite willing to take as many quires of the paper as I can carry and sell them (for a penny) in any thoroughfare in London." Whether Shaw actually did this is doubtful, but his attitude is clear.[14]

Shaw's play, *Mrs Warren's Profession*, may be viewed as a response to this public outcry—in the Preface Shaw specifically identifies Mrs. Warren's profession with "the White Slave Traffic" (p. 182)—and as an attempt ideologically to frame the ensuing debate that took place between reformists on how best to tackle this freshly exposed social issue.

The Liberal Response:
The Problem of Tainted Choices

> My principle has always been to let individuals alone, not to
> pursue them with any outward punishment . . . but to attack
> *organized* prostitution, that is when a third party, activated by the
> desire of making money, sets up a house in which women are
> sold to men.
>   —Josephine Butler[15]

Stead's newspaper, *The Pall Mall Gazette*, was closely associated with the
Liberal Party. Classical liberal ideology began as a protest against feudal
privilege. "Liberals criticized the political and economic privileges of the
landed aristocracy and the unfairness of a feudal system in which social
position was determined by mere 'accident of birth'."[16] This vein of protest
is continued in Stead's editorial. Angered by debates in the House of
Lords, where certain members objected to the pending (and much delayed) "Law Relating to the Protection of Young Girls" in terms of protect-
ing the "historic privileges of the upper-class rake,"[17] Stead fixed upon
the profligate aristocracy as the driving force behind the white slave trade.
Likewise, Josephine Butler was "scathing in her condemnation of the sexual proclivities of the privileged." "Without exception," observes Irwin,
Butler declared that "the destroyers of women were the aristocrats."[18]
   Stead's approach was also typically liberal in that he considered prostitution to be a private matter of contract between two consenting adults. John
Stuart Mill, for example, had famously argued in *On Liberty* (1859) that
"fornication" (a typical extension of the meaning of prostitution in the
mid-nineteenth century), while considered by society to be a "social evil,"
was basically "a case of self-regarding conduct," and therefore "must be
tolerated." Mill allowed, however, that pimping was a more complicated
issue.[19]
   The simple point of Stead's campaign, of course, was to ensure that both
consenting parties to this "contract" were, indeed, adults. Stead was careful not to give moral approval to prostitution. But should this choice be
made, despite wise counseling and frank discussions of sexual matters, then
the decision was regretful but legitimate, and no longer could be identified
as sexual slavery. "The streets," Stead insisted, "belong to the prostitute as
much as to the vestryman."[20] William Acton also reluctantly agreed that a
woman "if so disposed may make profit of her own person, and that the
State has no right to prevent her."[21]
   The Victorian sexologist, Havelock Ellis, attempted to make a similar
point by declaring that "the white slave traffic is not prostitution; it is the

commercialized exploitation of prostitutes. The independent prostitute, living alone, scarcely lends herself to the white trader. It is on houses of prostitution, where the less independent . . . prostitutes are segregated, that the traffic is based. Such houses cannot exist without such traffic. There is little inducement for a girl to enter such a house, in the full knowledge of what it involves, on her own initiative. The proprietors of such houses must, therefore, give orders for the 'goods' they desire, and it is the business of procurers by persuasion, misrepresentation, deceit, intoxication, to supply them."[22] The implication was that while "independent" prostitution is analogous to other forms of private enterprise, "white slave traffic" is akin to organized crime.

Finally, while liberal reformers were willing to acknowledge economic distress as part of the problem of prostitution, and, indeed, generally expected prostitutes to be recruited from the most financially hard-pressed sectors of society, they placed even greater stress on the importance of moral education. Their economic analysis typically terminated at the point of advocating changes that would somehow return these unfortunates to the status of ordinary, decent workers, often with a preference expressed for "training in domestic service and other forms of work that were subject to direct patriarchal supervision or parental discipline."[23]

Acton, for example, asked, "Is it any wonder that 'urged on by want and toil, encouraged by evil advisers, and exposed to selfish tempers, a large proportion of these poor girls fall from the path of virtue?' "[24] Poverty, in other words, precedes "the fall" by making these women vulnerable, but it is their moral weakness, their susceptibility to "evil advice" that is finally determining. Likewise, at the 1877 Geneva Conference on the "Abolition of Government Regulation of Prostitution," which was largely inspired by Josephine Butler, it was resolved, in classically liberal terms, that the "insufficiency of women's wages in industrial occupations" would be best remedied by the establishment of "equal laws, by the improvement of morals, by the abolition of regulated prostitution, and by the spread of general and professional education for women."[25]

This liberal position forms the basis of the discussion in Act II of Shaw's play. In Act I it had been established that Vivie Warren, while intelligent and resourceful, has remained quite innocent of her mother's profession although she is suspicious that something is being kept from her. In Act II, she takes advantage of the fact that her mother is visiting for a few days to confront her, asking pointedly, "Who is my father?" (p. 244). Mrs. Warren refuses to answer directly. Instead she launches into a harrowing account of her youth that provides some clue as to why the issue might be in doubt. Mrs. Warren confesses that while a teenager she became a prostitute, using the money she earned to go into partnership with her sister, Liz, in setting up in a "high class" brothel in Brussels (p. 248).

Here, Shaw is deliberately linking Mrs. Warren's fate to the wider scandal of the white slave trade. Her circumstances are not torn directly from the pages of Stead's articles, however. Kitty, although young at this time, was not legally under age, nor was she press-ganged or hoodwinked into prostitution. Clearly, Shaw is not interested in presenting Mrs. Warren in sensationalist terms that might lead his audience to sentimentalize over her. Kitty Warren made her own decisions, although admittedly not in circumstances of her own choosing. Her choices were tainted, limited to selecting among a variety of evils. The point Shaw wishes to stress, however, is that in her own untutored way Kitty was nonetheless abiding by cherished liberal principles when she finally decided to become a prostitute. As she explains in her own words,

> MRS WARREN: . . . Why shouldnt I have done it? The house in Brussels was . . . a much better place for a woman to be than in the factory where Anne Jane [Mrs. Warren's half-sister] got poisoned. None of our girls were ever treated as I was treated in the scullery of that temperance place, or at the Waterloo bar, or at home. Would you have me stay in them and become a worn out old drudge before I was forty?
> VIVIE: No; but why did you choose that business? Saving money and good management will succed in any business.
> MRS WARREN: Yes, saving money. But where can a woman get the money to save in any other business? . . . Do you think we were such fools as to let other people trade in our good looks by employing us as shopgirls, when we could trade in them ourselves and get all the profits instead of starvation wages? Not likely.
> VIVIE: You were certainly justified from a business point of view.
> MRS WARREN: Yes; or any other point of view. . . . Liz and I had to work and save just like other people. . . .
> VIVIE: Mother: suppose we were both as poor as you were in those wretched days, are you quite sure that you wouldnt advise me to try the Waterloo bar, or marry a laborer, or even go into the factory?
> MRS WARREN: Of course not. . . . How could you keep your self respect in such starvation and slavery? And whats a woman worth? whats life worth? without self respect! Why am I independent . . . when other women that had just as good opportunities are in the gutter? Because I always knew how to respect and control myself. . . . No: I never was a bit ashamed really. (pp. 248–51)

For Josephine Butler or Alfred Dyer, another noted investigator of the white slave trade, the fact that Mrs. Warren, even at the outset, avoided being held in bondage to a brothel owner or a pimp would have pointed up the inadequacy of Shaw's social analysis.[26] But the fact is, Shaw was not especially interested in depicting the very worst that prostitution could do to women. Instead, he was more concerned with examining specifically liberal arguments as to how an initial decision to enter the sex trade could be legitimized. And since all liberals were agreed that the condition of slavery could not be condoned, it follows that in order to explore those arguments, Mrs. Warren had to avoid that particular fate.

If it is allowed, however, that in some circumstances prostitution might represent a better alternative to work in "the whitelead factory," then Shaw's presentation of Mrs. Warren's preference falls into place. (This further suggests that Carpenter's aforementioned comment, that prostitution represents an ultimate example of the bartering of human lives, is too generalized. It might be true of the "enslaved" prostitute, but otherwise there were many "honest" working women, in Shaw's opinion, who faced worse conditions.) Mrs. Warren's decision is one of self-interest in precisely the sense lauded by liberals, namely, that given the alternatives, this is the decision that best preserves her self-respect and puts her most fully in control of her own life. ("I always knew how to respect myself and control myself.") In insisting upon controlling her own body, for example, rather than letting others trade in her "good looks" by "employing [her] as a shopgirl" to "get all the profits," Kitty Warren exhibits a fine sense of liberal proprietary rights. Moreover, in prospering as a prostitute, she has, ironically, developed certain of those Puritan instrumental values that were early associated with the development of liberalism. She is thrifty, calculating, hard working, and, although vulgar, not self-indulgent to the point of risking her savings or her investments. For "a poor girl," she informs her daughter, with delightful irony, prostitution is "far better than any other employment open to her" providing "she can resist temptation" (p. 250). Speaking on Mrs. Warren's behalf, Shaw even goes so far as to claim that her resort to prostitution was her best chance of keeping not only her "body" but also her "soul" together (p. 181). Finally, Mrs. Warren's own solution to the dilemmas she faced as a young woman is also typically liberal: "It cant be right, Vivie, that there shouldnt be better opportunities for women. I stick to that" (p. 250).

The Socialist Response:
The Problem of Tainted Money

. . . it is self-evident that the abolition of the present [capitalist] system of production must bring with it the abolition of the community of women springing from that system, that is, of prostitution both public and private.

—Marx and Engels, 1848[27]

When, in *The Origins of the Family, Private Property and the State* (1884),[28] Engels came to elaborate on his and Marx's earlier, brief comments on the condition of women, his focus, not surprisingly, was on private property relations as the determining factor. Thus, in the socialist analysis, the particular problem of prostitution is closely linked to the development of monogamy, which, in turn, is tied to the wider development of private wealth, inheritance, and the consequent need of men to constrict the powers and mobility of women in order to ensure otherwise unknowable lines of paternity. "In order," states Engels, "to guarantee the fidelity of the wife, that is the paternity of the children, the woman is placed in the man's absolute power" (p. 737). This "world historic defeat of mother right" (p. 736), however, is not accompanied by any real, compensating restriction on the male's freedom of sexual activity. A double standard of sexual propriety has thus "from the very beginning stamped on monogamy its specific character as monogamy only for the woman, but not for the man" (p. 746). It followed that prostitution must be viewed as a necessary outgrowth of monogamy, as "inseparable opposites, poles of the same social conditions . . ." (p. 746).

More particularly, the transformation of traditional hetaerism into commercial prostitution was to be seen as the product of monogamy's development within specifically capitalist commodity relationships, which increasingly put all social life, including sexual life, on a cash basis. From this vantage point, Engels further suggested that the selling of sexual favors is little different from the selling of other labor services characteristic of capitalism. Wage labor in general was likewise compelled by the circumstances created by private property ownership and in its own way was also dehumanizing and alienating. Much earlier, in *The Economic and Philosophic Manuscripts* (1844), Marx had suggested that "prostitution is only a specific expression of the general prostitution of the labourer."[29] Perhaps the supreme irony of this situation, as Engels noted in *Origins*, is that it is the married woman who most profoundly prostitutes herself, for unlike the professional prostitute and the day-laborer, who sell their services only on a piecemeal basis, the married woman "sells herself into slavery once for all" (p. 742).

Although Engels's work quickly became recognized as a classic within socialist circles, it did not address directly the particulars of the public debate on the white slave trade that was developing at its time of writing. That task fell to another noted socialist, August Bebel. Bebel's study, originally entitled *Woman and Socialism* (1879) but better known under its later title,

Women in the Past, Present and Future (1883), was fat on fact but thin on theory. In this regard, it is best viewed as a supplement to Engels's work. Only in the latter part of his book does Bebel attempt a distinctly socialist explanation, but then he does so in terms sufficiently abstract that it is largely left to the reader to make the connection between the general analysis and the particular conditions facing women, including prostitutes.

Nonetheless, these concluding chapters are significant because they give a sweep to Bebel's analysis similar to that found in Engels's account, which helps, in turn, to distinguish the socialist position from that of the liberal. Liberals, as already indicated, are alert to the connection between prostitution and economics. But this connection is seen as having limited explanatory value. Other distinct factors, like moral character, legislative initiatives, and so on, have to be taken into account. But for Engels and Bebel, morality is also class bound. And so is a nation's politics, its religion, and its law. This is not to say that economic factors rule absolutely, but they do significantly shape these other domains of social life. Moreover, having drawn a parallel between "sex-labor" and wage labor, it is also apparent that for the socialist the problem of prostitution cannot be treated in isolation. Liberal ameliorative action might reduce the number of prostitutes, but if they should return to the home, they would possibly face a patriarchal enslavement "worse than prostitution."[30] On the other hand, should they enter the factory and even receive "better payment" they would remain wage-slaves. Consequently, this would not "conquer" for them "their human status and dignity."[31] Clearly the socialist analysis points to the need for a much more radical undermining of market relationships than is contemplated by the liberal.

Shaw was knowledgeable about the works of both Engels, whom he had met personally,[32] and Bebel. Bebel's book had been serialized in Annie Besant's socialist magazine, *Our Corner,* at the same time as Shaw's novel *The Irrational Knot.*[33] Act III of *Mrs Warren's Profession* attempts the same kind of broadening of analysis that is apparent in these socialist works.

Vivie Warren has been temporarily appeased by her mother's description of the extenuating circumstances that led her into a life of prostitution. Indeed, she has declared her mother "stronger than all England" for resisting the taboos that would have prepared her for a slow death in the whitelead factory (p. 251). Act III opens with Frank viewing Vivie arm-in-arm with her mother, a sight that so alarms him that he feels compelled to warn Vivie that her mother is a "bad lot, a very bad lot" (p. 259). The transition from this kind of liberal moralizing to a more socialistic account that stresses not so much personal failings but the corruption of the social system as a whole is quickly effected, however, by Crofts's propositioning of Vivie.

Sir George Crofts is Mrs. Warren's business partner. (It would have pleased Stead and Butler that Shaw almost makes Crofts an aristocrat by giving him a baronetcy). Fittingly, his marriage proposal is entirely a business deal. He assures Vivie that he is "a safe man from the money point of view" and that the measure of his affection is that he will "pay hard money" for what he values (p. 261). Initially, Vivie is bemused by Crofts's bluntness, but when pressed is adamant in her refusal. Crofts, sensing Vivie's moral righteousness, decides to reveal the truth about her mother, namely that she is not, as Vivie had supposed, retired and living on her investments, but is still actively involved in running several Continental brothels, the profits from which have helped to pay for Vivie's education and upkeep. Enjoying the shock value of his revelation, Crofts next lectures Vivie on the "ways of the world," suggesting that beyond the issues of vice or virtue, business is business.

> VIVIE: My mother was a very poor woman who had no reasonable choice but to do as she did. You were a rich gentleman; and you did the same for the sake of 35 per cent. You are a pretty common sort of scoundrel, I think. That is my opinion of you.
> CROFTS: Ha! ha! ha! ha! Go it little missy, go it; it doesnt hurt me and it amuses you. Why the devil shouldnt I invest my money that way? I take the interest on my capital like other people: I hope you dont think I dirty my own hands with the work. Come! You wouldnt refuse the acquaintance of my mother's cousin the Duke of Belgravia because some of the rents he gets are earned in queer ways. You wouldnt cut the Archbishop, I suppose, because the Ecclesiastical Commissioners have a few publicans and sinners among their tenants. Do you remember your Crofts scholarship at Newnham? Well, that was founded by my brother the M.P. He gets 22 per cent out of a factory with 600 girls in it, and not one of them getting wages enough to live on. How d'ye suppose they manage when they have no family to fall back on? Ask your mother. And do you expect me to turn my back on 35 per cent when all the rest are pocketing what they can, like sensible men? No such fool! If youre going to pick and choose your acquaintances on moral principles, youd better clear out of this country. . . . As long as you dont fly openly in the face of society, society doesnt ask any inconvenient questions; and it makes precious short work of the cads who do. (pp. 264–65)

Here Shaw has used Crofts to illustrate an analysis as sweeping as is found in socialist indictments. Capitalist society offers no protected or privileged standpoint from which to judge others. Even those who are not investors or landlords, but must work in order to live, are compromised. Paralleling Marx's argument (above) that "prostitution is only a specific expression of the general prostitution of the labourer," Shaw, although with his middle-class sympathies suitably in evidence, likewise suggests that there exist "great prostitute classes of men: for instance, the playwrights and journal-ists, to whom I myself belong, not to mention the legions of lawyers, doc-tors, clergymen, and platform politicians who are daily using their highest faculties to belie their real sentiments" in order to make a living.[34] And in the play itself, Vivie's boyfriend, Frank, represents someone who is seeking marriage largely because, as he puts it, having "neither brains nor money," he had "better turn [his] good looks to account by marrying somebody with both" (p. 228). According to Shaw, marriage is a social institution spoiled by its capitalist integument: "All attractive unpropertied women," he opined, contract "marriages that are not more or less venal" than is prostitution (p. 181).

Capitalism thus operates as a totality, no part of which can be successfully reformed in isolation. As a Fabian, Shaw is not about to abandon reformist politics, but the long-term aim is not merely to tinker with the system but to transform it. At minimum, states Shaw, the reduction of market coercion would require "industries guarded by a humane industrial code and a 'moral minimum' wage"; ultimately, it would require the principle of "equality" to be established as the "permanent basis of social organiza-tion."[35]

A further implication of Shaw's analysis is that engaging in a specifically reformist socialist politics takes courage—a Fabian Realpolitik[36]—since the reformist is unable to delude himself or herself into thinking that he or she is somehow unaffected by the taint that attaches to everyone else in the system. This is why the system must be reformed from within rather than from without (for there is no real "without," no moral high ground), and will likely be changed in ways that are never purely successful or uncompro-mised.

Finally, this understanding of capitalism's complicity, although it may be faulted for lacking a definite point of determination, at least has the advan-tage of being one step up from a crude conspiracy theory, to which certain other early socialist organizations were prone, including the Social Demo-cratic Federation, which in the 1890s was viewed as a rival of the Fabian Society. Shaw's analysis requires of capitalists not wide-eyed collusion and evil intent, but mere selective cognizance and truncated sympathy, which is a much more plausible understanding of the workings of social power. As Shaw remarks in the play's preface, when these various groupings are added together "you get a large and powerful class with a strong pecuniary interest to protect Mrs Warren's profession, and a correspondingly strong incentive to conceal, *even from their own consciences* . . . the real sources of their gain" (p. 208).

The Radical Feminist Perspective:
The Problem of Tainted Sexuality

> Intelligent women are revolted by men's commerce with white
> Slaves. It makes them regard men as inferiors. . . . The disparity
> between the moral standards of men and women is more and
> more destroying women's respect and regard for men.
> —Christabel Pankhurst, 1913[37]

In the final Act, Vivie has fled from both Crofts and her mother ("the
unmentionable woman and her capitalist bully" [p. 266]) and has entered
a business partnership with her friend, Honoria Fraser. The major event of
Act IV is a second confrontation between Vivie and her mother. Mrs. Warren has arrived at Vivie's office seeking reconciliation. As a mother she
attempts to convince Vivie that she still has her daughter's best interests at
heart. She wants to make connections with "the big people, the clever people, the managing people" on Vivie's behalf (p. 282). She also wants Vivie
to continue accepting an allowance from her, which Vivie has refused to
do since becoming aware that her mother is still in the prostitution business despite the fact that her circumstances no longer require this sorry
choice.

Vivie is unimpressed. She has no interest in the idle, fashionable life
that her mother is offering. She is also unmoved, dismissing her mother's
entreaties as "a few cheap tears." Nor is she to be pressured into feelings
of familial duty. To her mother's plea—"I want my daughter. Ive a right to
you. Who is to take care of me when I'm old?"—Vivie simply replies, "I
dont want a mother" and bids her good-bye, forever (p. 284).

The coldness, even cruelty, of Vivie's response has perplexed many commentators. The reason for her disavowing her mother is not clear. Later,
Shaw himself felt compelled to explain her behavior as an unthinking,
purely emotional reaction to her mother's past neglect, to which she now
responds in kind. Shaw likely took some delight in knowing that his own
authorial imprimatur would not be held credible by most of the critics
who knew his plays (p. 199).[38] Even the few, like Eric Bentley, who were
sympathetic to this kind of interpretation, cautioned that although the reaction might be emotional, it was in all probability not pure in the way
Shaw implied. Bentley suggests that in this final scene Shaw was subconsciously rejecting his own neglectful mother, whom he blamed for his feelings of desolation.[39]

One issue is clear, however. It is not socialist principle that motivates
Vivie. Shaw does not, for example, send Vivie to work among the poor, as

he was later to send Barbara Undershaft to London's East End to work at a Salvation Army shelter.[40] Barbara has to learn through bitter experience about capitalism's complicity. But Vivie, perhaps because she is not "burdened" with Barbara's missionary zeal, seems quickly to adjust to Crofts's lessons on the ways of the world and goes ahead with her plans to go into business with Honoria Fraser. Her actuarial work, while not unseemly like her mother's brothels, nonetheless will be a part of what Shaw condemns as capitalism's "anarchical scramble for money."[41] Vivie's profession thus offers little defense against charges of hypocrisy, if it is the case, as is often alleged, that her renunciation of her mother is founded on the fact that the capitalist enterprise of Crofts and Warren continues as a money-making operation. (Additional support for this contention that Vivie's profession provides no safe moral haven also might be found in Shaw's prefatory remarks on gambling. Shaw describes gambling "as a moral evil" worse than prostitution, where bookmakers "play the odds" in order to try "to get other people's money without working for it" [p. 202]. Actuarial work might be considered an akin form of risk calculation.)

Significantly, then, the socialist perspective has no agent within the setting of the play. Vivie, who is initially stunned by Crofts's revelations as to capitalism's workings—"I feel among the damned," she confesses (p. 266)—does undergo a change of outlook, but she does not become a socialist as a result. For a brief moment she wishes that she had the "courage" to "spend the rest of [her] life in telling everybody—stamping and branding it into them until they feel their part in its abomination," but she admits such cause-fighting is not within her (p. 275). Vivie's own resolution of her problem is more personal, but in its implications, no less political.

A clue to the real source of Vivie's anguish is provided in an earlier scene when Vivie is visited by Frank. Frank has come to tell her that he is not, as Crofts had insinuated, her half-brother (a plot complication that is not a concern here). This fact, however, falls flat since Vivie apparently never took Crofts's goading seriously. Moreover, it quickly transpires that Vivie has no intention of marrying Frank, nor, indeed, of ever marrying (p. 284). In an earlier draft of the play Shaw had been even more explicit, giving to Vivie the lines, "Frank was the most unbearable thought of all, for I knew that he would force on me the sort of relation that my mother's life had tainted for ever for me. I felt that I would rather die than let him touch me with that in his mind."[42]

In this regard, the fact that Vivie has her own career and income becomes especially significant. Earlier arguments condemning marriage (and wage labor) as a form of legalized prostitution had insisted that such contracts were the product of women's economic vulnerability. But this is not Vivie's situation. The socialist indictment is not directly relevant to her particular case. In his "Biographers' Blunders Corrected," Shaw himself indirectly concedes this point when he comments,

> When Mrs Warren says that "the only way for a woman to provide for herself decently is for her to be good to some man that can afford to be good to her" she includes marriage, as you say; but she also points out that women with lucrative talents are independent of both marriage and prostitution as means of obtaining something better than a starvation wage. But this is only because exceptional talents have a scarcity value.[43]

Vivie is one of these "exceptional talents." Why, then, her refusal to marry? Why has she chosen to isolate herself, "for the rest of [her] life" in her Chancery Lane office, preparing for a life where "there is no beauty and no romance" (pp. 267, 273)? What makes this decision comprehensible is to recognize that Vivie has become aware that prostitution, above and beyond any liberal or socialist considerations, is the crystallization of male/female relations, putting into high relief men's pervasive and persistent desire to dominate women. Such domination ultimately spoils any contract (even one she might have struck with the seemingly genial Frank) and goes deeper than any situation of "mere" economic inequality. Looking back on the white slave trade, Emma Goldman had come to a similar conclusion: "Nowhere is woman treated according to the merit of her work, but rather as a sex. It is therefore almost inevitable that she should pay for her right to exist . . . with sex favors."[44] To which Kathleen Barry, a present-day feminist, has added the interesting observation that "unlike other institutions, in prostitution and marriage there is no one place where collective protest against these institutions can be lodged. Instead, through the colonization of women they permeate the whole society in individual relationships."[45] This, too, seems to be Vivie's conclusion.

In this light, Vivie's otherwise somewhat puzzling parting jibe at her mother, that she is "a conventional woman at heart" who has "lived one life and believed in another" (p. 286), becomes clearer. Mrs. Warren is not conventional in the same sense as is her sister Liz. She loves "work and excitement" too much to be a lady in a cathedral town (p. 283). Vivie acknowledges this. Consequently, this cannot be the point of her criticism. Mrs. Warren, no doubt, is being more conventional in wanting her daughter to live the life of a lady, even if she cannot, and perhaps in her "saying one thing and doing another" there may be found an element of the hypocrisy to which Vivie alludes. But this hardly seems to warrant Vivie's contempt. However, if it is appreciated that in her youth Mrs. Warren had railed against the power that men exercised over women, yet ultimately has engaged in a business the very purpose of which is to surrender women to men for a price, Vivie's disgust becomes more comprehensible. Here Mrs. Warren's living one life while believing in another is not merely evidence of misplaced motherly concern, but perpetuates the very system of patriarchy that will disempower her daughter despite her education and her middle-class advantages.

Like the modern-day radical feminist, Vivie seems to be struggling toward an understanding of gender as "the most fundamental of all social divisions . . . not only in politics and public life or in the economy, but in all aspects of social, personal and sexual existence"[46] Against this kind of male drive to domination, Vivie's income and career offer little protection. Hence Frank, who represents patriarchy's threat to her personal life, and Mrs. Warren, who represents patriarchy's public, albeit seamy, presence, are both banished by her.

Such separation, however, is only a negative act, and there is, despite Vivie's defiant attitude at the very close of the play, a sense of loss. The resolution of Vivie's dilemma is not part of the play. Nor is it clear that Shaw had a resolution in view. He is not willing to contemplate lesbianism, or even homosocial lifestyles, as a solution. It is doubtful, for example, that Vivie's mannish behavior in the opening Act is meant to carry this implication. But with no other options even hinted at Shaw seems to be at an impasse. In fairness to Shaw, it must be acknowledged that radical feminism, which has remained troubled to this day by the politics of separatism,[47] was, at the turn of the century, a fledgling doctrine, offering to Shaw little that was of substance. The historian Elizabeth Sarah has described radical feminist views during this period as "a sporadic and isolated impulse."[48] Shaw was thus unavoidably experimenting here. Once he had sensed the idea, however, he seemed to be at a loss as to how to develop it. Ultimately, it was a line of thought he chose not to pursue. *Mrs Warren's Profession* was, in fact, the last of his "Plays Unpleasant." Thereafter, while the battle of the sexes is continued in his plays, even to the point, arguably, of eclipsing earlier socialist themes, he never again allowed any of his heroines an honorable retreat to an office of her own.

Notes

1. Emma Goldman, "The Traffic in Women," in Alix Kates Shulman, ed., *Emma Goldman: The Traffic in Women and Other Essays on Feminism* (Ojai, Calif.: Times Change Press, 1970), p. 20.

2. Charles Carpenter, *Bernard Shaw and the Art of Destroying Ideals: The Early Plays* (Madison: University of Wisconsin Press, 1969), p. 49.

3. Melinda Corey and George Ochoa, *Encyclopedia of the Victorian World* (New York: Henry Holt, 1996).

4. Linda Mahood, *The Magdalenes: Prostitution in the Nineteenth Century* (London: Routledge, 1990), p. 53.

5. See Herbert Tingsten, *Victoria and the Victorians* (London: George Allen & Unwin, 1972), pp. 67–68.

6. William Burgess, *The World's Social Evil* (Chicago: Saul Brothers, 1914), p. 29.

7. Ibid., p. 21.

8. Statement of the Ladies National Association, 31 December 1869, quoted in Kathleen Barry, *Female Sexual Slavery* (Englewood Cliffs, N.J.: Prentice Hall, 1979), p. 14.

9. August Bebel, *Woman in the Past, Present and Future* (London: Zwan, 1988), pp. 94–95. First published 1879.

10. Bernard Shaw, Preface to *Mrs Warren's Profession*, in *Plays Unpleasant* (Harmondsworth, Middlesex: Penguin, 1982), p. 184. Subsequent citations from this play (1893) and its preface (1902) are from this edition and appear parenthetically in the text.

11. See Bramwell Booth, *Echoes and Memories* (London: Hodder & Stoughton, 1925), and Barry, *Female Sexual Slavery*, ch. 2.

12. See Mary Ann Irwin, " 'White Slavery' as a Metaphor: Anatomy of a Moral Panic," in *Ex Post Facto: The Journal of the History Students Association, San Francisco State University* 5 (1996): 7. Accessed at www.sfsu.edu/~hsa/wslavery

13. Ibid., pp. 19–20.

14. See Michael Holroyd, *Bernard Shaw, Vol. 1: 1856–1898, The Search for Love* (London: Chatto & Windus, 1988), p. 290.

15. Quoted in Barry, *Female Sexual Slavery*, p. 25. Emphasis in the original.

16. Andrew Heywood, *Political Ideologies* (London: Macmillan, 1992), p. 16.

17. Irwin, " 'White Slavery' as a Metaphor," p. 8.

18. Ibid., p. 14.

19. J. S. Mill, *On Liberty* (Harmondsworth, Middlesex: Penguin, 1974), p. 169.

20. Irwin, " 'White Slavery' as a Metaphor," p. 19.

21. Steven Marcus, *The Other Victorians* (New York: W.W. Norton, 1974), p. 5.

22. Quoted in Burgess, *World's Social Evil*, p. 76.

23. Mahood, *Magdalenes*, p. 73.

24. Marcus, *Other Victorians*, p. 7.

25. Josephine Butler, *Personal Reminiscences of a Great Crusade* (London: Hyperion, 1976), p. 171. First published 1911. See also Burgess, *World's Social Evil*, pp. 231–32.

26. But see Nicky Roberts, *Whores in History* (London: HarperCollins, 1992). Roberts claims, as against these contemporary accounts but more in line with Shaw's position, that even though brothel whores "had to pay outrageously inflated prices for clothes, make-up, hairdressing and other facilitites," they still "enjoyed a better standard of living than their sisters in 'honest' work" (p. 237).

27. Karl Marx and Friedrich Engels, "Manifesto of the Communist Party" (1848), in R. Tucker, *The Marx-Engels Reader* (New York: W. W. Norton, 1978), p. 488.

28. Reprinted in Tucker, *Marx-Engels Reader*, p. 737. All subsequent citations are from this edition and appear parenthetically in the text.

29. Karl Marx, "The Economic and Philosophic Manuscripts," in Tucker, *Marx-Engels Reader*, p. 82.

30. Bebel, *Woman in the Past*, p. 55.

31. Marx, "Economic and Philosophic Manuscripts," p. 80.

32. Michael Holroyd, *Bernard Shaw, Vol 3: 1918–1950, The Lure of Fantasy* (New York: Random House, 1991), p. 484.

33. Holroyd, *Shaw*, vol. 1, p. 290.

34. Shaw, Preface to *Plays Unpleasant* (1898), pp. 26–27.

35. Ibid., pp. 27, 7.

36. See John Allett, "Bernard Shaw and Dirty Hands Politics," *Journal of Social Philosophy* 26: 2 (Fall 1995): 32–45.

37. Christabel Pankhurst, "The Government and the White Slavery" (1913), quoted in Barry, *Female Sexual Slavery*, p. 31.

38. The preface was written in 1902, almost a decade after the play.

39. Eric Bentley, *Bernard Shaw* (Toronto: Fitzhenry & Whiteside, 1985), p. 179.

40. See Bernard Shaw, *Major Barbara* (Harmondsworth, Middlesex: Penguin, 1960), First performed 1905.

41. Shaw, Preface to *Plays Unpleasant*, p. 7.

42. Nicholas Grene, *Bernard Shaw: A Critical View* (New York: St. Martin's Press, 1982), p. 160.

43. Bernard Shaw, *Sixteen Self Sketches* (London: Constable, 1949), p. 101.

44. Goldman, "Traffic in Women," p. 20.

45. Barry, *Female Sexual Slavery*, p. 230.

46. Heywood, *Political Ideologies*, p, 235.

47. See Marilyn French, *Beyond Power: On Women, Men and Morals* (New York: Summit Books, 1985), pp. 446–48.

48. Elizabeth Sarah, "Female Performers on a Male Stage: The First Women's Liberation Movement and the Authority of Men, 1890–1930," in S. Friedman and E. Sarah, eds., *On the Problem of Men* (London: The Women's Press, 1982), p. 150.

Sidney P. Albert

EVANGELIZING THE GARDEN CITY?

> GBS's play turned out to be a dance of devils—amazingly clever,
> grimly powerful in the second act, but ending as all his plays end
> (or at any rate most of them) in an intellectual and moral
> morass. A.J. B[alfour] was taken aback by the force, the horrible
> force of the Salvation Army scene, the unrelieved tragedy of
> degradation, the disillusionment of the Greek professor and of
> Barbara—the triumph of the unmoral purpose, the anti-climax
> of evangelizing the Garden City! I doubt the popular success of
> the play. It is hell tossed on the stage, with no hope of heaven.
> —Beatrice Webb[1]

Beatrice Webb's abhorrent reaction to *Major Barbara*, as recorded in her
diary, has frequently been quoted in connection with this drama. Although
ostensibly attributed to the Prime Minister, the assessments are plainly hers
as well. Her evangelizing allegation alludes to the Garden City movement
that was burgeoning in the period immediately preceding the writing of
Major Barbara in 1905. The movement emerged from a century during
which an array of proposals for model communities—both utopian and
concrete projects—flourished. It culminated, in 1903 and 1904, in the establishment of an experimental Garden City at Letchworth in the county
of Hertfordshire where Shaw was living at the time (at The Old House,
Harmer Green, Welwyn) and where he established residence permanently
a year or so later (at Ayot St. Lawrence). The movement went on to attain
international importance in the subsequent thinking of city planners and
urban sociologists.

The problem of housing had long occupied Bernard Shaw, an interest
that found expression in his first play, *Widowers' Houses*, completed in 1892.
Mrs. Webb undoubtedly was aware that, unlike other Fabians, Shaw was by
no means inimical to the Garden City movement. Hence the venting of her
moral ire, based on her conviction that Shaw, in his presentation of Andrew

Undershaft's armament factory community of Perivale St. Andrews, was portraying a Garden City and "evangelizing" it—spreading its gospel. But are her contentions warranted? Is it true that Perivale St. Andrews is a Garden City? And does *Major Barbara* really preach the gospel of the Garden City?

Germane to a search for satisfactory answers to these questions are an examination of the Garden City conception in its nineteenth-century evolution and a comparison of the products of that evolving notion with what is said about the town of Perivale St. Andrews in the play.

The problem of providing adequate community housing harks back at least to Plato's design of an ideal city, modeled on a heavenly pattern, which inspired the Stoic and Christian idea of a city of God. A whole tradition of Utopias proceeded from this beginning: "From Plato and the man who saw the city 'descending out of heaven from God' to St. Augustine's *De Civitate Dei*, from Sir Thomas More and Campanella's *City of the Sun* to the day before yesterday, when the latest idealist described the city of tomorrow, men have imagined some beautiful and well governed city in which they could live the whole term of their lives in happiness and peace."[2] The continuity of Perivale St. Andrews with that tradition becomes immediately evident with Cusins's exuberant introduction of the factory town in the third act of *Major Barbara*: "Everything perfect! wonderful! real! It only needs a cathedral to be a heavenly city instead of a hellish one." Lady Britomart's report of the presence of the William Morris Labor Church disposes of that deficiency. Hence Cusins's response, "Oh! It needed only that. A Labor Church!"[3] Still, Shaw has furnished relatively spare concrete details about Perivale St. Andrews. Some of these are sketched in the stage directions at the opening of the scene:

> *Perivale St. Andrews lies between two Middlesex hills, half climbing the northern one. It is an almost smokeless town of white walls, roofs of narrow green slates or red tiles, tall trees, domes, campaniles, and slender chimney shafts, beautifully situated and beautiful in itself. The best view of it is obtained from the crest of a slope about half a mile to the east, where the high explosives are dealt with. The foundry lies hidden in the depths between, the tops of the chimneys sprouting like huge skittles into the middle distance. Across the crest runs an emplacement of concrete, with a fire-step and a parapet which suggests a fortification, because there is a huge cannon of the obsolete Woolwich Infant pattern peering across it at the town.* (157)

In the previous scene Undershaft had pictured it as "a spotlessly clean and beautiful hillside town" with two Methodist chapels, "a Primitive one and a sophisticated one," and a poorly patronized Ethical Society (154). It also had the aforementioned William Morris Labor Church. Other particulars emerge in the wave of overwhelmingly laudatory reactions by Undershaft's guests to their first encounter with the place, introduced by Cusins's salute to it. Their responses are reminiscent of the ejaculations of surprise and discovery that attend the utterances of visitors arriving at a Utopia. Their successive paeans to the place reveal that the town has a nursing home, libraries, schools, a Town Hall with a ballroom and banqueting chamber, a splendid restaurant serving inexpensive meals, and, among its economic benefactions, a pension fund, a building society, and "various applications of co-operation." Stephen Undershaft finds it all a "triumph of modern industry." He is struck by "the wonderful forethought, the power of organization, the administrative capacity, the financial genius, the colossal capital it represents." To Cusins "it's all horribly, frightfully, immorally, unanswerably perfect." Lady Britomart, uninterested in the "ridiculous cannons" and the "noisy banging foundry," lays claim to the orchards, gardens, and houses with their furniture, kitchen ranges, linen, and china (162). Undershaft arrests their escalating ardor with a stark reminder of the peril posed by the precarious industrial foundation of the town: "A sufficient dose of anxiety is always provided by the fact that we may be blown to smithereens at any moment" (160). This arcadia houses a munitions factory as well as its workers. If it be a model town, it certainly is one fraught with explosive potential.

The rash of utopias and proposals for urban reform that burst forth in the nineteenth century reflected, as prospective cures, the ailments that plagued English community life as it underwent rapid urbanization in the wake of changes wrought by the Industrial Revolution. In the course of a century, the population of England grew from ten million to thirty-seven million.[4] Congestion, dirt, squalor, and ugliness infected the cities and spread to the suburbs and surrounding country. "A blight that had its origin in England's dark Satanic mills, as William Blake called them, laid its diseased fingers on the new cities and stultified the further development of the old ones."[5]

William Morris, in his 1884 lectures on "Art and Socialism," vividly described this blight:

> The spreading sore of London, swallowing up, with its loathsomeness, field and wood and heath . . . mocking our feeble efforts to deal even with its minor evils of smoke laden sky and befouled river; the black horror and reckless squalor of our manufacturing districts; . . . not only are London and other great commercial cities mere masses of sordidness, filth, and squalor . . . ; not only have whole counties of England, and the heavens that hang over them, disappeared beneath a crust of unutterable grime, but the disease . . . spreads out all over the country. . . .[6]

Compare Undershaft's indictment in Act III of *Major Barbara*: "Poverty blights whole cities; spreads horrible pestilences; strikes dead the very souls of all who come within sight, sound, or smell of it. . . . [T]here are millions of poor people, abject people, dirty people, ill fed, ill clothed people. They poison us morally and physically: they kill the happiness of society . . ." (172). Small wonder, then, that "about two-thirds of our utopias should have been written in the nineteenth century," a century that Shaw judged to be "on the whole, perhaps the most villainous page of recorded human history."[7] These utopias, along with a number of concrete schemes for town-building and the actual establishment of model towns by several industrialists, form the nineteenth-century backdrop for the Garden City movement.

As early as 1801 Thomas Spence published *The Constitution of Spensonia, A Country in Fairyland Situated Between Utopia and Oceania*, a work advocating a program in which all land would become public property, with houses and workshops built at public expense. Another pioneer was the socialist Robert Owen, who influenced many of the early Fabians, including Shaw, and who has been called "the earliest contributor to the housing movement."[8] As manager and partner in large cotton mills at New Lanark, near Glasgow, he built a successful model industrial village, then went on to offer plans for creating "Villages of Co-operation" that were to engage in both agriculture and industry. Owen's attempts to have his theories put into practice in Scotland and in the United States foundered. But this utopian prophet of the practical and exponent of unpopular and unsuccessful causes left a lasting legacy, for "he played a decisive part in the beginnings of almost every valuable development of the age."[9]

James Silk Buckingham in his *National Evils and Practical Remedies*, published in 1849, included a design for a modern town, to be called "Victoria" after the young queen. His elaborate proposal, which anticipated the idea of a Garden City, included founding a Model Town Association that would build a community in keeping with the latest discoveries in architecture and science and maintain a balance between the agricultural and manufacturing classes.[10]

Edward Gibbon Wakefield's *Art of Colonization* (1849), combining some of the ideas of Owen and his predecessors, proposed a systematic approach to colonizing in distant lands by having communities organized from the beginning to perform all necessary urban functions.[11] In 1875 Sir Benjamin Ward Richardson (1828–96), a physician interested in sanitary reform, submitted an outline of an utopian city called *Hygeia*, in which the mortality rate could be reduced to a minimum. Applying scientific theories of his day, he made provision for efficient sanitation, gardens to help space houses, glazed bricks instead of germ-carrying materials, and kitchens at the top of houses with all smoke fully consumed.[12]

In contrast to these untried or unsuccessful schemes, a number of industrialists did in fact build model towns, at least two of which were known to Shaw, whose fictional Perivale St. Andrews is itself the project of a successful manufacturing firm. The first industrial settlement, felicitously, had a literary inspiration. Benjamin Disraeli, in his novel *Sybil*, first published in 1845, described a marvelous rural factory built by an opulent Mr. Trafford, who adjoined to it an attractive village surrounded by gardens, where he himself resided. The example of Disraeli's philanthropic employer directly animated Titus Salt, a mill owner who had made a fortune as the first manufacturer of alpaca fabrics. The earliest industrialist in Britain to establish a model factory, he also erected a model village near his "palace of industry" mill, with dwellings designed to be "a pattern to the country." The factory village was built on a site chosen "for the beauty of the situation and the salubrity of its air." Eight hundred well-constructed houses, with rent within the means of working people, were built for a population of three thousand. The place was named Saltaire.[13]

A dominant feature of the factory was a 250-foot chimney that became an outstanding landmark, giving "the effect of a bell tower or an Italian campanile." Fuel economizers were installed in the flue to remove "all annoying effluvium." At the official opening of "the Works" it was compared to "a fortified town, rather than a building destined to the peaceful pursuits of commerce." Attention was also called to "the long line of underground boilers which lie smouldering, as it were, at the foot of this huge commercial temple." Among the village buildings were a Congregational Church, a Wesleyan Chapel, factory schools, an infirmary, and a fourteen-acre recreational park adorned with two 32-pounder guns.

Unlike Robert Owen, whose plans miscarried in large measure because of his boldly expressed opposition to religion and divorce, the respectable Titus Salt, a Nonconformist Congregationalist, made provision for his employees to have places of worship of their own preference. He granted sites for chapels to the Wesleyans, the Primitive Methodists, the Baptists, and the Roman Catholics, and a room for meetings to the Swedenborgians. The paternalistic employer was willing to allow his employees to embrace a variety of beliefs, provided they were religious beliefs, but he did prohibit public houses, for which the Saltaire Club and Institute, a sort of community center, was to substitute. The entire populace of Saltaire was thoroughly dependent upon the philanthropic factory owner, but he apparently enjoyed considerable public esteem. "Perhaps no manufacturer of his time made so deep an impression on his employees or was so respected," Cecil Stewart reports.[14]

Notwithstanding the apparent absence of any mention of Sir Titus Salt in Shaw's writings, Saltaire is suggestive of Perivale St. Andrews in a remarkable number of respects. There are its scenic beauty, the campanile-like chimney, the smoke removal, the comparison to a fortified town, the guns, the underground boilers, the schools, the infirmary, and the variety of churches. The Primitive and Wesleyan Methodist churches, in particular, correspond to the Primitive and "sophisticated" Methodist chapels in Undershaft's city.

There is a further parallel that a summary judgment by Stewart brings to the fore: "Salvation, education, and sanitation, these three, seem to dominate descriptions of Saltaire, and if the greatest of these three is not sanitation, it is at least an important member of the trinity." Indeed, preoccupation with sanitation came to characterize prevailing conceptions of model communities in the nineteenth century: "It was not without significance that the eighteenth century saw the invention of the first valve watercloset, the widespread use of the handkerchief and the general adoption of the fork to supplement the knife and spoon. The Utopias that were to come in the end were all Utopias of spartan simplicity; Buckingham's Victoria, Owen's New Lanark, Salt's Saltaire and the rest, were all dominated by ideas of equalitarianism and efficient plumbing."[15] Apposite is this spirited exchange in *Major Barbara*:

> BARBARA. . . . [*Turning on him with sudden vehemence*] Justify yourself: shew me some light through the darkness of this dreadful place, with its beautifully clean workshops, and respectable workmen, and model homes.
> UNDERSHAFT. Cleanliness and respectability do not need justification, Barbara: they justify themselves. I see no darkness here, no dreadfulness. In your Salvation shelter I saw poverty, misery, cold and hunger. You gave them bread and treacle and dreams of heaven. I give from thirty shillings a week to twelve thousand a year. They find their own dreams; but I look after the drainage.
> BARBARA. And their souls?
> UNDERSHAFT. I save their souls just as I saved yours. (171)

Undershaft attends here both to sanitation and to salvation, essaying to preempt Barbara's special concern with the latter. Education, the third member of the trinity, is of course personified by Cusins, who is, additionally, an egalitarian.

In the absence of any direct evidence that Shaw patterned Undershaft's community after the city of Salt, these marked similarities may be no more than coincidences. Yet an indirect connection is possible, for Saltaire led to other kindred projects. As Mumford puts it, "the work of Sir Titus Salt at Saltaire, in the eighteen-fifties, paved the way for later settlements such as those of Krupp at Essen, Cadbury at Bourneville [*sic*], and Lever at Port Sunlight."[16]

Bournville and Port Sunlight, founded by George Cadbury and Sir William Lever, respectively, were the best known of the model towns established by industrialist reformers. In 1879 George and Richard Cadbury moved their growing chocolate and cocoa factory from Birmingham to a country site nearby. There they undertook to provide well-built cottages, not—as in the case of Saltaire and Port Sunlight—exclusively for the firm's employees, but for working people in and around Birmingham as well. The venture came to include hospitals, schools, technical schools, libraries, recreational facilities, and parks, all enhanced by a pension fund and sickness benefits.

Their factory, however, built in 1879, has no significant resemblance to Undershaft's, nor do the Bournville bungalows—built chiefly of red brick, with rough-cast and half-timbered walls, green slates, and red tiles[17]— precisely match the houses of Perivale St. Andrews, whose roofs are also of green slate and red tile, but whose walls are white, not red. Bournville did have a Friends' Meeting House, its first ecclesiastical building, erected in 1905, the year of *Major Barbara*'s composition, and a Musical Society with a band, orchestra, and choir.[18] Thus, while as model towns Bournville and Perivale St. Andrews do have several institutions and a few physical characteristics in common, their similitude is unexceptional.

During the period of Bournville's development, its counterpart, Port Sunlight, entered the scene. In 1887 William Hesketh Lever (afterward Viscount Leverhulme) purchased land in the vicinity of Liverpool as a new location for his soap works and set about building, as a form of profit-sharing, a model village that he named Port Sunlight, after the "Sunlight Soap" that the Lever Brothers firm manufactured. It was the autocratic Lever himself who laid out the basic plans of Port Sunlight. Of him, one biographer writes, "In all Lever's enterprises an impatient, tumultuous, raging energy took hold of him at ever-increasing tempo to the end of his life, and which generally scared everyone around him."[19]

The standard of working and living conditions at Port Sunlight was high. There were inexpensive restaurants as well as separate social clubs for men and women. Diverse cultural and recreational facilities were available, including a library, a theater, and a concert hall. Voluntary societies promoted interest in literature and art as well as in dramatic and musical performances. Lever gave encouragement to the Philharmonic Society in the village despite having practically no ear for music, unlike the fictional Undershaft, who played the trombone in "the Undershaft orchestral society," a comparable organization.

Christ Church, a Gothic building of dark red sandstone, opened in 1902 as a virtually nondenominational village church, reflecting Lever's conviction of the futility of theological dispute. The congregation included Anglicans, Nonconformists, Unitarians, and some agnostics. In typically un-

orthodox fashion Lever had a well-known radical clergyman and member
of the Independent Labour Party placed in charge of the church. All the
same, a minister who once nested there confessed, "I sometimes feel that
I am intended to be an advertisement for Sunlight Soap more than for the
Kingdom of God."[20] Although the soap works were concealed from view at
one end of Port Sunlight, its presence, like that of its paternalistic owner,
was pervasive. Palpably "the spirit of soap" dominated the whole village.
As an admiring associate reported, "You could no more escape from its
influence than from the odour (not at all an unpleasant one) permeating
it from the factory plant."[21] A different perspective was afforded by a union
official, who wrote, "No man of an independent turn of mind can breathe
for long the atmosphere of Port Sunlight. . . . The profit-sharing system not
only enslaves and degrades the workers, it tends to make them servile and
sycophant. . . ."[22]

Soap and munitions differ as industrial products, yet the inhabitants of
Perivale St. Andrews, like those of Port Sunlight, are persistently reminded
of their relation to the kind of commercial enterprise in which they are
engaged. Moreover, Undershaft intimates that the armaments he makes
have ablutionary properties. In the first act, contending that the Salvation
Army's motto, "Blood and Fire," could be his own, he declares, "My sort
of blood cleanses: my sort of fire purifies" (88). His Act III assertions about
cleanliness have already been noted in connection with the Saltaire paral-
lels. Again, each industrial domain was dominated by a powerful big business baron (with a relatively quiet partner) whose dynamic and forceful
personality established its firm impress on the factory town. Of the two,
Lever would appear to have been the less artful in his control: "Powerful,
and in many ways subtle, as Lever's mind was, he was perhaps at his weakest
in dealing with the finer shades of human rights and preferences, and . . .
the problems of social relationships which were involved. Nothing could
disguise the fact that benevolent as the scheme was, it was despotic benevo-
lence." To some extent the subsequent history of the enterprise mitigated
this judgment: "The Port Sunlight experiment was a bold venture, a conception with vision, imagination and a genuine concern for human welfare. Its gains were great and its influence beneficial."[23]

Concurrently, a succession of less prominent model industrial villages
sprang up in England and on the Continent. In Delft a leading Dutch
industrialist and social reformer, van Marken, set up a model village along
the lines of Port Sunlight.[24] Cocoa and chocolate manufacturers, in particular, appear to have been stirred into action to provide improved living quar-
ters for their employees. Those in England who undertook these
enterprises were, like Cadbury, Quakers. Whether emulating his example
or joining the growing Garden City movement, a spate of what might be
called "chocolate cities" were added to the model housing menu at this

time. One of these, the Joseph Rowntree Village Trust, founded in December 1904, established the attractive Garden City of New Earswick, near the Rowntree cocoa works, in the vicinity of the city of York.[25] As an adjunct to their large chocolate factory, Messrs. Russ, Suchard et Cie. built a garden village known as Serrières on the shores of Lake Neuchâtel in Switzerland.[26] In France the Messrs. Menier constructed the model village of Noisiel, near Paris, adjacent to their cocoa and chocolate factory.[27] In the United States in 1903, chocolatier Milton S. Hershey developed the privately owned community of Hershey, Pennsylvania, as a chocolate manufacturing utopia. Unabashedly designating two of its first streets Chocolate Avenue and Cocoa Avenue, he furnished the town with worker homes, a hotel, an electric street-railway, a pavilion in a park, restaurants, a lake, new schools, a zoo, baseball and football teams, a band, and an amusement park.[28]

But Perivale St. Andrews is linked to a factory that produces not chocolate, but steel for armaments. Comparable communal programs in businesses like Undershaft's did in fact then exist on the continent and very likely were known to Shaw. In 1900 the Labour Co-partnership Association in London published *Twenty Years of Co-partnership at Guise*, an English translation of a small French book publicizing the industrial community of Jean Baptiste André Godin at Guise in France.[29] Godin (1817–88), a steel manufacturer, modeled his settlement on the theories of Charles Fourier, which in turn reflected the ideas of Robert Owen. Godin's cooperative social organization, the Familistère, was, according to Mumford, "one of the first efforts at collective workers' housing *and* community building."[30] Convinced that the "capitalist has no moral right to use his fortune for personal aggrandizement," Godin was credited with showing "*practically that it pays the capitalist, in a pecuniary sense, even*, to organize industries associatively; to build palaces for the workers. . . ."[31]

Even though Godin's iron foundry town was publicized in London in the early 1900s and Shaw, to be sure, was familiar with the thought of Fourier,[32] little in the physical description of the Familistère in 1900 invites direct comparison with Undershaft's city, ruling out any likelihood that it could have appeared in the guise of Perivale St. Andrews. The case is otherwise with projects emanating from another steel works, one of the world leaders in the industry that Undershaft represents.

Indeed, one of the outstanding developments in community housing took place in the munitions industry itself. Over a period of years, the Krupp firm at Essen in Germany introduced the largest industrial dwelling program in Europe. Two brief reports about it were published in London in the year that *Major Barbara* was written, the more descriptive one appearing early in the year. A. R. Sennett, in his two-volume 1905 work on garden cities, wrote glowingly of "this extensive ultra-urban industrial centre," created by the "brothers Krupp." The other, a more detailed account of the

Krupp "colonies" in the vicinity of Essen, appeared in a brief article by Budgett Meakin in April 1905. Meakin told of the gradual improvement in worker accommodations, from ungainly barracks built after the wars of 1859–62 to more recent "ideal" garden cottages, all picturesque, half-timbered, one-story buildings. At Essen 4,300 separate dwelling places were then available for Krupp workers.[33]

In their housing colonies the Krupps built—and bore the entire expenses of—playgrounds, a church, and private nondenominational elementary schools for children of the firm's employees. By 1902 a staff of seventeen was giving free instruction to 1,050 children. The Krupp welfare plan was an extensive one, including sickness relief funds, hospitals, homes for the aged, pension funds for officials and manual workers, widows' and orphans' funds, and life insurance. At the same time, the relief fund and charitable operations incurred vehement criticism, for the business profited from them as much as the workers benefited. Taking over workers' consumer cooperatives modelled on Robert Owen's ideas, Alfred Krupp converted them into the Krupp Consumers' Institutions, a private million-dollar department store operation. As William Manchester observes, he transformed Essen "into the largest, most stable company town in history."[34]

The welfare services of the company expanded under Friedrich Alfred (Fritz) Krupp, Alfred's son, who succeeded his father as Cannon King in 1887. He founded a hospital for "Kruppians," and after his death in 1902 his widow Margarethe (Marga) added hospitals for wives and daughters, contributed $750,000 to needy families, and established a visiting nurse service. The concern also had an elaborate cultural project. The Krupp Reading Room had 28,000 volumes in 1902. The Krupp Cultural Union, formed in 1899, included a literary circle, an amateur orchestra, a mixed choir, a chess society, and a shorthand school, and by 1902 had 1,050 members. Critics of the Cultural Union maintained that its sole utility was to blunt the minds of those who belonged.[35]

The scale of the housing and social activities of the House of Krupp was clearly much greater than in the provisions of the manufacturers previously examined. It could really have elicited from Stephen Undershaft the kind of effusive praise that Perivale St. Andrews inspired in him and with it, perhaps, his concomitant concern lest the "pampering" weaken the workers' characters. There is at least one other significant symptom of consanguinity with Undershaft's business: "In the Chinese-Japanese War of 1894 both sides were privileged to kill each other with the same Krupp guns. This was another peculiarity of the weapon trade in Fritz Krupp's time: it stood above warring nations. Rather than getting entangled in alien quarrels, the firm upheld its proud and prosperous neutrality and impartially sold its goods to every buyer."[36] Thus the Krupps could readily have subscribed to the creed of the Armorer enunciated by Undershaft: "To give arms to all men who offer an honest price for them, without respect of persons or principles" (168).

Internally, the influence of the munition works penetrated deeply into the social and economic life of its employees. Cannon King Alfred had undertaken to establish a "welfare firm" almost a century before modern corporations began their industrial-relations programs, but the "Kruppians" who received the various benefits were treated like children and had to meet the standards of performance, obedience, and usefulness set by the company's owner. They owed allegiance "to their boss, their firm, and their state, in that order." The tenants of the "colonies" or "workers' villages" were subject to complete and continuous control by Krupp's "supervision officers," extending even to their personal relations and their reading matter. Nor were they allowed any voice in public affairs. Alfred Krupp wanted a faithful "pure race of Kruppians" for his skilled labor force and was willing to offer a good measure of wage and job security in return. As Manchester points out, "of course, a man dismissed from his job lost everything, including his pension." Muhlen, however, reports that after Alfred's death a court order changed this "modern bondage."[37]

Like Andrew Undershaft, Fritz Krupp had two daughters, the younger one named Barbara after the legendary patron saint of gunners and armorers. The elder sister, Bertha Antoinette, married Gustav von Bohlen und Holbach, who became the next head of the firm. The Kaiser granted him permission to assume the name Krupp (and pass the name on to subsequent eldest sons) so that, much as Adolphus Cusins became Andrew Undershaft's son-in-law, namesake, and successor, Gustav Krupp (von Bohlen und Holbach) succeeded to his father-in-law's name and authority. But in this case fact followed fiction since the Krupp marriage took place in 1906, the year after *Major Barbara* was written. There is another odd parallel between Gustav and Adolphus. Lady Britomart's acerbic comment about the latter—"A man cant make cannons any the better for being his own cousin instead of his proper self" (165)—could as aptly have been said of Gustav, the offspring of a father and mother who were cousins.[38]

All the same, the German pair were, *au fond*, quite unlike the Shavian couple. Known to the world later as Big Bertha (as was a Krupp cannon named after her), the plain-looking wealthiest heiress in Europe was sixteen years younger and at least a head taller than the "undistinguished" attaché whom the Kaiser had selected to be her consort. The bridegroom, in Muhlen's description, was a mediocre and "subaltern-minded little man," suited to be an "excellent second-in-command to any domineering, strong-willed wife," as was Bertha Krupp. About the unemotional, unimaginative Gustav, Manchester expresses doubt "that he entertained a single, original thought in his entire life."[39] No second Cusins he, nor did Bertha really replicate salvationist Barbara.

Manchester observes that the years between November 1902 and August 1906 "stand apart" in the Krupp dynasty's history. This was the interregnum from the presumed suicide of Fritz Krupp (after a major homosexual scandal) and the succession to ownership of his daughter Bertha, upon reaching her majority at twenty-one. During this interval Fritz's queen-like widow, Marga, ran the firm as her daughter's trustee, mainly devoting herself to its welfare realm.

Among those well aware of the Krupp family in these years, according to Manchester, were its critics,

> as George Bernard Shaw demonstrated brilliantly in December 1905 when his *Major Barbara*, a thinly veiled satire largely based on the Krupps, opened in London. In the play Barbara is substituted for Bertha, the head of the munitions family is named Sir Andrew Undershaft, and Bertha-Barbara is given a pacifist brother called Stephen. Stephen complains, "I have hardly ever opened a newspaper in my life without seeing our name in it. The Undershaft torpedo! The Undershaft quick-firers! The Undershaft ten-inch! The Undershaft disappearing rampart gun! The Undershaft submarine! and now the Undershaft aerial battleship!"
>
> Shaw is uncanny. Although he could not possibly have had access to Alfred's correspondence, the "disappearing rampart gun" is straight out of the Kanonenkönig's last mad scribbles about the *Panzerkanone* [armored gun or stationary tank], and while he couldn't have penetrated Germaniawerft's secret pens in Kiel, his submarine reference came less than a year before the launching of the U–1 there. Moreover, the discussion in Act III about the family's nursing home, libraries, schools, insurance fund, pension fund, and building society bears an extraordinary resemblance to Marga's memoranda to the Vorstand [Directors], now filed in the Krupp archives.[40]

Free of Manchester's blithe assumptions and his manifest errors—dubbing Undershaft a knight and Stephen a pacifist—Maurice Valency considers Undershaft's vast industrial complex to be "reminiscent of the Krupp empire" widely publicized during that period. Valency, too, adduces in support of this judgment the welfare program, model villages, and social benefits developed under Fritz Krupp as well as the 1906 marriage of Bertha to Gustav von Bohlen und Halbach and the latter's assumption of management of the Krupp works.[41]

Stanley Weintraub, in greater detail, joins these writers in discerning a correspondence between the business and family circumstances of Undershaft and the Krupps. Citing and concurring with Manchester, he deems Barbara a substitute for Bertha, quotes Stephen on the Undershaft armaments, and finds Shaw uncanny in prefiguring the U-1 and other concealed Krupp weaponry awaiting production. To these matchings he adds the third-act references to "the Undershaft nursing home, libraries, schools, insurance and pension funds, and building societies" as Krupp counterparts and marvels at the even more uncanny parallelism of the Barbara Undershaft and Bertha Krupp marriages. He concludes that "the possibility that Shaw was, among other things, satirizing Krupp dynastic problems cannot be overlooked."[42]

Further, Weintraub directs attention to lines inserted in the 1907 German edition of *The Perfect Wagnerite*, wherein Shaw employs the conduct of Alberich in *The Rhinegold* to illuminate economic developments. According to the Shavian analysis, Alberich discovers that greed is not the way to make money in the millions. To do so he "must make himself an earthly Providence for masses of workmen, creating towns, and governing markets." In consequence by 1876 "he was well on his way towards becoming Krupp of Essen, or Cadbury of Bournville, or Lever of Port Sunlight." In a subsequent paragraph (not mentioned by Weintraub) Shaw asserts that since Alberich's work is necessary work, even proletarians victorious in the class struggle would have to carry on the political and industrial toil "now being done . . . by our Romanoffs, our Hohenzollerns, our Krupps, Cadburies, Levers and their political retinues." In a later edition of the book Shaw deletes "Cadburies" and adds "Carnegies" and "Pierpont Morgans." Eventually he obliterated all these names, substituting, in the first passage quoted above, "becoming exoterically a model philanthropic employer and esoterically a financier," and in the second, "now gets itself done somehow under limited monarchs, despotic presidents, irresponsible financiers, and bourgeois parliaments."[43] For his part, Weintraub fully recognizes that there were other paternalistic industrialists who could serve as possible prototypes for Undershaft, including George Cadbury, Alfred Nobel, and Andrew Carnegie. The list could easily be extended to include others. Undershaft is manifestly a composite.

Before leaping to the conclusion that Perivale St. Andrews represents a Shavian portrait—satiric or otherwise—of the Krupps at Essen, it is essential to take into account some of the salient differences between the two realms. Although both operate as paternalistic armament establishments, their owners' personalities and managerial methods are markedly dissimilar. The thoroughgoing authoritarianism of the German firm—exercising almost total control over the lives of its workmen and requiring absolute and unswerving allegiance to their employer—is in sharp contrast to the deft hierarchically cascading modus operandi that Undershaft articulates in the play. Besides these there are the already noted disparities in the juxtapositioning of Gustav-Bertha with Cusins-Barbara. Pairing Barbara Undershaft with Bertha Krupp also involves rejecting any possible link between the play's eponymous heroine and her namesake, the younger daughter, Barbara Krupp, who became engaged in the same time period to Baron Thilo von Wilmowsky, a governmental solicitor. Unlike Gustav, the Baron was an authentic member of the Prussian nobility and had "an unusual degree of independence of mind." He brought valuable contacts to the Krupp works, whose management he too joined.[44]

The ineluctable fact that the composition of *Major Barbara* preceded by a year the comparable occurrences in Germany leads to crediting Shaw with "uncanny" anticipation of the future, but a simpler explanation beckons. The Krupps have to be viewed not in isolation, but in a wider global context. Thus, impressive as are some of the similarities of the Essen bill of fare to that at Perivale St. Andrews, they are by no means unique in that regard. As with the other model communities surveyed here, the Krupp kingdom shared with Shaw's fictional town certain generic features of the model housing schemes of the time, features that were equally common components of a continuously evolving movement.

The same considerations apply to the industrial and munition analogues of the Krupp and Undershaft-Lazarus business enterprises. As epigraph to the opening chapter of their book on the international armament industry, *Merchants of Death*, Engelbrecht and Hanighen quote Undershaft's armorer's creed. In a chapter devoted to British arms manufacturers they relate how the Vickers firm sold munitions to both sides during the war between Russia and Japan and that its chief competitor Armstrong-Whitworth sought to do the same, first with Argentina and Chile when tensions grew between those countries, and later with China and Japan. Vickers, after purchasing both the Naval Construction and Armament Company and the Maxim-Nordenfelt Company in 1897, became the chief producer of guns in the world.

Recounting political machinations by arms dealers of the era, the authors comment, "From these stories, it would seem that Shaw's Undershaft was perhaps not such a gross exaggeration after all. Indeed, some of the opinions of arms merchants, uttered out of the range of meddlesome reporters' ears, could well be lifted from the dialogues in *Major Barbara*." Of Frenchman Eugène Schneider—then "one of the most powerful cannon merchants in the world"—they write, "Like Bernard Shaw's Undershaft, he could well boast 'when other people want something to keep my dividends down, you will call out the police and military.' "[45]

The same applies to the weapon analogues since torpedoes, quick-firing fieldpieces, ten-inch howitzers, and disappearing mountings were all extant in British ordnance prior to 1905.[46] And even though the Krupps' construction of the first German submarine (authorized in the previous year) took

Fig. 6.   The Woolwich Infant, from *Illustrated London News*, 11 June 1887. The caption below the illustration reads "Firing the 111-ton gun at Woolwich (The largest gun in existence)."

place in 1906, submarines were already undergoing intense development in the late nineteenth century. "By 1900 six navies owned a total of ten submarines with another eleven under construction. . . . By the turn of the century, therefore, the submarine after over a hundred years of development was accepted as a warship with a future."[47]

In addition, there is the British Woolwich Infant, mentioned by Stephen in the first act as an appellation applied disparagingly to him by others and which looms over the play's final setting as a palpable presence and symbol. The Woolwich Infant was a 111-ton breech-loading naval gun built by Sir W. Armstrong, Mitchell and Company, "the largest gun in existence" according to a detailed description and captioned photograph of the cannon in the *Illustrated London News* of 11 June 1887.[48] That Shaw was in good measure conversant with contemporary and earlier developments in armaments is evident not only from Undershaft utterances in the text, but also from references in the draft manuscript of *Major Barbara* to disappearing carriages, to the replacement of muzzleloaders by breechloaders, and, in a canceled passage, to the adoption of the Undershaft system of sighting field guns by the governments of Sweden, Germany, and Italy.[49] It would seem that the playwright was a great deal more canny than uncanny.

Shaw's bracketing of Krupp, Cadbury, and Lever is another strong indication that his focus was not narrowly confined to a single industrialist and town to the exclusion of the others. Each of their communities sought to provide social and economic advantages as well as improved housing facilities, usually within the confines of the purposes, paternalistic or philanthropic, of the controlling entrepreneur. In like manner, Perivale St. Andrews reflects the social philosophy of the millionaire capitalist Undershaft.

But these industrial communities have additional relevance in laying the groundwork for a more important development, the Garden City movement. In Mumford's words,

> Hence a final paradox: the most lasting benefits in the suburban pattern of development came from a handful of industrialists who . . .—sometimes quite literally—stuck to their guns. Godin at Guise, Krupp at Essen, Salt at Saltaire, Cadbury at Bourneville [*sic*], Lever at Port Sunlight, all heralded at the beginning of the nineteenth century by the hardheaded fanaticism of Robert Owen—these men made a sound contribution to urban life. They accepted the vital principles of romanticism, the delight in nature, the concern for children, the interest in healthy rural sports, as a basis for a new type of community development. But they did not forget the factory: they united the domestic and the industrial scheme in the same general frame. In this handful of exemplary developments, the foundation for a new attack upon the problems of housing and city development were finally laid: they paved the way for the new biotechnic conception of a balanced urban environment—what was first called the Garden City.[50]

The Garden City idea received its explicit formulation in the work of Ebenezer Howard (1850–1928). In 1898 Howard published in London a book entitled *To-morrow: A Peaceful Path to Real Reform*. A revised edition was issued in 1902 with the new title, *Garden Cities of To-Morrow*, a work destined to become a veritable bible of English town planning.[51]

The term "Garden City" had been used before Howard wrote his book. Much earlier Chicago, Illinois, was referred to as the Garden City, and Christchurch, founded in 1850, was called the Garden City of New Zealand. In 1869 Alexander T. Stewart, a millionaire merchant who headed a large New York dry goods store (which later became Wanamakers) was the first to name a place Garden City. He gave that name to a residential suburb he established on the town lands of Hempstead, Long Island. But it was Howard who gave the term a technical meaning, one that was widely ignored or violated, however, as the garden city gained international popularity as *Cité-Jardin, Gartenstadt, Cuidad-jardín*, and *Tuinstad*.[52]

Howard undertook to resolve the problem arising from the continuous streaming of the growing population into already overcrowded cities and the accompanying depopulation of rural areas. The problem, as he saw it, was one of restoring the people to the land by uniting the social attractions of large cities with the hygienic benefits of rural life. In his famous and frequently reproduced diagram of the three magnets, he conceived of town and country as two competing magnets attracting people with the town-country proposed as a third alternative, combining the advantages of active town life with the beauty of the country.[53]

He envisaged the Garden City as a complete, coherent, and planned social unit formed on community-owned land under a common authority. All increments from the increase in land values would accrue automatically to the community. The population would be limited and the city's size and growth controlled by a permanent surrounding belt of country land reserved for agricultural or recreational use. This inviolable green belt would serve to cut off the encroachment of other towns, promote local food production for a nearby market, and provide an attractive environment. The growth of the city was to be encouraged up to the point of making a maximum contribution to the social and economic life of the people. Rational provision for needed growth would require the establishment of another garden city with like limitations. Howard envisioned a cluster of towns in a planetary system, with small towns built around a central city, each separated from the others by green belts but readily connected by handy transportation routes.

The bulk of Howard's book is devoted to practical considerations requisite to launching a garden city, including revenue, finance, engineering, agriculture, administration, and municipal enterprise. The actual scheme he presents is designed merely to illustrate his ideas. The sketches accompanying the text carry admonitions that they are diagrams only and that actual plans would vary with the site. He writes of "this plan, or if the reader be pleased to so term it, this absence of plan. . . ."[54]

Howard further proposes the acquisition of a six-thousand–acre estate with a town occupying one thousand acres near the center, and with six boulevards dividing it into six equal parts. The larger public buildings—town hall, theater, museums, library, hospital, and concert hall—are situated in the center, surrounded by a public park. Running around the Central Park is a glass arcade, the "Crystal Palace," containing a shopping center and a winter garden. Circular tree-lined avenues further divide the town. The wide central avenue constitutes an additional park of 115 acres, providing sites for schools and churches, the denominations to be determined by the beliefs of the inhabitants. Facing the various avenues and boulevards are the houses, with common gardens and cooperative kitchens. Variety in architecture and design is contemplated. The community's population is set at 30,000. On the outer ring of the town are factories, warehouses, dairies, markets, coal and lumber yards, all fronting on a circular railway that surrounds the town. All machinery is to be electrically driven to reduce smoke and to cut the cost of electricity for other purposes. Around the whole city is the agricultural belt with a population of two thousand residing on five thousand acres.[55]

Howard called his conception of the garden city "a unique combination of proposals."[56] It brought together in a novel way the views of Spence, Owen, Fourier, Wakefield, Buckingham, Henry George, and Richardson. Howard's contribution lay in the originality of the synthesis rather than in specific details embodied in his proposals.

It is noteworthy that none of these unique contributions of Howard figures importantly in Perivale St. Andrews. If anything, Undershaft's settlement seems closer to the paternalistic projects of the nineteenth-century industrialists than to the model city outlined in *Garden Cities of Tomorrow*. However, since the book had practical consequences in which Shaw himself was to a certain extent a participant, these ramifications also need to be examined before rendering judgment on the question of linkages.

The initial public reaction to Howard's book was hardly favorable. Political conservatives and reformers alike, including some of the Fabians, considered its proposals Utopian or impracticable. The review of the book by the secretary of the Fabian Society, Edward R. Pease, in the *Fabian News* of December 1898, is concordant with Beatrice Webb's later derogation of the Garden City:

> His plans would have been in time if they had been submitted to the Romans when they conquered Britain. They set about laying-out cities, and our forefathers have dwelt in them to this day. Now Mr. Howard proposes to pull them all down and substitute garden cities, each duly built according to pretty coloured plans, nicely designed with a ruler and compass. The author has read many learned and interesting writers, and the extracts he makes from their books are like plums in the unpalatable dough of his Utopian scheming. We have got to make the best of our existing cities, and proposals for building new ones are about as useful as would be arrangements for protection against visits from Mr. Wells' Martians.[57]

Nonetheless the work gained its supporters, especially since Howard had incorporated features in the scheme that were attractive to representatives of divergent points of view. Its semi-municipal character appealed to socialists, its land reform to liberals, and its utilization of private enterprise in solving housing problems to conservatives.

At the same time, Howard did not confine his efforts to the writing of his book. An eloquent speaker with a powerful voice, he lectured on behalf of his proposals all over Britain during the last two years of the century. Under the title, "The Ideal City Made Practicable, A Lecture Illustrated With Lantern Slides," he preached the "Gospel of the Garden City" as "the peaceful path to real reform," proclaiming that humanity was moving inevitably toward a higher future stage of brotherhood for which the sole suitable environment would be the Garden City. Setting about winning the support of social reformers, "he assembled a broad coalition of backers that ranged from 'Back to the Land' agrarians to George Bernard Shaw," in the words of Robert Fishman, who adds that Howard "made his ideas the basis of a movement which, fifty years after his death, continues to grow. As one of Shaw's characters in *Major Barbara* observes, absolute unselfishness is capable of anything."[58]

Howard proved to be a successful organizer. In 1899 he founded the Garden City Association to work for the implementation of the Garden City idea.[59] Cadbury and Lever, whose own industrial villages were well publicized at the time, became sponsors and active participants in the Association, having been persuaded that the Garden City was an extension of their own ideas and a vehicle for disseminating them throughout the nation. Although not subscribing to their paternalism, Howard recognized the need for the financial support that these men could render. Early Association conferences were held both at Bournville and Port Sunlight. The Bournville event, in September 1901, attracted more than 1,500 urban officials. One of them was G.B.S., "an early supporter of the Garden City movement," attending in his capacity as a St. Pancras vestryman.[60] At the time the Garden City Association had 13,000 members.

As a result of Howard's efforts, the Garden City Pioneer Company, Limited, was launched in June 1902 to seek possible sites for a Garden City, and in September 1903, First Garden City, Limited, purchased a tract of land in Hertfordshire, thirty-five miles north of London, and established Letchworth (Garden City), the first Garden City. This body later became the Garden Cities and Town Planning Association and finally the Town and Country Planning Association. In 1919 Welwyn Garden City, a second Garden City, was initiated two miles southeast of Welwyn in southern Hertfordshire, twenty miles from London. Welwyn is the post office address of Ayot St. Lawrence, which Shaw made his country home in 1906, but this garden city was established long after the composition of *Major Barbara*. Still, Welwyn was only some fifteen miles south of Letchworth, which was struggling into existence at that early date.

As already indicated, Bernard Shaw differed from some of his fellow Fabians in regarding neither Howard nor his book and work with disfavor. For many years their friendly association with one another was all but ignored in the literature about Shaw, including the principal biographies,

although collateral references to Shaw appeared in the Garden City literature. The contributions of Purdom, Osborn, and the relatives of Howard
in *Shaw the Villager and Human Being* have filled in some of the lacunae. In
his Shaw biography Michael Holroyd summarizes their relationship within
the confines of a single paragraph.[61]

The careers of these two contemporaries (who were virtually neighbors)
ran parallel and crossed at a number of important junctures. Ebenezer
Howard, six years older than Shaw, was by occupation a shorthand reporter,
working primarily in the law courts and Parliament. His keen interest in
mechanical invention led to his inventing a shorthand typewriter upon
which, Purdom tells us, he "spent many years and much money of his
friends." Among the contributors to this endeavor was G.B.S.[62] But Howard's career was markedly dissimilar to Shaw's, for neither his inventive
efforts nor his devotion to the Garden City cause brought him fortune to
accompany his fame.

In 1879, three years after his return to England following five years
abroad in America, Howard joined the Zetetical Society, where he met
James Lecky, Bernard Shaw, and Sidney Webb. Lecky, who first brought
Shaw to the Society, became a lifelong friend of Howard's. Purdom conjectures that the Society may have served to make a speaker of Howard, much
as it helped Shaw discover his platform capabilities. Purdom also reports
that "Shaw became greatly interested in Howard's subsequent ideas, but
Webb did not."[63]

The thought of each man reflected responses to common intellectual
influences. When Henry George came to London to lecture, beginning in
1881, his eloquence had a profound impact on the thinking of both. It
"changed the whole current of my life," said Shaw.[64] The effect on Howard
was similar. Both men turned avidly to *Progress and Poverty* and became earnest land reformers. In time, each came to incorporate into his own thinking a congenial residue of George's doctrine.[65]

Two other American thinkers, Thomas Davidson and Edward Bellamy,
strongly influenced Howard and, at least in the case of Davidson, indirectly
affected the direction of Shaw's Fabian Socialism. In a letter to Kingsley
Martin in 1947, Shaw wrote of the Fabian Society,

> It was founded by a Rosminian philosopher named Davidson, and
> was excessively unfabian, dreaming of colonies of Perfect Lifers in
> Brazil, and discussing the abolition of money and the substitution
> of passbooks, or constitutional Anarchism and all sorts of nonsense
> at each other's lodgings.
>   It split into a political section led by Hubert Bland, calling itself
> the Fabian Society, and a Fellowship of the New Life with Perfection-
> ist views.[66]

The "Rosminian philosopher" was Thomas Davidson (1840–1900) a Scottish-born American peripatetic philosopher who edited and translated the works of Rosmini-Serbati and wrote that Catholic social reformer's biography. After fifteen years in Canada and the United States, Davidson's peregrinations brought him to Great Britain. Having founded his Fellowship of the New Life in the United States, he proceeded to do the same in London in 1883.

This organization "suited Howard's enthusiastic but puritanical and moralistic nature," much as its offshoot, the Fabian Society, attracted Shaw. Davidson, too, had a housing scheme: he proposed that the Fellowship sponsor "a co-operative industrial, educational, and residential settlement in the neighbourhood of London." Purdom believed that Howard was influenced by this project.[67]

"Ideal communities were in the air,"[68] and the most popular one had the most decisive impact upon Howard's own conception. It was Edward Bellamy's *Looking Backward*, published in London in 1889, a year after its publication in America. That utopian novel of Boston in A.D. 2000 "played a larger part than is commonly recognized in the inspiration of the rising British working-class movement. Its two basic assumptions—that technological advance could emancipate men from degrading toil, and that men are inherently co-operative and equalitarian—were the essence of Howard's own optimistic outlook. . . ."[69] Archibald Henderson, Maurice Colbourne, Eric Bentley, and Julian B. Kaye have proclaimed that Shaw, too, was indebted to Bellamy, although there seems to be no acknowledgment of such a debt in Shaw's own writings.[70] The only reference to Bellamy that I can find in Shaw's oeuvre is in the Preface to *Three Plays for Puritans* (1900), where he decries the "love interest" in *Looking Backward*, although neither the book nor its author is mentioned by name.[71] Bellamy wrote "An Introduction to this American Edition" for *Socialism: The Fabian Essays*, the title given to the American edition of the *Fabian Essays in Socialism*, edited by Shaw. Oddly, he makes no mention of Shaw in his Introduction.[72]

Shaw has been depicted both as an early supporter and as an early critic of the Garden City movement. Paradoxically, both interpretations appear to be true. Among others, Fishman, as already indicated, has him favoring the movement from the outset, although he does report that at the Bournville conference Shaw "expressed the frustration of his fellow officials when he remarked that outlawing slums meant 'that you turn a great mass of people out into the streets without homes. Do you suppose that sort of reform is popular with the very class of people you intend to benefit?' "[73]

Conversely, Frank Jackson quotes Shaw as evincing scorn to a friend: "I got the Garden City book when it first appeared (the author had sent it, I suppose), glanced at the maps, and said, 'The same old vision.' "[74] This

Shavian judgment, it turns out, is excerpted from a September 1899 letter to the playwright Edward Rose, which contains this added comment:

> It is of course possible that the threat of legislation against factories in London might drive a few big & philanthropic firms to combine & buy land with the object of placing their "hands" thereon in a model township. . . . Join the association by all means & follow its fortunes & discussion: they will be more convincing & instructive than anything I could write; but dont contribute a farthing more . . . than you are positively eager to lose. Of course an artificial city, so to speak, is no more impossible than a canal is: in fact, Eastbourne & many other places are such cities; but the thing should be kept clear of philanthropy & utopian socialism because people (the tenants) will not stand being kept in a nursery.

Within two months Shaw again wrote to Rose:

> On Monday Ebenezer the Garden City Geyser lectured in Hindhead Hall, with a magic lantern giving views of that flourishing settlement in the manner of Mr Scadder in Martin Chuzzlewit. I had to make a speech, which had so fell an effect, in spite of my earnest endeavors to help him over the stile, that the audience declined to hold up a single hand for his resolution. Finally the chairman put it again, coupling it with a vote of thanks, when, the situation becoming too poignant, I ostentatiously held up my paw, on which the others followed suit and Eb was saved. I pointed out that the manufacturers were ready enough to go into the country; but that what they went there for was cheap labor. I suggested that half a dozen big manufacturers building a city could give good wages, and yet get so much of them back in rent and shop rent, or in direct butcher, baker, and dairy profits, that the enterprise might pay them all the same. At this the Hindhead proletariat grinned from ear to ear, and concluded that I was the man who really understood the manufacturing nature, the Geyser being a mere spring of benevolent mud.

In his speech Shaw had also declared that schemes like Howard's had come to his notice at least once every seven years.[75]

These letters indicate that, at least initially, Shaw viewed the Garden City idea with a kind of benign skepticism. But his recorded public statements about Howard are for the most part laudatory.[76] Purdom, in his account of the public response to Howard's Garden City plan, asserts, "Among the large number of eminent and well-known people who applauded the idea were [*sic*] Bernard Shaw, who said that 'nothing private enterprise can do appears to me more likely to succeed than this idea of organizing new cities!' " When Howard was knighted in 1927, Shaw was invited to a dinner in Welwyn Garden City to celebrate the event. In a letter of apology for his absence, he wrote, "Sir Ebenezer should have had a barony for the book, an earldom for Letchworth, and a dukedom for Welwyn, and I am not going to congratulate him on such an inadequate acknowledgement of his great public service as a knighthood."[77] Again, at Howard's death in May 1928, Shaw wrote to A.C. Howard, Sir Ebenezer's son: "He was one of those heroic simpletons who do big things whilst our prominent worldlings are explaining why they are Utopian and impossible. And of course it is they who will make money out of his work." In 1941 he concluded a letter about Garden Cities to Sir Frederic Osborn with this observation: "I knew Ebenezer Howard personally and mentioned him in my play called *John Bull's Other Island* nearly forty years ago. An amazing man, whom the Stock Exchange would have dismissed as a negligible crank."[78]

Since, as a Socialist, Shaw was committed neither to private enterprise nor to its successes, this testimony by itself falls short of being a ringing endorsement of the Garden City idea. Still, there are the insistent asseverations of Purdom (in Chappelow's *Shaw the Villager and Human Being*), who relates that when the Garden City Association was founded in London as an experimental project, "Shaw attended one of the early conferences called to discuss it and spoke strongly in its favour." Beyond that, "Bernard Shaw had a very direct and lifelong interest in the building of Garden Cities. . . ." And once again, "Shaw's connection with the Garden City movement spanned almost the whole of his life in this country. He recognized that the Garden City was one of the formative ideas of the century."[79]

It is evident that Shaw read and was well informed about the Garden City movement. But he also had another kind of interest in the Garden Cities—interest derived from investments in these enterprises. In the *Intelligent Woman's Guide to Socialism and Capitalism* he admitted to holding "a good deal of stock" in the garden cities, and in *Everybody's Political What's What?* he wrote, "Near by where I live, a private company purchased such an estate and built a Garden City on it. Its cost was not raised by a public rate; it was subscribed by private speculators. I was one of them, and am accordingly now a British landlord as well as an Irish one."[80]

Undoubtedly he was alluding to Welwyn Garden City, the second Garden City, founded in 1919, for Shaw's profitable connection with that enterprise has been more fully documented. Purdom offers this account: "Welwyn Garden City was founded in 1919, not far from Ayot St. Lawrence, where Shaw lived, and he often cycled over before building began and in its early days. When the company needed capital for development he invested in it—probably one of the most successful investments he ever made, for when the Government took over the town in 1947, he, in common with other debenture holders, ultimately received £4 for every £1 of holding." He further notes that an article in the *Daily Express* reported that Shaw had 12,214 pound shares and that in the 1947 transfer of the Garden City to the Government, he received £14,770 in cash and, in addition, shares in a new trust valued at £23,000. Blanche Patch also reports that "he did accidentally pick up a few thousand pounds when Welwyn Garden City was acquired by the Development Trust, but there it was the idea he had backed, not the luck of the market."[81]

But Shaw's investment in garden cities began earlier. According to Osborn, "Bernard Shaw subscribed very heavily to the Howard Cottage Society [established in 1911] of which Sir Ebenezer Howard was Director and I [was] Secretary. He put many thousands into it—but only after he had made a very thorough personal enquiry into its finances and organisation, and asked me innumerable questions." The reminiscences of Howard's daughter, Mrs. F. E. Berry, suggest even earlier financial commitments by Shaw: "I'm not sure whether Bernard Shaw initially thought the Garden Cities movement was going very far. Shaw's interest was partly humorous, though he did contribute generously to the funds."[82]

Finally, Osborn adduces Shaw's own evaluation of his Garden Cities investments:

> I am one of those investors who like to see something for their money . . . instead of adding nothing to the country's fixed capital. I found the new garden cities just what I wanted. I saw waste places changed into pleasant and well planned dwellings and handsome markets by my spare cash. The investments never gave me a moment's anxiety or trouble: they were and are entirely satisfactory, both morally and economically. I am glad I foresaw their future when my neighbors were buying shares in South American railways which are now bankrupt.[83]

Since Welwyn Garden City was not founded until years later, whatever Shaw's long-term interest in garden cities came to be, only the first Garden City, Letchworth, could have any bearing on the composition of *Major Barbara*. Purdom recalls that "Shaw took a great interest in the growth of the place, and often lectured there."[84] The remark of Howard's daughter that Shaw's interest in the whole movement was partly humorous may have been prompted by his allusions to Howard and Letchworth Garden City in *John Bull's Other Island*. In the opening pages of that play, written in 1904, the year after the initiation of the Garden City, Shaw extracted topical humor from the avid promotion of the nascent community then emerging between the towns of Hitchin and Baldock:

BROADBENT. Have you ever heard of Garden City?

TIM. [*doubtfully*] D'ye mane Heavn?

BROADBENT. Heaven! No: it's near Hitchin. If you can spare half an hour I'll go into it with you.

TIM. I tell you what. Gimmie a prospectus. Lemmy take it home and reflect on it.

BROADBENT. Youre quite right: I will. [*He gives him a copy of Ebenezer Howard's book, and several pamphlets.*] You understand that the map of the city—the circular construction is only a suggestion.

TIM. I'll make a careful note of that [*looking dazedly at the map*].

BROADBENT. What I say is, why not start a Garden City in Ireland?

TIM. [*with enthusiasm*] Thats just what was on the tip o me tongue to ask you. Why not? [*Defiantly*] Tell me why not.[85]

Another Garden City reference occurs in Act IV:

> BROADBENT. . . . I shall bring money here: I shall raise wages: I shall found public institutions: a library, a Polytechnic (undenominational, of course), a gymnasium, a cricket club, perhaps an art school. I shall make a Garden city of Rosscullen. . . . (1015)

The use made by Broadbent of the Garden City as exemplar does invite comparison of Letchworth with *Major Barbara*, for if Perivale St. Andrews were patterned on an existent Garden City, Letchworth would certainly be the inevitable model.

The site at Letchworth "consisted of gently undulating land, practically all of it under cultivation, about 300 feet above sea level. The estate sloped away from a central plateau in every direction, giving at various points very fine views towards the south-west, west, and north-east." Its shape was "something like that of a pear."[86] (The name "Perivale," incidentally, means "pear valley.") Bisected by a railway, the two parts of the estate were physically separated. Since this reality could not be ignored in planning the city, the layout unavoidably had to depart from Howard's diagrams. Other factors brought about further divergence.

The architects Raymond Unwin and Barry Parker, in addition to planning New Earswick, were the designers of the Letchworth plans. Unwin, a member of the Fabian Society, had written "Cottage Plans and Common Sense," issued as *Fabian Tract 190* in 1902. A town planner well grounded in the sociological side of housing and an admirer of the ideas of William Morris, he played a prominent role in establishing the general lines of development for the Garden City and, later, in designing Hampstead Garden Suburb, begun in 1907. (Parker designed the garage that Shaw had built at Ayot St. Lawrence.)

By 1905 Letchworth was still in its early stages of actualization. Parker and Unwin's original plan of the city was first published in April 1904. It proposed a central square, sites for a public hall, museum, schools, places of worship, hotels, municipal buildings, post office, open spaces, and parks. Projected for thirty thousand inhabitants, it also reserved a rural belt surrounding the town. The design addressed the needs for drainage and utilities—water, gas, and electricity—and called for both industrial and residential expansion. An engineering firm, Ewart and Son, Ltd., took the first lease for a factory in 1903 although it was not built until 1911. All factories were to be located in an area east of the town.

The advent of industrial firms increased the demand for workers' houses. The Garden City Tenants Limited was registered in January 1905 to build homes for workers on a co-partnership basis. It became one of the first public utility housing societies in England. A distinctive feature of Letchworth was its workmen's cottages. The typical "Garden City cottage" is described by Purdom as "a white roughcast Tudor-like building with red tiles, gables, green paint, water-butts, and casement windows."[87] The colorful red tiles were a uniformly required roofing material for all domestic buildings.[88]

The only church that could have been erected by 1905 was Letchworth's first, the nondenominational Free Church, formed by members of all the nonconformist churches and built by the voluntary labor of the congregation.[89] The city's educational council opened a public nonsectarian elementary school in temporary premises in November 1905. Howard Memorial Hall, the first public hall, was built in 1906 in memory of Howard's first wife, who had died in 1904. A golf club was started in 1905. In the very early days a small orchestra was organized, but it was not until 1906 that some experienced theater people founded the Letchworth Dramatic Society. This became one of the first amateur companies in England to present serious drama to the public, including several of Shaw's plays.[90] Letchworth did realize most of Howard's central ideas, including the agricultural belt, permanent ownership and control under a single organization, diverse industries, workers' housing, active community interest, a fine health record, and plentiful open spaces and gardens.[91]

Can Letchworth Garden City have been the archetype of Perivale St. Andrews? Certainly in topography, in industrial foundation, in physical attractiveness, there appears to be little similitude between the two cities. There are the houses with walls of white and roofs of red tile in both, although Perivale St. Andrews also has roofs of green slate, and a few parallel institutions, but little else to suggest a significant correlation between the two cities.

A kinship between the two communities is discernible, however, via the Garden City idea rather than because of specific physiognomic or institutional equivalents. *Major Barbara* was written when Letchworth was a brand-new town. The Garden City had attracted people of independent minds, filled with enthusiasm. "It seemed to some of them," Purdom relates, "as though Morris' *News from Nowhere* was being realized, and that the hopes of man for a community free from the evils of the old cities were to be fulfilled."[92] Letchworth, together with the model towns that led up to it, was designed to eradicate urban evils. It is therefore reasonable to approach Perivale St. Andrews as belonging to the Garden City movement in the sense that it, too, is presented as a city seeking to realize one of the Garden City goals: "the highest attainable physical and intellectual advantage of town life, together with the freedom and healthfulness of residence in the country—these being secured in the interests of the industrial, professional, and commercial classes alike."[93]

What, then, of the question that Beatrice Webb's gibe raises. Is Shaw evangelizing the Garden City? This question really divides into two: (1) To what extent is Perivale St. Andrews a Garden City? (2) Is Shaw, in *Major Barbara*, preaching the gospel of the Garden City?

First, is Perivale St. Andrews a Garden City? Because of confusion in the use of the term, the Garden Cities and Town Planning Association, in consultation with Ebenezer Howard, in 1910 adopted the following definition: "A Garden City is a Town designed for healthy living and industry; of a size that makes possible a full measure of social life, but not larger; surrounded by a rural belt: the whole of the land being in public ownership or held in trust for the community."

The term "Garden City" has been confused with two other terms, "Garden Suburb" and "Garden Village." Osborn proposed to distinguish these as follows: "In these combinations the word Garden connotes simply a well-planned open lay-out. . . . The word Suburb is conveniently reserved for an outer part of a continuously built-up city, town, or urban area, implying that it is not separated therefrom by intervening country land. . . . The word Village implies small scale, detachment, and . . . a basis which is primarily agricultural."[94] Such stipulations, aiming at standardizing terminology, have appeared long after the time of *Major Barbara*'s composition. Nor have they been faithfully followed since. Nevertheless, they can help us make some useful distinctions. Bournville and Port Sunlight, for example, become garden villages rather than garden cities (although lacking an agricultural basis).

According to this definition, Perivale St. Andrews meets only part of the requirements of the Garden City. It is "a town designed for healthy living and industry" of limited size. Whether it has a rural belt or not is not clear, although the hills that bound it could be so regarded. But it undoubtedly lacks the desideratum of being built on publicly owned land. If the hills really separate it from London, then the appellation "Garden Suburb" is equally inappropriate under the definition given. It might, therefore, most aptly be called a "Garden Village," like Port Sunlight. No reference to any such term appears in *Major Barbara*, but in the film version that Shaw published in 1951, there is this brief passage:

> *The view from the window is of a green valley dotted with bungalows of various design: each with its verandah and garden.*
> LOMAX. Garden city notion, what?
> UNDERSHAFT. They call it a garden suburb.[95]

But whether it is a garden village or garden suburb, Undershaft's town can at best be described loosely as exemplifying the "garden-city concept." Under the absolute control of a capitalist owner who acquires all of its profits, it cannot be a true Garden City as Howard conceived of it. Yet it may be viewed as a kind of Garden City, for Shaw evidently drew upon the Garden City movement for at least some of the features of the Undershaft industrial colony.[96] All in all, it appears to be a distillate of the various model communities.

As for the second, and more determinative question, if Perivale St. Andrews belongs to the garden city genre, is that what the play is endorsing? In turn, this brings to the fore the issue of the role of Undershaft's community in the whole drama. More specifically, since *Major Barbara* is concerned with the salvation of mankind and society, is such salvation somehow to be found in the social and economic organization of this factory town? There are a number of reasons for believing that the drama expresses no such intent.

Notwithstanding Shaw's approbation of the Garden City movement and the work of Howard and his associates, there is evidence that he, like his Fabian confreres, found such enterprises insufficient for the social improvement that they envisioned. In *The Intelligent Woman's Guide to Socialism and Capitalism* Shaw made manifest what he took to be the virtues and the deficiencies in garden city enterprises. He points out that under capitalism the government has been called upon to contribute to some private enterprises because of their public utility. As a consequence,

> these garden cities, which are most commendable enterprises in their way, are nevertheless the property of rich capitalists. As I hold a good deal of stock in them myself I am tempted to claim that their owners are specially philanthropic and public-spirited men, who have voluntarily invested their capital where it will do the most good and not where it will make the most profit for them; but they are not immortal; and we have no guarantee that their heirs will inherit their disinterestedness. . . . The garden cities and suburbs are an

enormous improvement on the manufacturing towns produced by unaided private enterprise; but as they do not pay their proprietors any better than slum property, nor indeed as well, it is quite possible that this consideration may induce the future owners to abolish their open spaces and overcrowd them with houses until they are slums. (pp. 300–301).

In the same work Shaw specifically mentions Port Sunlight and Bournville twice. In one reference he declares that the cities of Russia, far from being ripe for Socialism, had barely begun urban civilization: "There were no Port Sunlights and Bournvilles, no Ford factories in which workmen earn £9 in a five-day week and have their own motor cars . . ." (p. 375). Listing many other accomplishments of capitalist civilization, he concludes that, when consummated in England, Socialism will cap a pyramid already constructed. "We must build up Capitalism before we can turn it into Socialism" is the moral he draws, with the attendant caveat that "meanwhile we must learn how to control it instead of letting it demoralize us, slaughter us, and half ruin us, as we have hitherto done in our ignorance" (p. 376).

The other reference occurs in the book's chapter on "Sham Socialism," where he warns against the consequences of big business and trade unions employing first-rate business brains and instituting scientific management:

> And when this is accomplished they will enslave the unskilled, unorganized proletariat, including, as we have seen, the middle-class folk who have no aptitude for money making. They will enslave the Government. And they will do it mostly by the methods of Socialism, effecting such manifest improvements in the conditions of the masses that it will be inhuman to stop them. The organized workers will live not in slums, but in places like Port Sunlight, Bournville, and the Garden Cities. Employers like Mr Ford, Lord Leverhulme and Mr Cadbury will be the rule and not the exception; and the sense of helpless dependence on them will grow at the expense of individual adventurousness. The old communal cry of high rates and a healthy city will be replaced by Mr Ford's cry of high wages and colossal profits. (p. 307)

These passages show transparently what Shaw considered to be the advantages and dangers, from a Socialist point of view, in the social and industrial reforms of the millionaire capitalists. Note, too, that the Garden Cities are interlinked here not only with the housing colonies of Lord Leverhulme and Cadbury, but also with the industrial policies of Henry Ford. The efficiency they achieve ultimately feeds their own private interests rather than the public good. Socialism can build upon their achievements only by assuring that their private power is supplanted by public control.

Are these views reflected in Shaw's playwriting? In *John Bull's Other Island* he does more than poke fun at the Garden City. Tom Broadbent, who is called by Father Keegan "an efficient devil that knows his own mind," explains his object early in the first act: "I'm going to develop an estate there [in Ireland] for the Land Development Syndicate, in which I am interested. I am convinced that all it needs to make it pay is to handle it properly, as estates are handled in England" (899). Broadbent appropriates the garden city idea to his own ends: "I shall make a Garden City of Roscullen," he says in the passage already quoted. "He is efficient in the service of Mammon, mighty in mischief, skilful in ruin, heroic in destruction," in Keegan's terse assessment (1016).

Daniel J. Leary has printed and discussed a passage that Shaw was compelled to cut from the play, in part to reduce its length. The passage contains a line in which Broadbent says "I'm going to try the Garden City dodge in Rosscullen" and has him contending that "social enthusiasm" is an "enormous force" with "solid money value." He has learned that "one of the greatest commercial discoveries of the age is the lot of work you can get out of people for nothing under the influence of philanthropic ideas. . . ."[97]

What, then, about *Major Barbara* and Undershaft, the entrepreneur of the Perivale St. Andrews establishment? The evidence thus far cited is, after all, external to the play, and it could be argued that Shaw is not always consistent. Is Undershaft, too, using Perivale St. Andrews for his private purposes? Is that community presented as a model for society, or as an unmet challenge?

Evidence that Shaw originally conceived Undershaft in such suspect fashion is to be found in the Derry manuscript where, at the opening of the final scene, Cusins tells Undershaft that the latter's workmen regard him "as a master of craft, wickedness, and tyranny" who profits greatly from the reading rooms, lecture theatre, canteen, pension and insurance fund, and other "paternal provisions for the good of their souls & bodies." Undershaft, in turn, admits that they see him getting more from them than they from him and "know that all these institutions for their benefit— especially the insurance and pension fund—enslave them far more effectually than if they could change their employment without losing anything but a few days wages."[98] It was a sound decision to delete and revise this segment, but these lines are in accord with the sentiments of Broadbent and with Shaw's elsewhere-articulated mistrust of the beneficence provided by model towns owned by industrialists.

While explaining how a snubbing hierarchy maintains discipline in his factory, Undershaft concludes, "Of course they all rebel against me theoretically. Practically every man of them keeps the man just below him in his place. I never meddle with them. I never bully them. . . . *The result is a colossal profit, which comes to me"* (155, emphasis added).

Undershaft—echoing the same welcoming of huge profits that Shaw later ascribed to Henry Ford—lets everyone know that this is, after all, a millionaire capitalist's city, just as in the first act he unabashedly proclaims himself "a profiteer in mutilation and murder" (89) and in the second act remorselessly reminds Mrs. Baines that he grows rich on the ravages of war (133). He demonstrates to his daughter that the salvation administered by the Salvation Army, and, indeed, all religion, is purchased at the price of dependence upon the capitalist millionaire. In Act III he explains to his son, Stephen, how his capitalistic control of government, police, military, and press enables him to dictate political and economic policy and to decide when war or peace is in his personal interest: "*I* am the government of your country. . . . When I want anything to keep my dividends up, you will discover that my want is a national need. . . . I am going back to my counting house to pay the piper and call the tune" (151).

Undershaft is the embodiment of power and efficiency, and his polity is dependent upon him, as is society in general. But he has provided advantages that must themselves be taken advantage of, and superseded. That supersession is provided for in the succession of Cusins to the factory ownership and Barbara's return, as his wife, to salvationist endeavors conducted at the higher economic level afforded by Perivale St. Andrews. The function of Undershaft's model city is to provide that improved environment for the pursuit of human salvation, rid of the "bribe of bread," rid of poverty.

Beyond deploring *Major Barbara* for evangelizing the Garden City, Beatrice Webb judged it to be "hell tossed on the stage—with no hope of heaven."[99] Evidently she paid no heed—or gave no credence to—the climactic lines of Cusins and Barbara (as they were spoken in the original production, later revised slightly):

> CUSINS. The way of life through the factory of death!
> BARBARA. The raising of earth to heaven and of man to God, the unveiling of an eternal light in the Valley of The Shadow.[100]

A few days later she did set down in her diary Shaw's defense (in person) of the play against her attack. "He argued earnestly and cleverly, even persuasively, in favour of what he imagines to be his central theme—*the need for preliminary good physical environment before anything could be done to raise the intelligence and morality of the average sensual man.*"[101] This argument, which is the part of Undershaft's teaching that Barbara and Cusins do come to accept, failed to convince Mrs. Webb. While underscoring Shaw's whole thesis, she apparently missed the need for additional emphasis on the word *preliminary*. The Garden City, or some other such venture that takes care of basic physical needs, is an essential prerequisite to the improvement of human life and character.

Undershaft's version of a "Garden City" is intended by Shaw to provide a more worthy arena for the contests for human souls. Hence the scarcity of details about its physical characteristics. It is proffered primarily as an appropriate setting for the drama of salvation, in contrasting juxtaposition to the second act's scene of poverty and misery in the existing economic environment of neglect.

Perivale St. Andrews is portrayed as needing only a cathedral, the equivalent of which it has, to be changed from a hellish to a heavenly city. Earth, heaven, and hell are figuratively deployed in this play much as in its predecessors, *John Bull's Other Island* and *Man and Superman*. In the latter the frontier of hell and heaven is held to be "only the difference between two ways of looking at things."[102] Perivale St. Andrews is such a frontier. It sits on a powder keg, but has the means to propel us to heaven or hell.

In *The Intelligent Woman's Guide to Socialism and Capitalism* Shaw wrote, "The rule that substance comes first and virtue afterwards is as old as Aristotle and as new as this book. The Communism of Christ, of Plato, and of the great religious orders, all take equality in material subsistence for granted as the first condition of establishing the Kingdom of Heaven on Earth" (p. 94). That is the Kingdom Shaw is evangelizing, not the Garden City. If it is to lead to that Kingdom, the Garden City, like other gardens, stands in need of constant and continuous cultivation.

Notes

1. *The Diary of Beatrice Webb: Vol. 3, 1905–1924: "The Power to Alter Things"*, ed. Norman and Jeanne MacKenzie (Cambridge: Harvard University Press, 1984), p. 13. Also in Beatrice Webb, *Our Partnership*, ed. Barbara Drake and Margaret I. Cole (London: Longmans, Green, 1948), p. 314.

2. C. B. Purdom, *The Garden City: A Study in the Development of a Modern Town* (London: J. M. Dent & Sons, 1913), p. 1.

3. Bernard Shaw, *Collected Plays with Their Prefaces*, ed. Dan H. Laurence (London: Max Reinhardt, 1971), 3: 158, 162. Subsequent references to *Major Barbara* are to this edition, with page numbers noted parenthetically in the text.

4. Cecil Stewart, *A Prospect of Cities* (London: Longmans, Green, 1952), p. 168.

5. Lewis Mumford, *The Culture of Cities* (New York: Harcourt, Brace, 1938), p. 148.

6. William Morris, *Architecture, Industry, and Wealth* (London: Longmans, 1902). Quoted in Frederick R. Hiorns, *Town-Building in History* (London: Harrup, 1956), p. 331. See also pp. 318–23.

7. Lewis Mumford, *The Story of Utopias*, Compass Books Edition (New York: Viking, 1962), p. 115; Bernard Shaw, Preface to *Three Plays by Brieux* (London: A. C. Fifield, 1911), p. x.

8. Lewis Mumford, *The Culture of Cities*, p. 392. On Shaw's Owenism, see *Our Theatres in the Nineties* (London: Constable, 1932), 3:355–56, where he asserts that "modern Fabianism represents the positive stage of Owenism." Reprinted in *Bernard Shaw: The Drama Observed*, ed. Bernard F. Dukore (University Park: Penn State University Press, 1993), 3: 1035.

9. A. L. Morton, *The English Utopia* (London: Lawrence & Wishart, 1952), p. 131. See also A. J. Brown and H. M. Sherrard, *An Introduction to Town and Country Planning*, revised by the original authors and J. H. Shaw (New York: American Elsevier, 1969), pp. 273–74.

10. Harold Orlans, *Utopia Ltd: The Story of the English New Town of Stevenage* (New Haven: Yale University Press, 1953), pp. 6–7.

11. Lewis Mumford, *The City in History: Its Origins, Its Transformations, and Its Prospects* (London: Secker & Warburg, 1961), p. 515; F. J. Osborn, *Green-Belt Cities: The British Contribution* (London: Faber & Faber, 1946), pp. 176–77.

12. Sir Benjamin Ward Richardson, *Hygeia: A City of Health* (London: Macmillan, 1876). See Purdom, *The Garden City*, pp. 12–14, and Stewart, p. 169 n.

13. Stewart, pp. 152–53; Purdom, *Garden City*, p. 14. The descriptive information about Saltaire is drawn primarily from the detailed account in Stewart, pp. 148–67 (Chapter 8: "A Pillar of Salt").

14. Stewart, pp. 156–60.

15. Stewart, pp. 161, 112.

16. Mumford, *The Culture of Cities*, p. 393.

17. *Bournville Housing* (Publication Department, Bournville Works, 1922), p. 16.

18. Iolo A. Williams, *The Firm of Cadbury 1831–1931* (London: Constable, 1931), pp. 221–29; *The Bournville Village Trust 1900–1955* (Bournville, Birmingham: Bournville Village Trust, n.d. [ca. 1955]), p. 16.

19. Harley Williams, *Men of Stress: Three Dynamic Interpretations, Woodrow Wilson, Andrew Carnegie, William Hesketh Lever* (London: Jonathan Cape, 1948), pp. 276–77.

20. Quoted from Angus Watson, *My Life* (London: Ivor Nicholson & Watson, 1937), in Charles Wilson, *The History of Unilever* (London: Cassel, 1954), 1:150. Also quoted, uncredited, in W. S. Adams, *Edwardian Portraits* (London: Secker & Warburg, 1957), pp. 152–53.

21. Wilson, 1:149, quoting Watson, pp. 137–38. See also Williams, *Men of Stress*, p. 279.

22. Quoted in Wilson 1:150, and, in part, in Adams, p. 152.

23. Wilson, 1:148, 151.

24. Wilson, 1:146; A. R. Sennett, *Garden Cities in Theory and Practice* (London: Bemrose & Sons, 1905), 1:391–93.

25. Ewart G. Culpin, *The Garden City Movement Up-to-Date* (London: The Garden Cities and Town Planning Association, 1913), p. 39; *The Garden City*, Official Organ of the Garden City Association, September 1906, p. 169; Walter L. Creese, ed., *The Legacy of Raymond Unwin: A Human Pattern for Planning* (Cambridge, Mass., and London: MIT Press, 1967), pp. 1, 7, 52, 98. Unwin and his partner, Barry Parker, were the planners of New Earswick. In his Introduction to the latter work, Creese draws an interesting comparison of Unwin with Shaw and of the former's town plans with the latter's dramas.

26. Sennett, 1:381–84.

27. *The Garden City* (March 1906), pp. 41–42.

28. Roy Bongartz, "The Chocolate Camelot," *American Heritage* 24:4 (June 1973): 4, 92.

29. Reported in the second edition of the book, titled *Twenty-eight Years of Co-partnership at Guise*, translated from the French of Mmé. Dallet, M. Fabre, and M. and Mmé. Prudhommeaux by Aneurin Williams (London: Labour Co-partnership Association and Letchworth, Herts.: Garden City Press, 1908). Aneurin Williams was active in the Garden City Association as well as in the Labour Co-partnership Association.

30. F. J. Osborn, *Green-Belt Cities*, p. 176: Mumford, *Culture of CIties*, p. 393.

31. Marie Howland, Translator's Preface, in M. Godin, *Social Solutions* (New York: John V. Lovell, 1886), p. iv. (Emphasis is Howland's.)

32. See Bernard Shaw, *The Political Madhouse in America and Nearer Home* (London: Constable, 1933), p. 59: "We knew all about Fourier and Proudhon and Blanqui in France."

33. Sennett, I:393–94; Budgett Meakin [James Edward Budgett], "The Evolution of Ideal Industrial Housing," *The Garden City* 13 (April 1905): 41–42.

34. William Manchester, *The Arms of Krupp 1587–1968* (London: Michael Joseph, 1969), p. 179; Norbert Muhlen, *The Incredible Krupps: The Rise, Fall, and Comeback of Germany's Industrial Family* (New York: Henry Holt, 1959), pp. 65–66; Gert von Klass, *Krupp: The Story of an Industrial Empire*, trans. James Cleough (London: Sidgwick & Jackson, 1934), pp. 269–71; Bernhard Menne, *Blood and Steel: The Rise of the House of Krupp* (New York: Lee Ferman, 1938), pp. 120–22. Menne maintains that Alfred Krupp "frequently lagged behind" his time in the welfare treatment of his employees. See also p. 259.

35. Klass, pp. 270–71.

36. Muhlen, pp. 90–91.

37. Manchester, p. 179; Muhlen, pp. 65–67.

38. Muhlen, pp. 103–4; Klass, pp. 275–81; Peter Batty, *The House of Krupp* (London: Secker & Warburg, 1966), pp. 122–24; Manchester, pp. 285–89.

39. Muhlen, pp. 104–5; Manchester, p. 288; Batty, pp. 123–27.

40. Manchester, p. 282. In a remarkably misleading footnote, Manchester quotes Shaw's assertion that a London daily deplored *Major Barbara* as "a tasteless blasphemy" in 1905 and reports it as a reaction allied to the work of the Krupp firm's publicity men. The statement, made first in the play's 1907 preface—*not* "a quarter-century later" (in a 1930 reprinting)—referred to the newspaper's objection to "the despairing ejaculation of Barbara," in no way related to the Krupp firm's "journalistic Hessians."

41. Maurice Valency, *The Cart and the Trumpet: The Plays of George Bernard Shaw* (New York: Oxford University Press, 1973), pp. 249–50.

42. Stanley Weintraub, "Four Fathers for Barbara," in Stanley Weintraub and Philip Young, eds., *Directions in Literary Criticism: Contemporary Approaches to Literature* (University Park: Penn State University Press, 1973), pp. 203–5, reprinted in Weintraub, *The Unexpected Shaw: Biographical Approaches to G.B.S. and His Work* (New York: Frederick Ungar, 1982), pp. 150–53.

43. Shaw, *The Perfect Wagnerite: A Commentary on the Niblung's Ring* (Leipzig: Bernhard Tauchnitz, 1913, rpt. 1920), pp. 182–85; (New York: Brentano's, 1909, rpt. 1916), pp. 104, 106; *Major Critical Essays* (London: Constable, 1932), Standard Edition, pp. 242–43. The Brentano edition has only "Krupp of Essen or Carnegie of Homestead" in the first passage. Concerning Shaw's repeated revisions, see Dan H. Laurence, *Bernard Shaw: A Bibliography* (Oxford: Clarendon Press, 1983), 1:A31c.

44. Klass, p. 280; Muhlen, p. 106; Menne, p. 275.

45. H. C. Engelbrecht and F. C. Hanighen, *Merchants of Death: A Study of the International Armament Industry* (New York: Dodd, Mead, 1934), pp. 118, 121, 123. See also Donald McCormick, *Pedlar of Death: The Life of Sir Basil Zaharoff* (London: Macdonald, 1965), p. 76.

46. Fairfax Downey, *Cannonade: Great Artillery Actions of History, The Famous Cannons and the Master Gunners* (Garden City, N.Y.: Doubleday, 1966), pp. 219–22; Ian V. Hogg, *A History of Artillery* (London: Hamlyn, 1974), pp. 94–97; Engelbrecht and Hanighen, *Merchants of Death*, pp. 97–98; Menne, p. 256. As for the "aerial battleship," this is probably a Shavian allusion to the dirigible-type airship, undergoing active development early in the century but not yet seriously viewed as having offensive military capability. The Krupps in particular were cold to such use, focusing instead on anti-aircraft guns. Menne, p. 256; Air Marshall Sir Robert Saundby, *Air Bombardment: The Story of Its Development* (New York: Harper Brothers, 1961), pp. 4–6.

47. Vice Admiral Sir Arthur Hazlet, *The Submarine and Sea Power* (New York: Stein & Day, 1967), p. 15.

48. Brigadier O. F. Hogg, *Artillery: Its Origin, Heyday and Decline* (Hamden, Conn.: Archon Books, 1970), p. 85, reports that in 1870 a 35-ton muzzle-loading gun for turret ships was known as "the Woolwich Infant."

49. *Bernard Shaw, Major Barbara: A Facsimile of the Holograph Manuscript*, Introduction, Bernard F. Dukore (New York: Garland Publishing, 1981). British Library Add. Ms. 50616D, fol. 53, p. 185; 50616E, fol. 37, p. 225; 50616B, fol. 53, p. 53.

50. Mumford, *The Culture of Cities*, pp. 217–18.

51. Citations are to Ebenezer Howard, *Garden Cities of To-Morrow*, ed. F. J. Osborn, introductory essay by Lewis Mumford (London: Faber & Faber, 1945).

52. Osborn Preface, Howard, pp. 26, 9.

53. Howard, pp. 45–47. See also Mumford, *The Culture of Cities*, pp. 394–98.

54. Howard, p. 56.

55. Howard, pp. 50–57.

56. The title of Chapter 10, Howard, p. 118.

57. Quoted by Osborn, Preface, Howard, p. 11 n.

58. Robert Fishman, *Urban Utopias in the Twentieth Century: Ebenezer Howard, Frank Lloyd Wright and Le Corbusier* (New York: Basic Books, 1977), p. 26. As interesting as it is to find Fishman indirectly linking the Garden City movement to *Major Barbara*, one wonders whether he was totally unaware that Undershaft's line about *genuine* unselfishness is addressed to Barbara "*in profound irony*" according to Shaw's stage direction, and prompts Cusins to call the millionaire "Mephistopheles! Machiavelli!" in an aside (121). It is ironic that Fishman should miss the Undershaftian irony.

59. Reference has already been made to its journal, successively called *The Garden City, Garden Cities and Town Planning*, and *Town and Country Planning*, London, 1903—.

60. Fishman, p. 61.

61. *Shaw the Villager and Human Being*, narrated and edited by Allan Chappelow (London: Charles Skilton, 1961); Holroyd, *Bernard Shaw, Vol. III, 1918–1950, The Lure of Fantasy* (New York: Random House, 1991), p. 16.

62. *The Building of Satellite Towns*, p. 26; Chappelow, pp. 183, 186–87.

63. *The Building of Satellite Towns*, p. 27. Purdom's account in Chappelow, p. 195, differs slightly from this earlier version. See also Shaw's report on Lecky and the Zetetical Society, "How I Became a Public Speaker," in *Sixteen Self Sketches* (London: Constable, 1949), p. 56.

64. *The Political Madhouse in America*, p. 62. See also *Sixteen Self Sketches*, pp. 58, 66. Shaw here mistakenly gives the date when he first heard George lecture as 1884 instead of 1882.

65. "Nobody has ever got away, or ever will get away, from the truths that were the center of his propaganda: his errors anybody can get away from," wrote Shaw in a letter to Hamlin Garland, 29 December 1904, printed in Archibald Henderson, *George Bernard Shaw: Man of the Century* (New York: Appleton-Century-Crofts, 1956), p. 216; also in Bernard Shaw, *Collected Letters 1898–1910*, ed. Dan H. Laurence (New York: Dodd, Mead, 1972), pp. 477–78. Howard records some of his differences with George in his book, p. 136.

66. Kingsley Martin, "G.B.S.," in C. E. M. Joad, ed., *Shaw and Society* (London: Odhams Press, n.d.), p. 35.

67. Purdom, *The Building of Satellite Towns*, pp. 27, 39.

68. Purdom, *The Building of Satellite Towns*, p. 27.

69. Osborn, Preface, Howard, p. 20.

70. Cf. Archibald Henderson, *Bernard Shaw: Playboy and Prophet* (New York: D. Appleton, 1932, pp. xx, 241; Archibald Henderson, *George Bernard Shaw: Man of the Century*, pp. 258, 278; Maurice Colbourne, *The Real Bernard Shaw* (New York: Philosophical Library, 1949), pp. 31, 38, 294; Eric Bentley, *Bernard Shaw, 1856–1950*, Amended ed (New York: New Directions, 1957), pp. 18–19, 32–33; Julian B. Kaye, *Bernard Shaw and the Nineteenth Century Tradition* (Norman: University of Oklahoma Press, 1958), pp. 146–52. See Douglas MacFadyen, *Sir*

Ebenezer Howard and the Town Planning Movement (Cambridge, Mass.: M.I.T. Press, 1970), pp. 21–22, for Howard's own report of his reaction to Bellamy.

71. *Collected Plays with Their Prefaces*, 2: 25.

72. *Socialism: The Fabian Essays* (Boston: Charles E. Brown, 1894).

73. Fishman, *Urban Utopias*, p. 61, citing "G.B. Shaw, 'Garden City Conference at Bournville,' " p. 17.

74. Frank Jackson, *Sir Raymond Unwin: Architect, Planner, and Visionary* (London: A. Zwemmer, 1985), pp. 62–63.

75. Shaw, *Collected Letters 1898–1910*, pp. 103, 118–19.

76. One that might be regarded otherwise is Stephen Winsten's report, in *Shaw's Corner* (London: Hutchinson, 1952), p. 40, of a conversation with Shaw: " 'What a dull prosaic man he was,' G.B.S. remarked. 'It's the dull people who are changing the face of the earth, while the bright ones rise like balloons and burst. I have always envied dull people and have tried to model my life on theirs.' " The thought expressed is not unlike that in Shaw's letter to Howard's son, quoted below. But it is so different in tone and spirit as to raise the question whether this recollected conversation truly reflects Shaw's estimate of Howard.

77. *The Building of Satellite Towns*, p. 5: *Garden Cities & Town-Planning* 17 (2 February 1927): 33.

78. Chappelow, p. 186; Osborn in Chappelow, p. 191. Also Osborn, *New Towns after the War: An Argument for Garden Cities* (London: J. M. Dent and Sons, 1918), Preface to 1942 rev. ed., p. 15.

79. Purdom, in Chappelow, pp. 195–96.

80. *The Intelligent Woman's Guide to Socialism and Capitalism* (London: Constable, 1928), p. 301. Subsequent citations of this work will specify pages in the text. *Everybody's Political What's What?* (London: Constable, 1944), p. 18.

81. Purdom in Chappelow, p. 197 and n.; Patch, *Thirty Years with G.B.S.* (New York: Dodd, Mead, 1951), p. 243.

82. Osborn in Chappelow, p. 190; Mrs. Berry in Chappelow, p. 179.

83. Osborn in Chappelow, p. 191, and in his *New Town* Preface, p. 15. This is from the October 1941 letter cited in note 78, above.

84. Purdom in Chappelow, p. 196.

85. *Collected Plays with Their Prefaces*, 2:899. Subsequent page references to *John Bull's Other Island* are given in the text.

86. Purdom, *Building of Satellite Towns*, pp. 56, 89.

87. *The Garden City*, p. 80. Cf. Purdom, *The Building of Satellite Towns*, p. 59.

88. Purdom, *The Garden City*, pp. 68–69.

89. *The Garden City*, p. 121; *The Building of Satellite Towns*, p. 74. Purdom gives the date of its construction as 1905 in his earlier Garden City book and 1906 in his later one.

90. Among the interesting items in Letchworth's subsequent history is the fact that V. I. Lenin took temporary refuge in the town, as did other Russian refugees. *The Building of Satellite Towns*, p. 488.

91. "All these set standards which were to influence the whole story of town planning and urban development for the next fifty years." Stewart, p. 179. Cf. Osborn, Preface, Howard, p. 13, and Mumford's judgment of Letchworth, that "because of its success in incorporating industries and in building workers' houses, the garden city became a focal point in the mind of social-minded planners and administrators throughout the world." *The Culture of Cities*, p. 399.

92. Purdom, *Satellite Towns*, p. 59.

93. From a pamphlet issued in 1901, two years before Letchworth was begun, quoted in *Satellite Towns*, p. 173. Purdom supplies no title for the pamphlet.

94. "A Note on Terminology" in Osborn, Preface, Howard, pp. 26–28. This "Note" also

appears in Osborn's *Green-Belt Cities*, Appendix II, pp. 181–82. See also Brown, Sherrard, and Shaw, pp. 276–77.

95. *Major Barbara: A Screen Version* (Baltimore: Penguin Books, 1951), pp. 137–38.

96. Margery M. Morgan, *The Shavian Playground* (London: Methuen, 1972), regards the Perivale St. Andrews setting as that of a Garden City—and even more suggestive of Cadbury and Bournville (p. 137 and n.). Michael Holroyd, *Bernard Shaw, Vol. III*, p. 16, sees Shaw as putting "Ebenezer Howard's dream-town . . . on the stage as Perivale St Andrews." Neither offers any apparent evidence or argument for these claims.

97. Daniel J. Leary, "A Deleted Passage from Shaw's *John Bull's Other Island*," *Bulletin of the New York Public Library* 74:9 (November 1970): 598–606.

98. *Major Barbara: Facsimile*, pp. 185, 187. British Library Add MS. 50616D, fols. 53–54.

99. Webb, *Our Partnership*, p. 314; also *Diary*, 3:13.

100. *Major Barbara: A Facsimile*, p. 324, British Library Add. MS. 50616A, fol. 76. The text is the same in the typescript of the original production.

101. Webb, *Partnership*, p. 315; also *Diary*, 3:14. Emphasis is Webb's. On 4 December 1905 she sent G.B.S. a conciliatory letter, beginning, "You made me doubt my own criticism of the ending of *Barbara* by your persuasive exposition of it." She still remained dissatisfied, complaining that he had not got his message across to the audience, perhaps because of the acting or "some lack of proportion to Undershaft's argument." She did laud the second act. *The Letters of Sidney and Beatrice Webb, Volume II: Partnership 1892–1912*, ed. Norman MacKenzie (London: Cambridge University Press, 1978), pp. 216–17.

102. *Collected Plays with Their Prefaces*, 2:687.

Bernard Shaw

"THE DARK LADY": G.B.S. REPLIES TO FRANK HARRIS

[The following interview appeared in the *Daily News*, London, on 24 November 1910. It was based on a partially published manuscript of Shaw's with corrections and additions made by William R. Titterton, a critic, journalist, and press agent. The occasion that prompted the Shaw article was the first production of *The Dark Lady of the Sonnets* by the Committee of the Shakespeare Memorial National Theatre at a Charity Matinee at the Haymarket Theatre, 24 November 1910, followed by another performance the next day. Shaw attended the first matinee performance and shared the author's box with Mr. and Mrs. Frank Harris. Harley Granville Barker was both director and actor, playing William Shakespear, while Hugh B. Tabberer played the Warden, Suzanne Sheldon played Queen Elizabeth, and Mona Limerick played Mary Fitton. According to Raymond Mander and Joe Mitchenson in *The Theatrical Companion to Shaw*, the play itself was suggested to Shaw by "Dame Edith Lyttleton, who was raising money for the, still projected, National Theatre" (pp. 138–39). Dan H. Laurence includes in *Collected Letters 1898–1910* a letter (21 November 1910) to Charles Ricketts, who designed the costumes and the setting for *The Dark Lady of the Sonnets*. Shaw discusses in that letter his ideas of how the music should be arranged to correspond with specific portions of the play and then notes some changes that he has made to the text itself.

Shaw's reference to Harris's play that he had read in manuscript is to *Shakespeare and His Love* (1910). Harris had also written two critical works on Shakespeare, *The Man Shakespeare* (1909) and *The Women of Shakespeare* (published in 1911). None of these publications won him scholarly acclaim.

The text is drawn from a transcription by Blanche Patch of Shaw's shorthand manuscript, now in the possession of Dan H. Laurence, by whose courtesy it is reproduced. Material set in brackets was deleted before publication, by Titterton, and is published here for the first time. Titterton's alterations appear in boldface type.—G.K.L.]

"I thought you'd be coming round," Mr. G.B. Shaw remarked to me (writes Mr. W.R. Titterton). "It's about Harris, of course. Well, [B]before I saw anything about your interview with [Frank Harris] **him,** let me do an act of justice. The theory that the lady of the sonnets was Mary Fitton was suggested and worked out neither by [Frank] **Harris** nor by me, but by the late Thomas Tyler. In the eighties Tyler and I worked every day in the reading room of the British Museum. He was interested in the Sonnets; and he often brought me a passage, and asked me what I understood by it. He was convinced that [a] "Mr. W.H.," the ["onlie begotten"] **'onlie begetter'** of the Sonnets, was the Earl of Pembroke; and this put him on the track of Mistress Fitton. [He kept me informed of every link in the chain of evidence as he wrought it from week to week.]

"The New Shakespeare Society, of which I was a member and a constant frequenter at that time, knew of his labours, and the Rev. W.A. Harrison gave him some clues[,]; but the idea was Tyler's, and all the work, down to his final trip to Cheshire to see whether the remaining scraps of colouring on the effigy on Mary Fitton's tomb [shew] **showed** her as a dark lady, was all done by Tyler, whose book on the Sonnets can be consulted [by anyone who wishes to study the case. The truth is] Shakespearean scholars were, and still are, rather shy of the theory; for, though [they think] the superstructure **of evidence** is ingenious and interesting, the foundation is no more than a guess[:] - I would not myself stake half-a-crown on it. But, should it ever be substantiated, all the honours must go to Tyler [; and Frank and I must stand aside with the rest of the crowd and take our hats off]. Tyler was a better scholar than either of us; and, as he lived and died without ["]having as much public notice["] in fifty years as we two have often had in a week, we are bound to make it clear that it is to him **that** we both owe the discovery of Mary Fitton." [If that point is quite clear I am now ready for cross examination.]

G.B.S. AS PROSPERO

[*Question.*] "Do you recognize Mr. Harris's account of your relations as a correct one?"

[*Answer.*] "Quite correct enough for all reasonable purposes. Much more correct than nine out of ten statements that appear in the Press. I mean as to the facts. Of course, I do not see them exactly as he sees them[;]**, and he does not see them exactly as I see them;** but there are very few literary men whose points of view would keep us close to one another."

[*Question.*] "Do you accept his estimate of your attitude towards him as [being one of] patting him on the head, for instance?"

[*Answer.*] "Yes, except as to the word 'contemptuous.' It is [only] natural [to] **for** me to pat Frank on the head[.]**:** My white hairs, my hard work, my exemplary habits give me the right to do it. Harris is one of the very few English authors who really care[s] for literature. [For] **If** he could only be as [kind to mediocrity doing its little best as he is] enthusiastic and delicately and penetratingly sympathetic [with] **to** men of genius [but]**,** **he** would be admitted to a very high place among men of letters. [But he has no mercy for mere respectability in art; but is reckless, violent, even coarse. And he has not served literature faithfully. When he wrote you he "drifted into other things", he mentions that he wrote two plays to my ten and wasted his time in finance, in founding journals of which he got tired in a week, in doing everything except the business he was born to do. The consequence is that it is not as easy as he thinks to get justice done to him. He has wounded the feelings of a great many people whose crime[,] was that they did not interest him as much as Shakespeare did. If only he would publish some thoroughly bad work, all the world would hear of him, because there would be something to abuse him about. But all the things he has published - his short stories and his Shakespearean studies are so good that nobody can say anything against them except that they are revolutionary, which he would take as the highest compliment - quite rightly. So they say nothing about them at all; and he has lived in the legends of a very superior **coterie** order then in the public eye.]

"I have always tried to encourage him, to praise him, to reform him, and to flatter him by stealing his excellent ideas[. But]**,** **but** there is no changing the man. Indeed, **in his literary capacity,** he is not a man in the normal sense[:]**;** he is a [sort of] monster compounded of Caliban and Ariel - an outrageous Caliban and a most delicate Ariel, on whom [the] good advice and **fatherly** pats on [his] **the** head [of the] **from a** steady going Prospero like [myself] **me** are quite lost."

"Did you write the unpublished criticism of his man Shakespeare?"

"Yes, I was so interested that I went on writing until the review was too long for an article. Besides, Harris was so splendid and so right and decent in his disposal of the unmentionable interpretation which has been put on the sonnets that I felt bound to say as much; and our family journals might not have liked it."

SHAKESPEARE MISREAD

[*Question.*] "Have you really stolen his Shakespeare?"

[*Answer.*] "Why should I? Not that his Shakespeare is not worth stealing, but Shakespeare is common property; and I can dramatise him **for myself** in half the time it would [cost] **take** me to steal Frank's [dramatics] **drama-**

tization. Besides, [Frank] **he** will never really understand Shakespeare. Frank has a most enormous capacity for pity: he is a sort of Parsifal - [quote from notes]; **'durch Mitleid wissend'***; and his pity for Shakespeare overwhelms every other consideration with him. But what did Shakespeare say? Listen[:]**!**

> There is no creature loves me**;**
> And when I die no soul will pity me.
> Nay, wherefore should they[,]**?** since that I **myself**
> [myself f]Find in myself no pity for myself.

HARD AS A DIAMOND

"This last [jibe] **jibing anticlimax, highly characteristic of Shakespeare,** is the side of [Shakespeare] **him** that Harris cannot [understand] **stomach.** Shakespeare, with all his humanity, was as hard as a diamond, and was a stupendous mocker and laugher. Mary Fitton might just as easily have broken the dome of St. [Paul's] **Peter's** in her little fingers as Shakespeare's heart. There is no suffering in Shakespeare. Tragedy swings him up instead of striking him down. He defies Frank's pity. No matter: Frank's genius is a genius for pity, a pride in suffering[,]**;** and he makes Shakespeare pitiable in spite of all the immortal William's jibes. **Now, I** pity Mary Fitton.

["But Mr. Harris says you don't understand women." Mr. Shaw smiled. "I don't pretend to", he said. "I have to fall back on the unromantic assumption that the female of the species is not so very unlike the male, whatever the male may think. It answers well enough to enable me to write possible plays about women. But Frank does very well at that work. There is a very fine story of his about Sophie - about the **Nihilist** saint and martyr who was hanged for assassinating Alexander II - Sonia I think he called her: her real name was Sophie. That story would have made the reputation of anybody but Frank Harris: no doubt it will make it in the long run, when Frank grows old and settles down, of which there are no present signs. I couldn't have written that story. Shakespeare certainly couldn't have written it. It is perhaps necessary to be taken in to a certain extent by women to write such things. Therefore if you want to know whether Harris or I knows most about women - an enquiry strangely unsuited to the decorum of the "Daily News," by the way - you had better consult some lady, as the question is one on which it is clear that we cannot offer an opinion without making ourselves ridiculous.]

"As to my portrait of Shakespeare, it will not be wholly mine. Both Mr.

---

*Shaw's reminder to "quote from notes" implies that he, not Titterton, added this quotation from *Parsifal*, but the German phrase does not appear on the transcription of his shorthand manuscript.

Granville Barker and Mr. Ricketts will have a hand in it this afternoon. You can read Frank's play - I read it myself in [MSS] **manuscript** long [ago] **before I wrote my own** - and then come to the Shakespeare Memorial National Theatre Matinee [this afternoon] and judge for yourself. **Thanks to you, I anticipate a good crowd. The General Election threatened to spoil everything, but now -**

> " 'Now all your enemies will come,
> There will not be room for them.' "

David Gunby

THE FIRST NIGHT OF
O'FLAHERTY, V.C.

The circumstances surrounding the writing and (non) performance of Shaw's play, *O'Flaherty, V.C.*, are well enough known. Based on the exploits of Lance Corporal Michael O'Leary, awarded the Victoria Cross for single-handedly killing eight German soldiers and capturing another fifteen, the play was conceived by Shaw both as a boost to a flagging Irish recruitment campaign and as a means of assisting the financially straitened Abbey Theatre. What Shaw produced, however—a play demonstrating that life in Ireland was so unpleasant as to make serving as a soldier on the Western Front a palatable alternative—proved unacceptable to Sir Matthew Nathan, Under-Secretary for Ireland, and to the authorities in Dublin Castle, and accordingly a production scheduled at the Abbey was first postponed and then canceled. Given not only the pessimism of Shaw's view of Ireland, but also of O'Flaherty's comments, such as "Dont talk to me or to any other soldier of the war being right. No war is right," and "Youll never have a quiet world til you knock the patriotism out of the human race," it is hardly surprising that the Dublin authorities saw in Shaw's recruiting play more prospects of rioting than of an increased flow of volunteers and that they applied pressure that resulted in the play's being withdrawn from production.

The circumstances surrounding the canceled Abbey Theatre production of *O'Flaherty, V.C.* are well known and documented, but those in which the play was first performed are less so, and what is in print is often inaccurate or misleading. The usually accepted facts are those given in the Bodley Head *Collected Plays*: "First presented by Officers of the 40th Squadron, R.F.C., on the Western Front at Treizennes, Belgium, on 17 February 1917, with Robert Loraine as O'Flaherty, supported by a cast of amateurs."[1] This statement presumably forms the basis of the brief reference to the first performance of *O'Flaherty, V.C.* in Michael Holroyd's biography: "Shaw's picture of Ireland as unmitigated hell . . . received its first presentation on 17 February 1917 at Treizennes in Belgium where Shaw attended a dress rehearsal. Robert Loraine was O'Flaherty and the other parts were played by officers of the Royal Flying Corps, while the men put on a performance of *The Inca of Perusalem.*"[2] Repeating the date and the Belgian location (both, as will be seen, wrong), Holroyd adds a further dimension to the problem by referring to the performance as "a dress rehearsal." If in the strict sense it was, when was the performance for which this was a rehearsal? Fortunately there is enough information, fragmentary as it is, to settle these points, but not enough to satisfy all the questions that might be asked about the first performance of *O'Flaherty, V.C.*

First, the place. Treizennes is correct, but it is in France, not Belgium, being a tiny hamlet two kilometers southwest of Aire, in Artois. Forty Squadron had been based there since its move to France at the end of August 1916, the airfield being in the grounds of a chateau owned by a M. Schatzmann, and the personnel accommodated in huts in the grounds, with the squadron office and Officers' Mess in the Chateau itself.[3]

Second, the date: 17 February. This cannot be correct since two *termini ad quem* rule it out decisively. One, 12 February, is established by the fact that on that date Robert Loraine left for England on leave, having relinquished command of 40 Squadron the previous day, after nearly a year as Commanding Officer. A farewell dinner, attended by his successor, Major L. A. Tilney, was held in his honor on the evening of Saturday, 10 February, and he left for England Monday morning.[4]

The second and earlier *terminus*, 5 February, is provided by Shaw's return to England on completion of his official tour of the Western Front, about which he wrote three articles in the *Daily Chronicle*, 5, 7, and 8 March 1917. Unfortunately Shaw did not long maintain his 1917 new year's resolution to keep a diary, but the itinerary given by Dan H. Laurence in Shaw's *Collected Letters 1911–1925* establishes when Shaw was at Treizennes:

> He departed for France and Belgium on 28th January, visiting Arras, St Eloi (where he met Philip Gibbs), Ypres, Bailleul, Etaples, Tirancourt (where he dined with Robert Loraine and Lady Gregory's son Robert), Montreuil (where he lunched with Sir Douglas Haig), St Omer, Amiens, the Somme front (where he had tea with General Rawlinson), Aire (where he visited Loraine's air squadron), and Boulogne (where he missed the scheduled ship and spent the night with Sir Almroth Wright, who was Consultative Physician at the military hospital there). He returned to England on 5th February.[5]

From this it is clear that the night Shaw spent "freezing . . . at Loraine's flying station"[6] was that of 3/4 February, and the first performance of

Fig. 7. (Left to right): Major Robert Loraine, Captain Denis Mulholland, and Captain Frederick Powell. Enlargement of part of a photograph of the officers of 40 Squadron, Royal Flying Corps, taken at Gosport, Hants., August 1916. Courtesy of Chaz. Bowyer.

O'Flaherty, V.C. must therefore have been on the evening of Saturday, 3 February 1917.

What of the circumstances under which the play was performed? In *Journey to Heartbreak*, Stanley Weintraub writes of "*The Inca of Perusalem*, done by the men, and *O'Flaherty, V.C.*, done by the officers," being performed "in the nearly empty mess,"[7] and this information is no doubt derived from Winifrid Loraine's biography of her husband, in which she quotes F. J. Powell, at the time Loraine's senior flight commander, as saying, "I sat behind him in the empty mess at this rehearsal."[8] But in a lengthy interview, taped by the Imperial War Museum in 1973, Powell gives a fuller account that seems to show beyond doubt that the plays were performed in a theater: "our C.O. was this famous actor-airman, Robert Lorraine [*sic*], and he found a hut: it was a Red Cross hut which he saw and he'd noted that nobody seemed to own it. And all the officers went off in cars. We dismantled the hut and we brought it back to our own aerodrome and built it again. We had a wonderful theatre. It had a stage. It would hold about 250."[9]

Fig. 8.   Captain Robert Gregory. Courtesy of Mrs. Catherine Kennedy.

It is not likely, either, that the theatre was "nearly empty" since there
were two squadrons based at Treizennes, and the personnel of the two,
ground crew, pilots, and (with 43 Squadron) observers as well would have
gone close to filling the auditorium, if all were attending. That attendance
was not restricted to 40 Squadron is attested by Harold Balfour, then a
flight commander with 43 Squadron, who recalls the evening in his memoirs:

> [Mr. Bernard Shaw] came to stay with our command and visited,
> naturally, his friend and old professional colleague, Robert Loraine.
> In his honour No. 40 Squadron performed two of Bernard Shaw's
> plays. I forget what they were, but I do remember that special cos-
> tumes were hired from England, and that these all arrived in due
> course safely, and the performance was a great success, eliciting I
> believe some praise from Mr. Shaw himself![10]

Besides the "special costumes . . . hired from England" were there sets also
for *O'Flaherty, V.C.* and *The Inca of Perusalem,* or merely the few props that
the two require? The question is worth asking because one of the officers

Fig. 9. Lieutenant Desmond de Burgh. Enlargement of part of a photograph of 40 Squadron pilots taken early May 1917.

of 40 Squadron was an artist of note, Robert Gregory, son of Lady Augusta Gregory, and a stage designer who had been involved in notable collaborations at the Abbey with Yeats.[11] Moreover it would have been a nice touch if Gregory had designed and painted sets since *O'Flaherty, V.C.* opens "*At the door of an Irish country house in a park,*" and we know from a letter of Shaw to Lady Gregory (14 September 1915) that Shaw based Sir Pierce Madigan's country seat on Coole and that the the opening scene "is quite simply before the porch of your house."[12]

Apt as it would have been, however, it seems unlikely that there were sets, for in a letter to his mother (14 January 1917) concerning the forthcoming performance of *O'Flaherty, V.C.*, Robert Gregory makes no mention of them (as surely he would have done): "We are doing O'Flaherty V.C. in about a week's time; I am playing the serving [crossed out] maid, Tessie; I think it will go well. The Inca of Perusalem is being played at the same time."[13]

What of the performance itself? In her biography of her husband, Winifrid Loraine quotes in a footnote F. J. Powell's account of Shaw's reaction to the performance: "He laughed throughout the performance and enjoyed himself at his own jokes, and at the end I leant over and said to him: 'I'm glad you appreciate our poor efforts at your play, sir.' He could scarcely speak for laughing. 'Do you know,' he said, 'if I had thought the stuff would prove to be as poor as this, I'd never have written it.' "[14]

This account, which forms the basis of Stanley Weintraub's in *Journey to Heartbreak* (p. 224), fails to clarify which of his plays Shaw was laughing so uproariously at, but the Imperial War Museum interview does so:

> We actually acted two unpublished plays of Bernard Shaw's and to
> our intense delight who should arrive to stay with us as a VIP for a

week but Bernard Shaw himself. At that time, I think it was in *John Bull*, I had seen an article from Bernard Shaw urging men not to enlist. And I said to Lorraine [*sic*], "You know, there is a job for a public assassin, a fellow trained by the Government to kill people like this." And one week afterwards who should arrive but Bernard Shaw himself. Lorraine introduced me and said, "Oh, Shaw," he said, "this is Powell. This is the boy who wants to shoot you." Shaw said, "How do you do? I am very pleased to meet you. And you know you might have chosen somebody worse."

We were acting a play, and Lorraine at dinner excused himself and said, "I've got to go down; we are doing a dress rehearsal for the men, *The Inca of Perusalem*, one of your plays, Shaw." He said, "Powell, will you bring Shaw down as soon as he's finished his meal?" So I took Bernard Shaw down to the theatre and I sat on a seat, just behind him, and I was worried to see that all the way through this play he roared with laughter. He roared so much that he actually cried and brought out a handkerchief to wipe his eyes. In those days, Shaw had a ginger beard, not white, but he was absolutely ginger, and I remember this beard wobbling up and down.

It struck me at the time that it was extremely bad form for a playwright to laugh until he cried at his own comedy, and I leant forward to him afterwards, when it was finished, and I said, "I am so glad sir that you appreciate our poor efforts at your play." He turned round, still wiping his eyes, and he said, "Do you know. If I had thought it was going to be anything like that I wouldn't have written it!"[15]

Powell's account is not absolutely to be relied upon, as witness his statement that Shaw was "with us as a VIP for a week," but again the details ring true.

What, however, of the reference to a "dress rehearsal" of *The Inca of Perusalem*? Was it? And if so, in what sense? The answer is to be found at the University of Guelph Library, which holds a "PROGRAMME of an Entertainment at THEATRE ROYAL on Wednesday 21st February."[16] Given by "No. 40 Squadron, R.F.C." and "*By the kind permission of the Commanding Officer*," it lists six items, three of them dramatic: *O'Flaherty, V.C.*, *The Inca of Perusalem*, and "A Vignette from a Shakespeare History" that clearly comprises excerpts from Act IV of *Henry V*. It seems evident that the producton of both Shaw plays had been arranged before Loraine knew that Shaw would visit Treizennes. The performances of *The Inca of Perusalem* and *O'Flaherty, V.C.* on 3 February were, then, "dress rehearsals," perhaps literally, perhaps in the common theatrical sense of preview performances before an official premiere that critics are invited to review.

It seems generally to have been assumed, as by Michael Holroyd, that

Fig. 10. Lt. William Morrice, in the photograph supplied by him in July 1916 when, after qualifying as a Royal Flying Corps pilot, he applied for his Royal Aero Club Certificate. Courtesy of the Royal Air Force Museum, Hendon, London.

Robert Loraine took the title role in *O'Flaherty, V.C.*, but the cast list in the Theatre Royal program appears to rule this out, for alongside Robert Gregory as Tessie we find Capt. D. O. Mulholland as O'Flaherty, Lt. W. Morrice as General Sir Pearce Madigan, and Lt. D. H. de Burgh as Mrs. O'Flaherty. The tall, angular scion of a distinguished Anglo-Irish family with a long history of military service, Desmond Herlouin de Burgh would have brought to the part of the harridan Irish mother an authentic brogue but also a comic inappropriateness of appearance, accentuated by that of O'Flaherty, since Denis Osmund Mulholland (affectionately known as "Little Mull") was small of stature, with a round face and soft features.

William Morrice, who played Sir Pearce Madigan, must have been a talented amateur actor, for Loraine also cast him in the title role in the excerpts from *Henry V* that presumably included Henry's great St. Crispin's Day's speech. The photograph of himself that Morrice submitted when applying for his Royal Aero Club Certificate, after qualifying as a pilot, shows a fashionably dressed young man well-suited to the role of the patrician General, but his accent may have been Scots (he was born in Glasgow).

One final aspect of the first performance of *O'Flaherty, V.C.* is worth investigation: the nervous state of Robert Loraine at the time of Shaw's visit. Winifrid Loraine's biography paints a vivid picture of a man at the end of his tether, broken by crippling losses among those he commanded and sustained only by will-power and alcohol:

> His days were spent in fear, his nights were panic—which one of the men he knew would be taken next? He could scarcely bring himself to attend an Inter-squadron Swimming Sports, because the boys who were laughing and striving in the pool, would be crossing the line next morning. Or would they know a next morning—they might be sent up to Hun-straf that evening.
>
> He, who had always preached the joy of battle, now hated the sound of it.
>
> During his last days with 40 Squadron, he had to force himself to enter mess of an evening. When possible, he surrounded his end of the table with visitors, officers from other messes, so that he should not miss certain "faces" too quickly. "Faces" he had probably been rehearsing between while in *O'Flaherty, V.C.*, during the day, and now no longer faces.[17]

Stanley Weintraub's account, relying heavily on Winifrid Loraine at this point, links playmaking to the need to obliterate the sense of loss: "Loraine had become a martinet for efficiency and duty in an attempt to provide a substitute for self-pity, and after the notes of the Last Post concluded each funeral ceremony for a downed flier, Loraine would urge on the nightly merrymaking in the mess, shepherding his young officers to the piano and commanding, 'Sing! Sing!' With an actor in command, it was inevitable that fragments from plays would be part of the entertainment. . . ."[18]

In fact, however, the losses that 40 Squadron had suffered since its arrival in France in August 1916 had been remarkably few: one pilot killed in a flying accident in August, two shot down and taken prisoner in November, and only one killed in action, on 17 January 1917.[19] The horrendous losses that undoubtedly did affect Loraine were those suffered by the corps reconnaissance squadrons forming part of 14 Wing, which he commanded in the spring and early summer of 1917, after his return from leave in England. During "Bloody April," as it came to be known, losses of aircraft and crews reached crisis proportions, and no doubt Winifrid Loraine's account refers to that period (the inter-squadron swimming sports, for instance, must have been a summer event, not held during the winter of 1916–17, one of the coldest on record).

Robert Loraine was indeed a martinet and pushed his officers and men hard, but there is no reason to assume that this was because of his distress over losses. The martinet major was, rather, part of Loraine's inveterate role-playing. Harold Balfour comments, for instance, "I saw Robert Lo-

raine under a variety of different circumstances during those months on
Trezenes [*sic*]. I never saw him other than being Robert Loraine 'the pioneer aviator' and Robert Loraine the actor."[20] And Fred Powell is quoted
as saying, "You felt that the officer was a conception of what he felt the
part to be. Loraine, the man, was full of understanding. But outwardly he
remained a disciplinarian to the last inch of him."[21]

Powell also recalled, in his Imperial War Museum interview, how Loraine
played the part of Major:

> He had just been promoted Major. But of course being an actor, the
> actor on stage always had an eyeglass, and who should acquire an
> eyeglass but of course Robert Lorraine [*sic*]. When I was on one of
> my leaves in London I bought from Harrods a whole box of plain
> eyeglasses with broad black ribbons. When I returned to the squad-
> ron I issued each one of these ribbons and eyeglasses to the officers.
> That night at dinner everybody wore an eyeglass. I must say that
> Lorraine was quite good. He took it in good part. He didn't com-
> ment at all. He didn't even try to say that he had a defective eye . . .
> and for that I admired him.[22]

Arthur Tedder, then a Royal Flying Corps Captain stationed near Treizennes, but later to become Marshal of the Royal Air Force Lord Tedder,
wrote to his wife on 2 October 1916 about a dinner he had attended at
which "The 'Actor Airman' was present and being opposite the general
had of course to act up to it. He was really extraordinarily funny with his
eyeglass and 'air.' "[23] Tedder, whose wife, Rosalinde, was a close friend of
Shaw's secretary, Ann Elder, and who had met Loraine pre-war, comments
in a letter on 16 October that "the 'Actor Airman' . . . is a bit of a fusser,"
and in another (18 September) writes, "He is an amusing fellow, but he
doesn't seem to be exactly liked by anyone much."

In yet another letter, incidentally, Tedder provides evidence of Loraine's
long-held intention to produce *The Inca of Perusalem*. On 26 October 1916
he wrote to his wife of dinner at Treizennes "with 'Bobbie' and our friends
of the 'Baby Eights' [i.e., 40 Squadron, which flew the single-seat F.E.8
scout]. Robert is extraordinarily funny at times," he continues,

> especially when he doesn't mean to be. I was talking to him—or
> rather, he to me—most of the time. After dinner, the others
> crowded round a piano and made a noise while we settled in a cor-
> ner seat at the other end of the room. Discussed many things—
> aviation and war and other things.
>   Then he produced a little play he's going to produce in his squad-
> ron—perhaps you've heard of it, *The Inca of Perusalem?* It's supposed

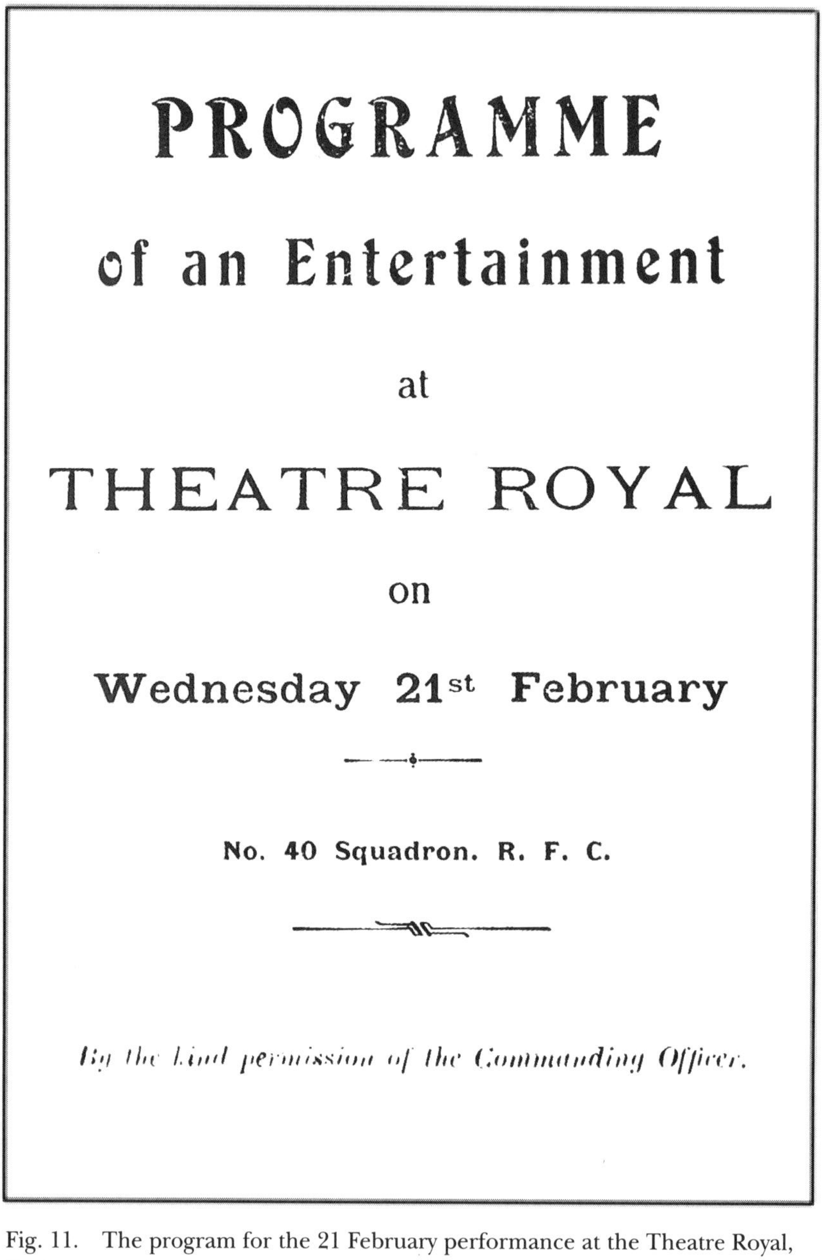

PROGRAMME

of an Entertainment

at

THEATRE ROYAL

on

Wednesday 21st February

———•———

No. 40 Squadron. R. F. C.

—————➤————

By the kind permission of the Commanding Officer.

Fig. 11.   The program for the 21 February performance at the Theatre Royal, Treizennes, of *The Inca of Perusalem* and *O'Flaherty, V.C.* Courtesy of the Dan H. Laurence Collection, Special Collections, University of Guelph Library.

1. OVERTURE. — Sergt. Major Donaldson's Band.

O'FLAHERTY V. C.

An interlude in the Great War

by Bernard SHAW.

CAST

O'Flaherty V. C.	Capt. D. O. Mulholland.
Genl. Sir Pearce Madigan	Lieut. W. Monnick.
Mrs O' Flaherty	Lieut. D. de Benon.
Teresa Driscoll	Capt. R. Gregory.

Scene. — Outside the house of Genl. Sir Pearce Madigan.

3. Song. — THE DEATHLESS ARMY.

Sgt. Major Donaldson.

---

4. The Inca of Perusalem

An absurd Historical Comedietta by a fellow of the Royal Society of Literature

CAST

The Inca	1 A. M. A. B. Penney.
The Archdeacon	Corpl. J. H. Smythe.
Hotel Manager	2 A.M.E.W. Manwaring.
Hotel Waiter	Corpl. W. A. Medlen.
The Princess	1 A. M. S. G. Cann.
Ermyntrude	Corpl. S. J. White.

Scene. — A Hotel Room

5. Dance.	2 Lieut. P. H. Smyth.

6. A VIGNETTE FROM A SHAKESPEARE HISTORY

CHORUS: Capt. D. O. Mulholland.

Gloucester	Capt.D.O.Mulholland.
Bedford	2 Lieut. W. B. Hills.
Westmorland	2 Lieut. P. H. Smyth.
Salisbury	Capt. R. Gregory.
Exeter	Lieut. D. de Benon.
King Henry V	Lieut. W. Monnick.

Scene. — The English Camp before Agincourt

LA MARSEILLAISE
GOD SAVE THE KING

to be anonymous, but he showed me writing on the front page and naturally I knew *GBS*'s handwriting. As a matter of fact, it couldn't be written by anybody else. Robert started reading it to me and got so lost in it that with very little encouragement he read right through it. It was awfully interesting and very witty. Rather a funny sight it would have been to an onlooker, I should think; the big chateau dining hall with long white table down the middle, up one end of the room a crowd of pilots round the piano shouting choruses, at the other end, in a corner seat beside a huge fireplace, the Actor Airman reading me GB's latest—and reading it very well too. I enjoyed the show.[24]

In fact, *The Inca of Perusalem* was not Shaw's "latest." That was *O'Flaherty, V.C.*, of which Loraine may well not have then received a script.

To sum up, there can be no doubt that *O'Flaherty, V.C.* was first played on 21 February 1917 in the theater at the Royal Flying Corps base at Trei-zennes, near Aire, but that the first performance was a dress rehearsal arranged for the benefit of Shaw on 3 February. Direction was by Robert Loraine, and the cast of 40 Squadron officers included Denis Mulholland (as O'Flaherty), William Morrice (as General Sir Pearce Madigan), Desmond de Burgh (as Mrs. O'Flaherty), and Robert Gregory (as the maid, Tessie). The production was costumed, but there were almost certainly no sets. Of Shaw's response to the production we have no record, save Harold Balfour's comment that "the performance was a great success, eliciting I believe some praise from Mr. Shaw himself," and of the R.F.C. audience's, nothing. It may not be too fanciful, however, to speculate that the audience at Treizenne responded as did the wounded soldiers to whom Shaw read *O'Flaherty, V.C.* later in 1917, at a hospital near Ayot St. Lawrence: "They gave me three cheers," Shaw wrote to Lady Gregory on 27 November, "and laughed a good deal; but the best bits were when they sat very tight and said nothing."[25]

Notes

1. Bernard Shaw, *Collected Plays with Their Prefaces*, ed. Dan H. Laurence (London: Max Reinhardt, 1970–74), 4: 984.

2. Michael Holroyd, *Bernard Shaw, Vol. 2: 1898–1918: The Pursuit of Power* (New York: Random House, 1989), p. 381.

3. See David Gunby, *Sweeping the Skies: A History of No. 40 Squadron, RFC and RAF, 1916–56* (Bishop Auckland: Pentland Press, 1985).

4. See *Sweeping the Skies*, p. 12. A reproduction of the signed menu for the farewell dinner

is printed in Harold H. Balfour, *An Airman Marches: Early Flying Adventures 1914–23* (Repr. London: Greenhill Books, 1985), p. 81.

5. Bernard Shaw, *Collected Letters 1911–1925*, ed. Dan H. Laurence (London: Max Reinhardt, 1985), p. 448.

6. G.B.S. to Harley Granville Barker, 28 February 1917, in *Collected Letters 1911–1925*, p. 457.

7. Stanley Weintraub, *Bernard Shaw 1914–18: Journey to Heartbreak* (London: Routledge & Kegan Paul, 1973), p. 224.

8. Winifrid Loraine, *Robert Loraine: Actor, Soldier, Airman* (London: Collins, 1938), p. 237.

9. Imperial War Museum interview, p. 24 (Reel 05).

10. Balfour, *An Airman Marches*, p. 86.

11. For Robert Gregory's career as artist and stage designer, see Richard Allen Cave, "Richard Gregory: Artist and Stage Designer," published as an Appendix (pp. 347–400) to Ann Saddlemyer and Colin Smyth, eds., *Lady Gregory: Fifty Years After* (Gerrards Cross: Colin Smythe, 1987).

12. *Shaw, Lady Gregory and the Abbey: A Correspondence and a Record*, ed. Dan H. Laurence and Nicholas Grene (Gerrards Cross: Colin Smythe, 1993), p. 94.

13. Quoted from the Gregory Family Papers by kind permission of the Librarian, Robert W. Woodruff Library, Emory University, and of Anne de Winton and Catherine Kennedy.

14. Winifred Loraine, *Robert Loraine*, p. 237.

15. Imperial War Museum interview, p. 24 (reels 05–06).

16. I am indebted to Dan H. Laurence for alerting me to the existence of this program and to the University of Guelph Library for permission to reproduce it.

17. Winifred Loraine, *Robert Loraine*, pp. 236–37.

18. Weintraub, *Journey to Heartbreak*, p. 224.

19. See Gunby, *Sweeping the Skies*, pp. 4–14.

20. Balfour, *An Airman Marches*, p. 70.

21. Winifred Loraine, *Robert Loraine*, p. 218.

22. Imperial War Museum interview, p. 17 (reel 04).

23. Tedder family papers (correspondence), quoted by courtesy of the Tedder family and Vincent Orange.

24. This must have been a printed rehearsal copy, i.e. an unpublished proof in which the deletions required by the Lord Chamberlain had been made (see Weintraub, *Journey to Heartbreak*, p. 130). Loraine did not receive a copy of the unamended text until mid November (*Journey to Heartbreak*, p. 131).

25. *Shaw, Lady Gregory and the Abbey*, p. 135.

Wendi Chen

THE FIRST SHAW PLAY ON THE CHINESE STAGE: THE PRODUCTION OF *MRS WARREN'S PROFESSION* IN 1921

Modern Chinese Spoken Drama (also previously known as "New Drama" and "Civilized New Drama" in contrast to traditional Chinese drama) owes its existence to Western drama. During the years of its gestation and development, it faced serious challenge and competition from indigenous traditional drama. One of the influences that shaped it was Bernard Shaw, particularly the production of *Mrs Warren's Profession* in 1921,[1] an event designed to revitalize the young and fragile New Drama. Although it did not have the success that had been expected, it left a permanent imprint in the history of the modern Chinese drama, even down to the end of the century.

During the early years of the development of Chinese Spoken Drama, the 1921 production of *Mrs Warren's Profession* was the only noticeable stage production of a Shaw play in China. Although there were productions of other plays in the following two decades—*Arms and the Man* in Nanjing in 1935 by the Chinese Drama Association[2] and others staged by university students on campuses[3]—these attempts did not have an impact on either dramatic development or the society as a whole. Hence the focus in this essay on the 1921 production as a significant historical event in modern Chinese drama.

Bernard Shaw first came to the attention of progressive Chinese intellectuals at a time when the general desire for social and cultural reforms was strong. Western culture, be it technology or ideology, held great promise for Chinese reformers. Drama was recognized as an effective medium for

disseminating new ideas and for mobilizing people in their efforts to reform backward traditions. Dramatists like Henrik Ibsen and Shaw were
greatly admired for their unconventional views and iconoclastic spirit. In
June 1918, *New Youth*, the most significant intellectual journal of the time,
published a special issue on Ibsen and also announced its plans to publish
a special issue on Shaw in December of the same year: "Xiao Bona [Ber-
nard Shaw], an English writer, is a first-rate living dramatist who is both
prolific and profound. The editorial board has decided to introduce his
masterpieces to the people of our country. The December issue will be
devoted to Xiao Bona. The first plays to be introduced will include *Man
and Superman, Major Barbara,* and *Mrs Warren's Profession.*"⁴ Although the
plan for the special issue never materialized, translations of Shaw's plays
were undertaken. In October 1919, ten months after the original announcement, Pan Jiaxin's translation of *Mrs Warren's Profession* was published in the literary magazine *New Tide* (*Xing Chao*, vol. 2, no. 1). Only
a little more than a year later, Wang Chongxian staged the first public
performance of the play in China. Clearly Shaw's play was thought to have
something to say to a China in the throes of social and cultural change.

Shaw's play was also intended to help save the "Civilized New Drama," a
name given to the newly imported Western drama in contrast to traditional
Chinese drama. Ever since the first appearance of this Civilized New Drama
(later renamed Spoken Drama because of its dialogue form), at the turn
of the century, this new drama had been given a very uneven reception
and began to suffer a serious recession in the latter half of the 1910s. Although it had enjoyed modest popularity during the final years of the Qing
Dynasty and the first few years of the Republic of China (approximately
from 1907 to 1914), by 1915, however, the New Drama started declining.
By 1918, only one theater in Shanghai (the birth-place and nurturing
ground for the New Drama) was still producing the New Drama, and it was
not long before it, too, closed its doors. By this time the New Drama had
obtained such a notoriety that the term Civilized Drama or New Drama
had acquired negative overtones. Ouyang Yuqian, one of the earliest advocates of the New Drama in China, reminisced many years later about the
embarrassing situation at the time: "For many years . . . 'Civilized Drama'
had become an easy target for satirical attack. If a stage performance was
done poorly, or appeared extremely radical or ludicrous, people would call
it 'Civilized Drama.' "⁵ Apparently it was not an auspicious moment for
attempting to stimulate general interest in the New Drama.

The decline of the New Drama was mainly caused by various cultural
barriers. The realistic acting style employed in the New Drama—its plain
modern dress instead of exquisitely designed traditional costume; plain
dialogue instead of stylized music and arias; the use of realistic props like
doors and windows instead of symbolic gestures to suggest such objects—

created the impression among many Chinese that the New Drama required no acting. Hong Shen, one of the early advocates of the New Drama, recalled later, "Unfortunately, some people mistook realistic acting for no acting at all, for something requiring no skill. They saw no need for singing, no obvious rules and techniques in acting. It seemed to them that an actor could do anything he wanted in Civilized Drama. Since acting seemed so easy, many wanted to take part. . . . That was the beginning of the end of the Civilized Drama."[6] Some would-be actors who did not have any aptitude for the art of acting misjudged their talents as well as the profession, which they took up for the wrong reasons, not artistic aspiration or professional devotion, but easy money and quick fame.

On the Chinese stage, the New Drama was turning into a new farce, costing actors respect and the New Drama its reputation. Since the New Drama was such a recent phenomenon, there were virtually no writers to provide acceptable scripts for actors and directors to choose from. Moreover, the Chinese theater had a tradition of not taking scripts seriously. Play writing was not considered a reputable literary activity in China before the twentieth century, and working scripts were often the products of the joint efforts of generations of directors and actors, so the absence of scripts did not at first seem to present a problem to directors and actors engaged in the New Drama. They simply resorted to their old art of improvisation in the absence of well-written full scripts, working on the basis of what were called "script outline plays." Ouyang Yuqian describes their theatrical practice in the following terms:

> "Script outline plays" refers to a practice in which an outline rather than a fully written play is used. The writer does not produce the full text of a play, but merely a synopsis of a story taken from a legend, a novel or simply from notes. He divides the plot into several acts, each involving a few characters. Sometimes specific entrances and exits are noted, sometimes not. Sometimes, certain particularly important lines are written down, sometimes not. Rehearsal means casting the roles, writing down the names of players underneath their respective characters, going over the plot and the sequence of entrances and exits. Once that has been done, the responsibility of script writer and director has been exhausted.[7]

What Ouyang described was considered the normal procedure in the profession. Actors who were ill-prepared for the performance would resort to buffoonery, for the laughter of the audience was considered a prime indicator of good acting.[8] However, such improvisation usually made the play appear ridiculous and nonsensical because it was either inconsistent with

or inappropriate to the conception of the play as a whole. Given this situation, it was no wonder that the New Drama became a butt for satire.

The core of the problem was the players' lack of understanding of the
major differences between the traditional Chinese drama and the imported New Drama. In the traditional Chinese drama, the emphasis had
been on physical movement, but in the Western-styled New Drama, the
emphasis was on verbal interaction between characters. In the traditional
Chinese drama, characters were grouped into types and plots fell into formulae so that characters' lines were loosely transferable from one play to
another, especially when the attention of the audience was focused on spectacle. The New Drama, however, relied heavily on words for arousing the
interest of its audience. If players retained their old style of acting, exagger-
ating their gestures while neglecting the importance of verbal exchange,
they would, as it were, fall between two stools and succeed only in making
themselves incoherent and even ridiculous. That was in fact what happened to the "old" actors in the "new" drama, to the traditionally trained
Chinese actors working in Western-style drama. The incompatibility between the old acting practices and the technical requirements for new plays
inevitably contributed to the failure of the New Drama.

The poor adaptation, or even distortion, of Western theatrical practice,
whether in plots or acting style, reached such a point that it alarmed a
number of drama reformers who became deeply concerned with the
deadly effect on the development of the *real* New Drama. Zheng Zhenduo
and Chen Dabei were dismayed at the degree of degeneration of the so-
called New Drama.[9] Song Chunfang warned that such "decadent performances could lead to the loss of our country, making us slaves to foreign
invaders,"[10] for the influence of theater on the whole society was too great
to be overlooked. Moreover, the failure of the New Drama was providing
an opportunity for traditional drama to make a strong come-back and re-
gain its popularity. As a result, the reform of the stage seemed more urgent
a task than ever to many progressive intellectuals.

As the national movement to modernize Chinese culture, known as the
New Cultural Movement, gained momentum during the May Fourth Movement, the need to reclaim the theater for educational and propagandistic
uses became more pressing. In May 1921, the People's Drama Society was
founded to assume the historical mission of drama reform. All thirteen
founding members were influential writers, dramatists, and actors.[11] This
liberal, intellectual, and reformist group published a new magazine called
Drama to disseminate new ideas and to introduce Western drama to China.
Their ultimate goal was to effect social reform. Shaw came to be a leading
influence in the drama society, which devoted considerable space to him in
its short-lived magazine. In its opening declaration, the Society's magazine
invoked Shaw as a model, with the following passage typical of the whole

statement: "Bernard Shaw once remarked, 'Stage is a platform for propaganda.' Although this might not be an absolute truth, we can at least say that the time for 'drama to be solely a pastime or entertainment' is gone forever. Theater occupies a very important position in modern society: it is a vehicle moving society forward; it is an X-ray machine exposing all the diseases of a society; it is a truthful mirror reflecting the people of a country in their nakedness. . . . China has never had such a theater before, but we are striving to build one now."[12] The social function of drama, hitherto primarily to entertain, was to be redefined. Drama was assigned an important social and political role. Such a direct, specific involvement of theater in current social affairs was not in the tradition of Chinese theater. It was a new concept and a new practice derived entirely from European realist practice of the late nineteenth century. Shaw, along with Ibsen and Romain Rolland,[13] were among the playwrights who contributed to the profound reshaping of modern Chinese theater, showing it a new direction and a new place in society.

It is significant that *Mrs Warren's Profession* was selected for public performance against this sociopolitical background—the decayed condition of the New Drama and the perceived necessity to change the theater into an institution for political propaganda. The objectives seemed clear in this undertaking: it was not a commercial endeavor but a cultural-political counterattack against the abuse of newly adopted Western drama as well as an effort to restore the proper status to the New Drama. Shaw, well known as an effective propagandist on stage, seemed to hold the greatest promise of being both an instructive model and, at the same time, through his "real drama," a means of rectifying the image of the New Drama.

The 1921 production of *Mrs Warren's Profession* was to prove an extraordinary event in the world of Chinese drama. Virtually all the participants were important figures in the dramatic profession, and all were enthusiastic advocates of the New Drama. Wang Chongxian (1888–1937), the director and leading actor (Vivie), was known as a staunch drama reformer who had started experimenting with the Civilized New Drama at the beginning of the twentieth century. As early as 1905, Wang organized a literary society called *wen you hui* (Society of Literary Fellows), whose main aim was to modernize the traditional acting style. In 1906, Wang, together with Zhu Shuangyun and others, organized the *kai ming yan ju hui* (Enlightenment Drama Troupe), which put on plays advocating reforms in politics, the military, religion, society, family, and education. In 1910, when Ren Tianzhi, another drama reformer who had studied in Japan, returned to Shanghai to organize a drama company for the New Drama, Wang supported Ren and joined his group called *jin hua tuan* (Progressive Drama Troupe). It was the first professional New Drama company in China. It lived up to its name by producing plays on various current social concerns in China, chiefly plays adapted from foreign novels and plays. In 1921, when the People's Drama Society was founded, Wang was one of the thirteen original founders. Wang was not only a passionate theater lover, but also a progressive intellectual, an enthusiastic social reformer—a thinker as well as an artist, somewhat like Shaw.

Xia Yueren (1878–1931) was the chief supporter that Wang sought. Xia was a nationally well-known figure, not only because of his close connections with celebrities—both his father and father-in-law were renowned Beijing Opera actors and his father-in-law, Tan Xinpei, was the most famous actor in China before Mei Lanfang—but also because of his professional achievements and his unbending character. A Beijing Opera actor, he occupied the prominent position of Chairman of the Shanghai Actors' Association. Personally he was famous for his courageous refusal to perform in the Japanese concession in Shanghai during the last years of the Qing Dynasty, an action that brought him tremendous respect from his fellow countrymen. He was also known for his pioneering efforts to modernize the Chinese theater. According to Hong Shen, Xia had gone to Japan early in the century and had studied with the Japanese dramatist Sadanji Ichikawa. On returning to Shanghai, he rallied other supporters of the modern drama and built the New Theater in a popular downtown area in Shanghai. It was the first technically modern theater in Shanghai— indeed, the first in all China—with a rotating stage for easy management of props. This theater provided a nurturing ground for the newly introduced realistic acting style, with props, modern costume, and a realistic style of acting.[14] Considering Xia's personal influence on the theater in Shanghai as well as in the country as a whole, the decision to produce Shaw's play here was significant.

The whole process of planning the production revealed extraordinary care and subtlety. As Hong Shen recorded, the decision to stage Shaw's controversial play was made in the spring of 1921 by Director Wang Chongxian, who then persuaded Xia Yueren, Xia Yuesan, and Zhou Fengwen, the leading actors of the New Theater, to collaborate with him. A great deal of effort and money was put into the project. As Wang later wrote, the usual practice of the theater was to advertise forthcoming performances in two newspapers—*Shen Bao* and *Daily News* (*mei re xin wen*), the two major Shanghai dailies. However, in the case of *Mrs Warren's Profession*, ads were put in five dailies and were scheduled to run for several more days than usual. The theater had never spent so much money on advertising before.[15] In addition, rehearsals took much longer than for other plays—an unprecedented period of more than three months. There were even three dress rehearsals. The total cost was more than 1,000 yuan, the equivalent of approximately 90,000 yuan in modern currency.[16] The care put into the production of the play and the expenses incurred in staging it demonstrated extraordinary dedication on the part of the theater to the promotion of experimental Western drama. This great expenditure of money and effort also suggested expectations of success, but the play ran for only three nights.

The opening night was set for a Saturday, the busiest night of the week for theaters in Shanghai. During the previous two years, as Wang recalled, the New Theater had staged *Live Buddha Ji Gong*, a popular Chinese comedy, every Saturday night. Box-office sales had always been good. The play took in as much as 1,400 yuan on some occasions, and even the least busy days brought in 500 yuan (with the average cost of a seat being less than one yuan). Shaw's play was scheduled to be performed both Saturday and Sunday nights. It took in 300 yuan on the first night and 313 yuan on the second, considerably less than the lowest previous receipts.[17] The tepid response from the general public revealed that there was still much to be done before Western drama would become popular in China.

The reaction of those who went to see the play was even less encouraging than the box-office receipts. On opening night, during the scene in which Vivie confronts her mother with the question of her parentage and Mrs. Warren tells Vivie about her past experiences, several fashionably dressed ladies walked out, with a number of others following shortly thereafter. When the curtain fell, three-quarters of the audience was gone. Wang noticed that several people occupying second- and third-class seats had left in a foul mood, uttering curses. The second night was no better. Had they not stopped the performance after the third night, the theater would have been empty, or, worse still, the audience might have rioted, as Wang later joked. The first performance of a Shaw play in China had turned out to be a complete fiasco, and the director, the theater, and the actors were totally dismayed.

Analyzing the causes of this failure, Wang Chongxian noted that the main factors were the audience, the players, and the media. First, the audience had been ill-prepared for such a play and had difficulty understanding it because the audience had no generic context within which to situate the play. Second, the players, being new to an authentic Western play and not having been trained in a realistic tradition of acting, did a poor job. Third, the media were unsupportive. Most of the papers honored the occasion by ignoring the play altogether, and only a few carried reviews consisting of superficial flattering comments.[18]

Various responses to the performance, such as the director's analysis and the critic's comments, suggest that the failure of the 1921 production seemed, to a large extent, the result of differences in the theatrical traditions of Western and Chinese drama. These differences led to difficulties in approaching the play both for the players and for the audience, with the former unsure about how to present it and the latter uncertain about how to comprehend it. The technical differences between Western and Chinese theater at the turn of the century were substantial, with the former differing from the latter, among other ways, by its radical de-emphasis of spectacle and music. In addition to these obvious differences in style, Western plays were usually more subtle and indirect in plot construction and characterization. Chinese plays tended to follow fixed formulae with easily predictable endings, and their relatively simple plots obeyed the commonly accepted laws of probability familiar to Chinese audiences. Moreover, the use of stock characters, clearly distinguished by costume and facial makeup, helped the audience to tell hero from villain. Characters even habitually introduced themselves to the audience at their first appearance on stage. Even if a particular audience happened to be unfamiliar with the plot, it never had to strain after the meaning. To Chinese audiences accustomed to such open and direct self-identification on the part of the characters, figuring out who is who in a Western play could be challenging and frustrating. As Wang Chongxian noted, some members of the audience were unable to understand Shaw's play at all; others could understand a little, but not enough to sustain their interest; and the rest could follow the plot but had trouble finding any real meaning in the play.[19] This was not entirely the fault of the audience. Afterward Wang Chongxian admitted that "in the case of *Mrs Warren's Profession,* it was our own fault. This was our first experiment, but we picked too difficult a play with which to challenge the audience; and they afterwards complained about their inability to understand it. We have ourselves to blame."[20]

The unfamiliar subject matter presented another difficulty for the audience. Chinese audiences were accustomed to watching plays based on familiar historical or legendary incidents and characters. Usually playgoers went to the plays they already knew, or at least knew about in terms of plot and character. They went to the theater to enjoy the spectacle and hear the singing, a tradition closer to Western music halls than to that of the legitimate theater. To encounter totally strange characters with strange names must have been intimidating. As Song Chunfang remarked, "In the minds of the people, there first had to be a Zhuge Liang[21] before there could be a sensational historical farce like *Zhuge Liang Getting Married;* there first had to be a Ji Dian before there could be a popular play like *Live Buddha Ji Dian.* But, what ladies in the audience could possibly have been acquainted with Mrs. Warren, the major character in Shaw's *Mrs Warren's Profession?* And who among the men who frequent brothels has ever heard of Mrs. Warren?"[22] Few people in the audience had read the play or even heard about the characters in *Mrs Warren's Profession* before attending the performance. The growing frustration of a bewildered audience that had nothing to fall back on is therefore easy to imagine. In traditional Chinese drama, the audience at least had a visual spectacle to watch and music and singing to listen to if the new plot grew momentarily unclear. However, there was nothing in Shaw's play to entertain the senses of an audience beyond a few people talking unintelligibly to one another. Worse still, to a Chinese audience, their conversations seemed interminable. Even a professor of literature who was well read in Western drama found the play intolerably long. "Just think," Song Chunfang complained, "there are only six people in the play who engage in mundane conversation for four and a half hours. At the beginning of the play, Vivie and Praed talk trivially for nearly 30 minutes. In the third scene, Mrs. Warren and Vivie talk for an hour."[23] If the conversation between Vivie and Praed in the opening scene seemed pointless to Professor Song, how could an average Chinese audience with no background in Western literature be expected to enjoy it? Song sympathized with people who had been brought up on a type of drama that he called "watching lanterns on horseback"[24] and felt that such an audience had good reason to dislike plays like Shaw's.

A Chinese play staged in the same theater at about the same time as *Mrs Warren's Profession* reveals what a Chinese audience was accustomed to. The New Theater had been performing *Live Buddha Ji Gong* on weekends for two years prior to its staging of Shaw's play. Based on a folk tale, *Live Buddha Ji Gong* portrays a monk endowed with a sense of justice and magic powers to punish the mean-spirited rich and help the down-trodden. The protagonist Ji Gong would have been known to everyone, literate and illiterate, young and old. Stories of his heroic deeds were familiar to all households. The play is immensely entertaining because of the playful personality of the main character, whose clever tricks, light-hearted humor, and strong sense of justice, accompanied with cheerful music and lyrics, provide the audience with considerable moral gratification and pleasure. The audience could identify with Ji Gong's distinctive Chinese personality, appreciate his humor, and count on the final triumph of justice, an outcome that was particularly meaningful to people living in a country where the legal system had never been strong. The audience was able to make various connections at different cultural, moral, and psychological levels while watching Ji Gong, something that they could not do while watching Kitty Warren, with whom they could not identify, much less grasp the point of her talk.

Critics tend to dismiss the audience as intellectually incompetent while ignoring various cultural barriers. Chen Dabei draws an interesting comparison when he says that "If you ask a person who is used to enjoying *Live Buddha Ji Gong* to come and see *Mrs Warren's Profession,* how can you expect to succeed? Inviting a person used to loud singing and melodramatic acting to see a representational play with little action and plain dialogue is like dragging a sick friend from a hospital bed to take part in a one hundred meter race."[25] Chen's comparison of the Chinese audience with a sick person in a hospital bed clearly shows his bias. What he ignored was the cultural incongruity between the audience and the play. The same thing would have happened if a Western audience had been introduced to *Live Buddha Ji Gong*. To introduce admirers of Ji Gong to Shaw's Mrs. Warren was to try to make them run not a one-hundred-meter race but take a leap across a giant cultural gulf.

Another critic, Song Chunfang, considered the construction of Western plays too complex for Chinese audiences: "Our audience is used to the direct self-introduction of characters saying things like 'I come from Sleeping Dragon Mountain. . . .' "[26] Song maintained that the Chinese audience, having formed a simple mind-set, was intolerant of more complex structures. "What's more," he continued, "Western plays often begin with disconnected dialogue that leaves the audience at a loss. As for Bernard Shaw and Brieux, schooled in the Dumas' tradition, they tend to engage in eloquent argument and lengthy discussion, which, to a Chinese audience, are both equally dry, consisting of boring lectures on philosophy, tending to put the audience to sleep."[27] Song's assumption of the Chinese audience's simple mind-set puts him in the same category as the audience, for he omits all discussion of the more complex issues of cultural tradition. Nevertheless, his point about differences in representational styles as well as in the construction of play scripts between the Chinese and Western plays is well taken.

Differences in acting styles between the Western and Chinese theatrical traditions created difficulties for the Chinese actors as well. Their "poor" or inappropriate performance, in turn, made the play difficult for the audience to understand. It was a daunting task for the actors to switch from the traditional Beijing Opera acting style to an unfamiliar Western acting style since they had to learn new ways of walking, standing, sitting, speaking, gesturing, and using facial expressions. In a word, it meant a thorough personal transformation, an awesome task for any actor. A Westerner observing the development of the new theater in China in the late 1920s commented on the difficulties of such a transformation: "Of all the phases of the actor's art in the ancient dramas, only two remain untouched by the new influences. The ritual of motion still requires that the warrior walk with 'the tiger's step,' pain is still represented by throwing the head back and gazing upward, and anger by staring eyes and hard breathing. And the female impersonator must still, of course, use the high falsetto voice. To give up these is to give up the fundamentals of the art. Many of the actors would not, others could not, change to the natural modern style."[28] Here Vera Kelsey mentions two fundamental elements in the acting tradition of the Beijing Opera—stylized gestures and cross-gender casting. These features make Beijing Opera unique in its presentation. To ask an actor trained in this school to give these up was to ask him to abandon the skills that he had spent all his life acquiring.

Even if an actor was able to overcome his emotional attachment to his old art, the acquisition of "the natural modern style" was not easy. Mei Lanfang (1894–1961), the world-renowned Beijing Opera actor, is a case in point. Mei started his theatrical training at the early age of eight. His teacher made him sing every required passage twenty or thirty times even though he had already learned how to sing it after the first six or seven times. As William Dolby remarks, "He acquired the extremely exacting skills of the *qingyi* actor, learning the appropriate way to walk, open and close doors, move the hands, point the fingers, flick and waft the sleeves, put on a slipper, throw up a hand in appeal to Heaven, raise the arm in lamentation, pace the stage, and faint into a chair. Walking on the short stilts or clogs . . . required arduous practice. Mei even practiced on the ice in winter. Through pain and blistered feet he neared perfection in that art. Later, under other teachers, he studied acrobatics, fighting and many other subjects."[29] After so many years of training and perfecting his art, art and artist became almost inseparable. What seemed natural to Western-educated, Western-influenced modern thinkers and reformers of China was not necessarily natural to traditionally trained actors and audience. To Beijing Opera actors, the old style was more natural than the newly adopted Western style. The actors playing in *Mrs Warren's Profession* were all Beijing Opera actors who had undergone training similar to Mei's.

Attempting to adapt to a Western style for the first time, the actors were understandably nervous. Wang Chongxian recalled that the actors were intimidated by the unfamiliar Western acting style and the playwright's great reputation and so became extremely nervous, forgetful, and unnatural in their performance. Although the director made sure that each actor memorized his own lines correctly, some actors did not bother to cope with the meaning of the play as a whole. They concentrated only on learning their lines by rote and recited them mechanically. When on stage, they sometimes forgot a line or an important phrase, thus reducing a good argument to a nonsensical speech and leaving the audience in utter confusion. On top of that, not all the players were able to speak Mandarin Chinese, which affected the performance as well as the attendance.[30] Despite the considerable length of time spent on rehearsing the play, the actors still found themselves ill-prepared for the performance.

What could be inferred from this case is the double jeopardy that the actors were confronted with, one cultural and the other technical. To begin with, they were culturally displaced, resulting in a sense of loss and confusion that eventually led to awkward, unnatural acting. With regard to both the script and the acting style, the actors were entirely disadvantaged, even disabled by their unfamiliarity with the Western tradition. For the actors in

Mrs Warren's Profession, the cultural and psychological alienation was real. Without understanding and identifying with the characters they were playing, the actors were reduced to mechanical robots. Technically, the familiar was also replaced by the unfamiliar. What used to come naturally to them on stage was subdued or denied. Instead, they had to follow what seemed to them an "unnatural" way of acting. As a result, what they presented was neither Chinese nor Western, "natural" to neither of the traditions.

As with the audience and the actors, the director also faced cultural obstacles. Eager to promote reform in the theater as well as in society in general, Wang selected a serious playwright and a play dealing with topical issues. Meanwhile, he overlooked the distinction between "serious" and popular plays. As a member of the traditional Chinese theater, Wang probably was not aware of such a distinction, for traditionally Chinese theaters, whether belonging to the Beijing Opera or to regional operas, served a mixed audience of the educated and uneducated, of the upper and lower classes. There were theatrical differences among regional operas, to be sure, but never differences of cultural hierarchy. Hence, Wang was unable to foresee the discrepancy between the play that he had selected and his audience, the majority of which was far more attuned to popular entertainment than to serious intellectual challenge. All he had foreseen was a relatively minor language problem. Wang recalled, "I was experimenting for the first time with *Mrs Warren's Profession*. Afraid that the audience might be made impatient by complex detail, I made the subtle parts more explicit (in addition, we provided the audience with a detailed description of the play in the program). I also changed certain expressions not natural to the Chinese ear, and shortened long speeches, in the hope that these changes would make it easier for the audience to understand, yet at the same time, I did not alter the original meaning."[31] These changes did not seem to have the desired effect, however. Wang failed to realize how large a gap there was between Chinese and Western theater.

Although the 1921 production of Shaw's play did not turn out to be a success, it eventually came to be considered a momentous event in the history of Spoken Drama in China. Tian Han, Chairman of the Chinese Dramatists Association in Mao's regime, acknowledged it in his speech at the commemorative celebration of Shaw's centenary in 1956: "That was the first time Chinese actors performed a Western play without the accompaniment of gongs, drums, and string instruments. Though the production was not a success, it was a significant event in the history of drama in China."[32] Its significance, as Tian perceived, was that it was the first experiment with the Western drama performed in a style closely resembling the Western one. Its impact on other aspects of the Chinese theater world and on the later course of Spoken Drama was to prove momentous.

The production introduced a new concept and a new problem into Chinese theater, namely the distinction between serious, intellectual drama and popular entertainment or, to use a Western term, the distinction between high-brow and low-brow theater. Chinese theater, ever since it had become accessible to the general public, had not made such a distinction. Dramatic performance meant entertainment for all. The failure of *Mrs Warren's Profession* made the director of the play realize that there was such a distinction and also that there was a need to resolve the problem of audience: should theater consider the needs of the majority or of the elite? His experience with Shaw's play taught him that stage production, if it was ever to reach a large audience, had to take the interest of the majority into consideration: "Theater cannot cut itself off from its audience. There can be no theater without an audience. Since the Chinese people consider theater-going to be pure entertainment, we have to provide them with entertainment in return for the money they pay. Otherwise they will feel cheated. If you insist on preaching to them, they will turn their backs on you."[33] To provide the audience with both entertainment and education, the New Drama had to seek a middle ground either by adapting Western drama to the Chinese audience or by educating the audience to appreciate Western drama. The conclusion he came to after much analysis was to *adapt* Western plays rather than *adopt* them. Wang summarized the lessons he learned from the production of *Mrs Warren's Profession* in these words: "Our future principle should be: we cannot always cater to the expectations of the general populace, nor can we cater to the needs of the highly-educated few. Instead, we must select simple, new ideas and weave them into an interesting and entertaining plot; in this way we will produce a play which the audience find so engaging that they will want to see it from the beginning to the end."[34] This was the principle that Wang later consistently followed. His play *A Good Son* (1923), although similar to *Mrs Warren's Profession* in theme, uses a familiar cultural setting (Shanghai), familiar characters (an ordinary Chinese family), and simple language to explore serious social problems such as the effect of an evil feudal system on individual lives. It proved to be both entertaining and educational, touching the audience psychologically through historical and cultural cords.

The 1921 Shaw production reaffirmed the method of adaptation when dealing with Western plays, the method that had been abused and made responsible for earning the New Drama a bad name, the method that drama reformers were eager to relinquish. The earliest attempts at producing Western plays had been undertaken by adapting the original to Chinese circumstances, often incurring radical changes such as characters' names, thematic emphasis, and even plots. Such free alteration of Western originals was a common practice in the 1910s. Sometimes poor adaptations made the original work hardly recognizable. The New Drama advocates were disturbed by these apparently irresponsible practices. While many of them were engaged in discussing drama reform on paper instead of putting their ideas into practice, Wang intended to demonstrate to his colleagues that it was possible to produce a Western play in the Western style. Had he succeeded in his attempt in 1921, later theatrical practices in China would have been radically different. His failure, however, ultimately confirmed the old methods of adaptation.

In 1924, three years after the unsuccessful production of *Mrs Warren's Profession,* Hong Shen directed Oscar Wilde's *Lady Windermere's Fan* for the Shanghai Drama Association. Hong took the lesson offered by the failed production of *Mrs Warren's Profession* to heart and adapted the play to meet the needs of a Chinese audience. According to Chen Meiying, "Hong Shen did not follow the script of *Lady Windermere's Fan.* He adapted the plot, the characters, the language, and the customs to make the play accessible to the Chinese audience; thus the play was understood and accepted by the audience."[35] Hong's production was a great success. All the seats were sold out for all performances. Additional performances had to be arranged because of the strong demand. Mao Dun recalls the production in his article, "Foreign Drama in China":

> At 2:00 p.m. on May 4th, 1924, the Drama Association organized by Hong Shen and his friends put on a public performance of Wilde's *Lady Windermere's Fan.* . . . On May 10th when it was again performed . . . all five hundred tickets were sold out in no time. Two hundred more tickets had to be added. It was performed in the auditorium of the China Vocational School. At 2:00 p.m. on May 18th, the last performance was scheduled to take place. Seats were limited to five hundred. There were so many people who could not get in that they sent representatives to request another performance. At 5:30 p.m. that same day, one more performance was arranged to meet the demand.[36]

The sharp contrast between Hong Shen's success and Wang Chongxian's failure shows what was acceptable to Chinese audiences. A foreign play delivered in a recognizably foreign form would be rejected whereas a foreign play presented in a recognizably Chinese form was welcome.

Adaptation thus became the order of the day during the following two decades. Western plays had to undergo a process of Sinicization in order to be appreciated by Chinese audiences. Edward Gunn, in his examination of the development of Spoken Drama during the Japanese war period in Shanghai, notices that "next to costume drama the largest trend was to adaptations of Western works, from *Gone with the Wind* to Shaw's *Pygmalion.* There were some that received less recognition than they should have, such as Huang Zuolin 's *Liangshang junzi* (from Molnar's *Doctor Ur*), and others that succeeded more than one might have expected, such as Huang's *Huangdao yingxiong* (from Barrie's *Admirable Crichton*), and Gu Zhongyi's simplified and sinified [*sic*] *King Lear,* titled *San Qianjin.*"[37] Gunn makes two points here. First, costume drama, that is traditional drama, was still predominant in the 1930s. Second, only adaptations of foreign plays were popular. These adaptations must have been heavily altered from their originals to meet the needs of Chinese audiences. The Chinese translations of the titles suggest shifts of focus and simplification of plot. The Chinese translation of Ferenc Molnar's *Doctor Ur* uses a Chinese proverb *liang shang junzi,* an allusion to a historical incident described in *A Biography of Chen Shi (he han shu: Chen Shi chuan)*. The allusion is to an incident in the household of Chen Shi (104–87), a high-ranking government official in the Han Dynasty. One night, a thief crept into Chen's house and hid on top of a rafter. Chen called him "*liang shang junzi* [Gentleman on the Rafter.]" The term became a synonym for thief. In this way, historical allusion transforms Molnar's doctor into a native Chinese. Barrie's *Admirable Crichton* became *The Hero on a Desert Island,* a title which is more explicit and specific than the original. *King Lear* was changed into *Three Daughters,* shifting the focus from Lear's tragedy to interactions among his three daughters, most likely eliminating the subplot concerning the fate of Gloucester's family. Gunn's speculation on the success of these adaptations is, "Perhaps it was the focus on domestic conflict that helped these plays impress their audience. Yet an important historical point about all such works is that they were adaptations, not translations; the latter form had virtually disappeared. Translations had never really captured more than a very limited audience."[38] Judicious selection of subject matter and representational style was crucial to the success of dramatic performances, but most important of all was the extensive work that went into the process of adaptation, de-nationalizing the characters on the stage to enable Chinese audiences to identify with them.

While the failure of the 1921 Shaw production confirmed the validity of adaptation, tailoring Western plays to fit Chinese audiences, it also demonstrated an urgent need to train competent actors for the New Drama. In traditional Chinese opera, the training of actors emphasized improving acting skills, the craftsmanship, rather than general education. The New Drama, as shown in the case of the production of Shaw's *Mrs Warren's Profession,* required something new of actors: the intellectual ability to process new ideas. Western plays such as Shaw's did not mean much to those actors who were seasoned in the old Chinese culture, much less make them identify with the characters they were playing. The result was mechanical recitation. Wang Chongxian recognized the problem and realized that in order to use drama to teach the audience, "we actors, if not striving to surpass the high-brow audience in learning, should at least not fall far behind them."[39] The old method of training actors was seen as inadequate because it focused only on the technical aspects, neglecting the education of actors in other necessary areas, such as literacy and culture. New Drama demanded that actors be intellectually and technically competent. It was no accident that a year later, the first drama institute was founded in Beijing. It was called the Beijing Institute of People's Arts. Wang Chongxian was actively involved in charting the direction of the new institute. His experience with the Shaw play had made him keenly aware of the lack of competent actors for Western drama, so his advice to the founders of this new drama institute was to train three kinds of dramatic professionals: performing artists, playwrights, and drama teachers. He felt it important to train teachers who could then help train more performers, writers, and teachers throughout the country to help ease the shortage of dramatic professionals. Education programs were thus set up in a nationwide effort to promote the New Drama. Drama reformers wanted to make sure that Western drama would find a home in this foreign land.

The audience's response to Shaw's *Mrs Warren's Profession* made it clear that actors were expected to be entertainers only and that as soon as they stopped entertaining, they failed. This led to a discussion of actors' social status. Lu Minghui published an article entitled "An Address to All Actors in Shanghai" in June 1921, calling on all actors of traditional plays to change their roles from mere entertainers to educators. Lu put his position in the following terms: "Actors and actresses in the West occupy a social position even higher than that of university professors. . . . Why are actors and actresses in China deemed lower in the social ladder than even prostitutes?"[40] Lu explained that actors and actresses in the West enjoyed a much higher social position than their Chinese counterparts because they participated in the production of much worthier plays: "Their plays make people think, and they employ higher aesthetic means to meet the spiritual needs of their audience; whereas Chinese plays are worthless because they are intended only to entertain and to make their audiences laugh. The wretched position of Chinese actors and actresses stems from their principle of 'entertaining people.' "[41] To Lu, this principle was the fundamental cause of all of China's theatrical ills, for it reduced actors to mere playthings for the audience, just as prostitutes were playthings for their clients. Lu called on all actors to rebel against such treatment: "If you want to rid yourself of such a monstrous humiliation, stop being a plaything for your audience."[42] Although Lu's generalization about Western theater may not be accurate, his analysis of the main cause of the Chinese actors' poor position was insightful. Chen Dabei also encouraged actors to reject base, vulgar, and harmful plays that they adopted merely to please their audiences' vulgar instincts. He urged them instead to take on the more noble responsibility of educating and elevating people: "We must ask ourselves: 'Why do I want to be an actor?' Since we have chosen to be actors, we should do our best to promote good over evil, the beautiful over the ugly. This is our duty today."[43] Only with the change of the theater's function and a consequent change in the role of actors would there be change in the social position of actors.

Switching the theater's role wholly from popular entertainment to social education meant, so the lesson of the Shaw production taught, a loss of audience and a consequent loss of profit. In the context of the questionable viability of the New Drama, the need to establish amateur drama companies came to be recognized, for as training grounds, the commercial theaters had proved to be obstacles rather than vehicles for the introduction of serious drama. Shortly after the production of *Mrs Warren's Profession*, Zheng Zhenduo wrote an article entitled "Initiation of an Enlightenment Movement" in which he strongly advocated founding amateur theaters. He argued that under the capitalist system, theaters were controlled solely by entrepreneurs whose primary interest was in profit. Regardless of possible moral degradation and aesthetic worthlessness, if there was profit to be made out of it, capitalists wanted the play to be performed. On the other hand, if there was no profit in a good play, it would be disregarded. Since actors were controlled by capitalists, they had no choice but to please their audiences and bring in profits for their masters. Zheng lamented, "You see, after they lost money on the production of *Mrs Warren's Profession*, they would not touch any more Western plays."[44] Zheng was convinced that this unhealthy dramatic atmosphere was a natural result of the dominance of commercial theaters. Unless amateur theaters were established, he contended, there would be no hope of changing the current situation. Zheng's concern was echoed by many progressive literary figures of the time.

The reform of theater regulations also became an urgent matter for advocates of the New Drama after witnessing the audience's restlessness during the performance of Shaw's play in 1921, when people simply left the theater. A "civilized" drama needed a "civilized" audience. Drama reformers also took on the task of educating audiences on how to conduct themselves appropriately in the theater. In May 1923, when the first group of drama students from the Beijing Institute of People's Arts put on their first public performance, Chen Dabei took precautions in this regard and issued a brief note in the program reminding the audience to behave properly. In this piece, called "Three Requirements for Tonight's Xin Ming Theater Audience," he details the important role that audiences were to assume in drama reform: "To promote a healthy new drama, it is imperative to have competent playwrights and directors, but without cooperative audiences and supportive critics, success is impossible."[45] Chen sets three basic rules for audiences to observe: "First, please don't applaud in the middle of a performance. . . . Even if there are occasions deserving applause, reserve it for the end of each act. . . . Second, please don't talk loudly in the middle of the performance. . . . Talking among members of the audience will make it hard to hear crucial speeches on the stage. . . . Third, please provide us with criticism after the performance."[46] A new theater atmosphere was thus in the process of being created.

Although in terms of box-office profits, Director Wang's production of *Mrs Warren's Profession* was an embarrassing failure, in terms of its impact on the theater world, few box-office hits would ever match this production. It left permanent marks on all aspects of the New Drama Movement, from the treatment of Western plays (adaptation or adoption), to the training of actors (elevating them intellectually, culturally, and socially), to theater management (forming amateur drama groups), and finally to audience needs and responsibilities (taking care of the needs of the majority as well as establishing theater regulations). Moreover, this Shaw production provides an important historical lesson about the clash of Eastern and Western culture. The significance of the event reaches beyond the realm of drama to the realm of culture and civilization.

Notes

All sources from Chinese publications are translated by the writer.

1. Two dates have been suggested for Wang Chongxian's production of *Mrs Warren's Profession*, the spring of 1921 and October 1920. The former date is cited in Hong Shen, "Introduction" to *An Anthology of New Literature and Art in China* (Hong Kong: Hong Kong Literature and Art Research Society, 1966), 9:33; the latter date is cited in Zhao Mingyi, "An Overview of Thirty Years of Spoken Drama Movement: 1907–1937," *Fifty Years of Spoken Drama Movement in China,* ed. Xing Ken (Macao: Spoken Drama Research Society, 1976), 2:24. I use Hong Shen's date here.

2. *Arms and the Man* was staged by the Chinese Drama Association in the Star Theater in Nanking in 1935. It failed to capture the interest of the public. Tian Han, Chairman of the Chinese Drama Association in the 1950s, attributed the failure to historical circumstances, to a time when the Chinese felt it hard to look at war from a romantic point of view, for the Japanese invasion of China had forced them to see the ugly reality of warfare.

3. Professor Cai Wenhao, in his commemorative essay entitled "Ideology and Aesthetics in Bernard Shaw's Dramatic Creation," *Zhong Shan University Journal,* Social Science Edition, no. 4 (October 1956), recalled that some students in Zhong Shan University put on *Pygmalion* during the War of Resistance against Japan. Ying Ruocheng remembered rehearsing *Arms and the Man* with a group of young students in Beijing University in the late 1940s. See "Director's Words," *Major Barbara Performance Program,* The Beijing People's Arts Theater Archive (June 1991), p. 2.

4. *New Youth* 4:6 (June 1918).

5. Yuqian Ouyang, "On Civilized Drama," *Fifty Years of Spoken Drama Movement in China* (Beijing: Chinese Drama Publishing House, 1985), 1:47.

6. Hong Shen, "Introduction," *An Anthology of New Literature and Art in China,* 9:14–15.

7. Yuqian Ouyang, "On Civilized Drama," p. 88.

8. Ibid.

9. See Zheng Zhenduo's criticism in "Initiation of an Enlightenment Movement," *Drama* 1:3 (July 1921), and Chen Dabei's in "Hasn't China's New Drama Done Enough to Satisfy the Audience?" *Dawn (shou guang),* 2:3.

10. Hong, "Introduction," p. 18.

11. The thirteen founders include Shen Yanbing, Zheng Zhenduo, Chen Dabei, Ouyang Yuqian, Wang Chongxian, Xu Banmei, Zhang Yuguang, Ke Yicen, Lu Bingxing, Shen Bingxue, Teng Ruoqu, Xiong Fuxi, and Zhang Jinglu.

12. Originally printed in the opening issue of the official journal of the People's Drama Society, *Drama* 1:1 (May 1921). Note that the statement attributed to Shaw in quotation marks is not a direct quotation. It is rather a summary of Shaw's view expressed in his various writings.

13. Other influential Western dramatists of the time include August Strindberg, Gerhart Hauptmann, Hermann Sudermann, Eugène Brieux, Anton Chekhov, Maurice Maeterlinck, and John Galsworthy.

14. Hong, "Introduction," pp. 12–13.

15. Ibid., pp. 33–34.

16. Mingyi Zhao, "An Overview of Thirty Years of Spoken Drama: 1907–1937," p. 24.

17. Wang Chongxian recorded his experience in producing Shaw's play in 1921 in his essay "You-you Talks about Drama," first printed in the Qing Guang Column of *shi shi xin bao* in late 1921. The present paper refers to Hong's "Introduction," p. 33.

18. Ibid., p. 34.

19. Ibid.

20. Ibid., p. 36.

21. Zhuge Liang (174–241) is one of the major characters in *Three Kingdoms,* a popular Chinese novel written by Luo Guanzhong (?1330–1400?). It depicts political and military intrigues among three ruling cliques headed by Liu Bei, Cao Cao, and Sun Quan. Many plays have used episodes from the novel, making all the major characters household names.

22. Hong, p. 36.

23. Ibid., pp. 36–37.

24. A Chinese proverbial expression, referring to the superficial act of looking at spectacles without seriously understanding the significance.

25. Chen Dabei, "Chen Dabei's Reply to Yang Minghui's Letter," *Drama* 1:5 (September 1921): 9.

26. Hong, p. 36.

27. Ibid.

28. Vera Kelsey, "The New Theater of China," *Theater Arts Monthly* 12:6 (June 1928): 434.

29. William Dolby, *A History of Chinese Drama* (London: Elek Books, 1976), p. 216.

30. Hong, p. 34.

31. Quoted in Hong, p. 37.

32. Tian Han, "Learning from the Great Masters of Realist Drama," *Guang Ming Daily* (27 July 1956), p. 2.

33. Quoted in Hong, p. 35.

34. Ibid.

35. Chen Meiying, "A Pioneer: Hong Shen," *Biographies of Chinese Spoken Drama Artists* (Beijing: Culture and Arts Publishing House, 1984), 1:185–86.

36. Mao Dun, "Foreign Drama in China," *Foreign Drama* No. 1 (October 1980): 2–3.

37. Edward Gunn, "Shanghai's 'Orphan Island' and the Development of Modern Drama," *Popular Chinese Literature and Performing Arts in the People's Republic of China: 1949–1979,* ed. Bonnie S. McDougall (Berkeley and Los Angeles: University of California Press, 1984), p. 51.

38. Ibid.

39. Quoted in Hong, p. 35.

40. Quoted in Hong, p. 31.

41. Ibid.

42. Ibid.

43. Ibid.

44. Zheng Zhenduo, "Initiation of an Enlightenment Movement," p. 6.

45. Chen Dabei, *Program* (May 1923), quoted in Hong, p. 30.

46. Ibid.

Rodelle Weintraub

TOO TRUE TO BE GOOD:
THE BOTTOMLESS ABYSS
FOLLOWING WORLD WAR I

Too True to Be Good is an enigmatic title chosen one might think for its punning on "too good to be true." But why? The "too true to be" is easily understood. From the opening curtain, with the Patient asleep and the measles Microbe ill, through the surreal events that follow, *Too True to Be Good* can be viewed as fantasy and as another of Shaw's Freudian-like dream plays.[1] More challenging is the "to be good."

A young woman who might otherwise be healthy has been made ill by her oversolicitous mother, who would now be described as suffering from Munchausen disease.[2] The life-size Microbe, blamed for her illness, claims that *it* has been made ill by the patient. The new night-nurse turns out to be a former chambermaid and one of a pair of burglars who intend to steal a valuable necklace. The rope of pearls is in plain view, *"heaped half in and half out"* of a black steel jewel box with its lid open (429.)[3] Yet the burglar, unable to see the necklace, tries to open the already-opened jewel box. After the patient springs from bed and floors him with a well-aimed kick, he decides to take her with him and have her steal her own jewelry. At the end of the act, when she has been cured, so has the Microbe.

The second and third acts take place in some unnamed British outpost that has both sandy beach and mountains. The three young persons from the first act are now tourists implausibly vacationing in a British army camp. The chambermaid has become the "Countess," the patient her servant, and the burglar her brother. The camp is actually run by Napoleon Alexander Trotsky Meek, a lowly private. The mother has offered a reward for her daughter, thinking that she is being held for ransom by brigands. While there are no brigands, a cavalry attack by the natives is repulsed by the firing of harmless flares. Leaving the operation of the installation to Meek, the Colonel devotes himself to his passion for "sketching in watercolors" (516). In the final act, both the patient's mother and the burglar's father arrive at the encampment. Sweetie, the chambermaid, commits herself to a Bible- and *Pilgrim's Progress*–reading Sergeant. The mother, having been struck on the head with the Colonel's umbrella, refuses to recognize her daughter. The daughter, who has wished that there were no mothers or daughters, but "only women" (509), goes off with her mother as a friend and companion. The play ends with Aubrey, the former burglar turned preacher, preaching "no matter whether I have nothing to say—" (528).

For all the characters in *Too True to Be Good,* the world as they knew it before 1914 "has crumbled like the walls of Jericho. . . . All is caprice: the calculable world has become incalculable . . ." (499–500). In the 1870s, the mathematicians Cantor and Dedekind discovered the set and divided the mathematical continuum, ushering in the modern age that, for nine-teenth-century rationalists, became incalculable. In 1927, Werner Heisen-berg and Niels Bohr showed that "discontinuity implies uncertainty in physics no less than in mathematics."[4] Shaw, who had met Einstein in 1921 and was interested in and well aware of developments in mathematics as well as in other sciences, made use of these findings. *Too True to Be Good,* written in 1931, depicts that discontinuity, fragmentation, uncertainty— modernism—as it affects characters representative of their time. Nothing could reflect that discontinuity and fragmentation more than a dream.

Shaw's other dream plays have the dream as a subtext that complements and illuminates the manifest play.[5] In *Too True to Be Good,* it is the manifest play that appears to be the dream. Only by analyzing and deciphering that dream can one find what could be the underlying dream. The manifest play appears to be a Freudian-type pre-oedipal problem-solving dream in which the child has to achieve independence from the overpowering, suffo-cating parent. Margery Morgan describes Harry Smiler, about whom Sweetie tells a story, as the id and the Elder as the superego. She says that the Sergeant's conflicting desires represent Shaw's "old theme of hypocrisy in terms of libido and inhibition."[6]

The curtain opens on what Shaw has described as *"One of the best bedrooms in one of the best suburban villas in one of the richest cities in England"* (429). The objects in that room, such as a fever thermometer in a tumbler of water, although appropriate to an invalid's bedside, could also be viewed as classic Freudian symbols,[7] the most interesting of which is the bedroom itself. The door is *"carefully sandbagged lest a draught of fresh air should creep underneath"* (429); the window is covered by curtains closed over a dark green blind. The room is dimly lighted by a small green-shaded lamp. It is hot; it is dark. The Patient is trapped within, awaiting her emergence into the world. Rather than merely representing a woman,[8] the bedroom could also signify a womb.

The heroine is asleep, feverish with measles. It is the Monster, a Microbe, that addresses the audience, complaining that the sick person has made *it* ill. The Monster insists that only when the Patient becomes well can the Microbe be healed, but the mother's efforts to prevent her daughter from dying have put the Patient into her state of illness. The Patient must separate herself from her mother before she dies from her mother's ministrations, as have her siblings before her. At the end of the first act, having jumped onto the bed, the now-healthy Microbe tells the audience that "The play is now virtually over; but the characters will discuss it . . . for two acts more. The exit doors are all in order" (456). The Microbe pulls up the covers and goes to sleep.

Shaw's language makes clear that the manifest play is the Patient's dream. In both the first act and the last act, the Patient repeatedly says that this play is her dream. The play begins with the Patient asleep. After she has awakened and attacked the burglar with the strength that no person who has been forced to be an invalid could have, the Nurse and Burglar discuss her being asleep, the Burglar saying, "Let her sleep. Wake not the lioness's wrath" (445), but they do awaken her. In the first act, her responses include, "I'm dreaming. . . . I'm dreaming that I'm perfectly well. . . . Go on with the dream. . . . Let nobody wake me. . . . in dreamland generosity costs nothing. . . . Lucky for you that I'm asleep. If I wake up I shall never get loose. . . . I'm going to make the most of this dream" (448, 451–52). In the last act, she says, "My dream has become a nightmare. . . . I want a world without parents: there is no room for them in my dream. . . . I have found myself out thoroughly—in my dream" (508–9, 512). So she has. By the end of the play, the Patient has escaped from her bedroom and the control of her suffocating mother. She has recovered physically and emotionally, and her conflicts with her mother have been solved. She has a matured personality and a name. No longer merely mother and daughter, these women can be friends, but when they exit the stage, the play does not end as it might were this the daughter's dream.

With one exception, all the characters depart, but the discussion continues. Aubrey, "A soldier who has lost his nerve, a thief who at his first great theft has found honesty the best policy . . ." (526), a preacher with neither Bible nor creed who must "preach and preach and preach . . . no matter whether I have nothing to say" (527–28), is left on stage preaching as the fog envelops him. For Aubrey, World War I "has been a fiery forcing house in which we have grown . . ." yet also one in which "we have outgrown our religion, outgrown our political system, outgrown our own strength of mind and character. . . . Their way [that of men of action] is straight and

sure; but it is the way of death; and the preacher must preach the way of
life. Oh, if I could only find it! . . . I have lost my nerve . . ." (527).

Shaw's final stage direction states that "*The audience disperses . . .*" (528).
In the first production I saw of *Too True,* a Penn State University Theatre
Department production directed by the late Warren Sylvester Smith in the
1950s, Smith had the curtains close behind Aubrey and the lights slowly
come up as Aubrey preached his final speech. Silence followed until the
audience realized that the play had ended, after which it erupted into applause. There was no rush for the exits. The audience dispersed.

David Foulkes, in *Dreaming: A Cognitive-Psychological Analysis,* claims that
"It is generally assumed that the sources of our dreams lie in what we know,
that their particular images can be traced back to whole units or bits and
pieces of memory and knowledge that we have acquired through experience."[9] The Patient's dream and the Patient as dreamer cannot explain
the Aubrey character. He, Meek, the Sergeant, and the Colonel discuss the
horrors of war and situations and strategies and weapons about which she
would have had neither knowledge nor experience. She would know little,
if anything, about their torment. Nor would she have any idea about the
work done by a chambermaid, or in a charity ward, or even that a woman
who has been imprisoned would have had ample opportunity to read and
learn the Bible. Could the Patient's dream, therefore, be a dream within
the true dreamer's dream?

It is the Monster who has the first and last speeches of Act I. It is awake
but ill at the opening curtain, healthy but asleep as the act closes. The
Monster has been made ill by the Patient and can be cured only if she be
cured. The play ends with Aubrey preaching his sermon to the audience
that had not followed the Monster's injunction to exit. Aubrey, the Sergeant, Private Meek, and the Colonel, all possibly different facets of Aubrey, as is the Monster, have in common that they have been made ill not
by a microbe but by their society.

Aubrey, rejecting his father's atheism, had secretly become ordained
while at university, but his wartime experience has destroyed his faith, leaving him unfit for the profession that has called him and for the society in
which he must live. He tells his father that stealing a necklace was

> Less than nothing, compared to the things I have done with your
> [and the nation's] approval. . . . I . . . dropped a bomb on a sleeping
> village. I cried all night after doing that. . . . I swooped into a street
> and sent machine gun bullets into a crowd of civilians: women, chil-
> dren, and all. I was past crying by that time.
>
> . . . You cannot divide my conscience into a war department and
> a peace department. . . . Do you suppose you can make a man the
> mortal enemy of sixty millions of his fellow creatures without mak-

ing him a little less scrupulous about his next door neighbor? (504–5)

In a dream, characters "split, double, multiply, vanish, solidify, blur, clarify."[10] Like Aubrey, the Sergeant is struggling to find his faith. Whereas Aubrey had been an officer and a gentleman, the Sergeant is from the working class and in the ranks. He reads the Bible and *Pilgrim's Progress*, not what one would expect an undereducated member of the working classes to choose. The Sergeant, preaching to Sweetie, as Aubrey preaches to everyone,

> used to believe every word of them because they seemed to have nothing to do with real life. But war brought those old stories home quite real. . . . And our government chaps are running about with a great burden of corpses and debts . . . on their backs, crying "What must we do to be saved?"
>
> . . . there used to be a peace of mind in the army. . . . But the war made an end of that. . . . We were not killing the right people in 1915. We werent even killing the wrong people. It was innocent men killing one another. . . .
>
> For the misery of it . . .
>
> For the devilment of the godless rulers of the world. . . . it was damnation. . . . What the gentleman here [Aubrey] said about our all falling into a bottomless pit came home to me. *I feel like that too.* [496, 512–13; my italics)

The Sergeant, who has lost his faith in soldiering, cannot afford to be an officer or to leave the army. Aubrey, having lost his nerve for flying, became an army chaplain. Then, losing his faith, he became shell-shocked and had to be invalided out. After being discharged as cured, he left the nursing home and shed his status as an officer to become a rather drifting civilian.

Another aspect of Aubrey is Private Meek, patterned after Lawrence of Arabia, who, like Aubrey and Meek, was "so warped by his wartime experiences that he cannot resume his life at the point where the war interrupted it. . . ."[11] Meek, like Lawrence, resigned his commission as a colonel to join the ranks. When asked how many commissions he has resigned, he says "Three, I think." He says that he prefers "the ranks. . . . I have a freer hand" (490). Lawrence resigned only one commission but joined the ranks three times, first joining the Air Corps as "Ross," then the Tank Corps, and yet again the Air Corps as "Shaw." He retired from the service when he reached the maximum age for the rank that he held rather than permit himself to be promoted. Two of Lawrence's brothers were killed in the war, as was Aubrey's brother. At an audience with King George V, when the

monarch offered a medal to Lawrence, he refused it. Aubrey, although he
accepted a decoration, is contemptuous of his "poorly designed silver
medal for committing atrocities . . ." (502). Aubrey's "incorrigibly superstitious mother" (507), who insisted that he learn three verses of the Bible
every day, seems to have been suggested by Lawrence's Calvinist mother.

Colonel Tallboys, needing the perks of his rank but happy to be relieved
of its responsibilities, could be, in the splitting of personalities made possible in dreams, an inversion of Meek—the former Colonel who relishes the
responsibilities of authority while refusing the rank. Tallboys, in discussing
the medal he craves, says that

> I have earned it, . . . ten times over. . . . I . . . have won real battles,
> and seen all the honors go to a brigadier who did not even know
> what was happening! . . . My turn today: Private Meek's tomorrow.
> . . . How I envy him. Look at me and look at him! I, loaded with
> responsibilities whilst my hands are tied, my body disabled, my mind
> crippled! . . . he, free to turn his hand to everything! . . . I have been
> driven to sketching in watercolors because I may not use my hands
> in life's daily useful business. . . . I see this man Meek doing every-
> thing that is natural to a complete man . . . whilst I . . . must . . .
> prevent myself going mad. I should have become a drunkard had it
> not been for the [water]colors.
> . . . How willingly I would exchange my pay, my rank, my K.C.B.,
> for Meek's poverty, his obscurity!
> . . . I once cut down an enemy in the field. Had I not done so he
> would have cut me down. It gave me no satisfaction: I was half
> ashamed of it. I have never before spoken of it. . . . (516–17, 520)

According to Freud, that which would be consciously unacceptable is banished from the conscious to the unconscious; that is, it is *repressed,* but
under the conditions of sleep, repressed ideas can slip past the censor. In
a dream, where one need not exercise "voluntary control over the flow of
conscious waking ideation,"[12] the Colonel can, and does, speak of it.

In addition to being a reflection of Lawrence, the Colonel, who paints
pictures to keep himself sane, may also have in him a suggestion of Winston
Churchill. A few years after World War I, in 1921, Lawrence became an
adviser on Middle Eastern affairs for Churchill when he was Colonial Secretary. After the disaster of Gallipoli in 1915, Churchill resigned his position
as First Lord of the Admiralty. On 18 November he crossed to France to
join the Oxfordshire Hussars as a Major. In January 1916 he was in the field
as Colonel of the 6th Royal Scots Fusiliers. In late April he was recalled to
England for a possible Parliamentary debate on Gallipoli. A combatant in
several colonial wars before he became a journalist and politician, Church-

ill began painting landscapes at Hoe Farm after resigning from the Cabinet in 1915 and continued painting while serving on the Western Front. After leaving France on 7 May, he tried "to find solace in painting."[13] Supported and encouraged by his ambitious wife, Clementine, Churchill would eventually redeem himself in World War II and earn for her the status of Ladyship that Colonel Tallboys's wife covets.

When Meek makes his entrance in Act II, he does so on a very noisy motorcycle. Lawrence, after becoming an enlisted man, would visit his friends and acquaintances, roaring up to their houses on his cycle, *Boanerges*—"a vociferous, loud-voiced preacher. . . ."[14] Among those whom Lawrence visited on his cycle was Churchill. Bunyan, in his autobiography *Grace Abounding*, speaks of being terrified by troubling dreams. In *The Holy War*, he invents the preaching captains of Emanuel's army, Credence and Boanerges. The Sergeant reads Bunyan; Aubrey is a preacher. Aubrey, Meek, the Sergeant, and the Colonel, four facets of the same Monster, are all multiples of the same individual and are all damaged by the wartime experiences that their society forced upon them.

The Patient and Sweetie are also different facets of a single character. The Patient, Miss Mopply ("Mops"), is a lady, yet she insists that she is not, for "there is no such thing as a lady. I have the instincts of a good housekeeper . . ." (511). Like Meek, she prefers the freedom allowed her as a servant to the restrictions of her rank. Sweetie has been a nurse and a hotel chambermaid and "has a conscience of a chambermaid and none as a woman" (472). Both Sweetie and Mops have loved Aubrey ("Popsy" or "Pops"), and both reject him, Mops having tired of him "sooner than Sweetie did" (512). Sweetie accuses Mops of really being in love with Meek, while Sweetie winds up with the Sergeant. The Sergeant tells Sweetie that "men and women have a top storey as well as a ground floor; and you cant have the one without the other" (495). Sweetie represents what Aubrey describes as "our lower centres" (474) whereas Mops is controlled by her "higher centres" (477).

Mrs. Mopply, the mother from whom her daughter must escape, recalls Lawrence's mother, from whom Lawrence did escape into the ranks, as well as Aubrey's domineering and religious mother. Lawrence's fanatically religious, "incorrigibly superstitious" mother could not find atonement for living with another woman's husband and bearing five sons out of wedlock. Mrs. Mopply has failed as a mother and only gains her sanity and her personhood when Tallboys bashes her on the head with his umbrella. This episode could also represent a repressed incest motif in that an umbrella can replace a penis, the Colonel being one representation of Aubrey and Mrs. Mopply being one representation of Aubrey's mother. Just as in *Simpleton of the Unexpected Isles*, where the English tourist is educated through sexual intercourse in the cave, Mrs. Mopply, having been struck on the head by the umbrella, is brought to her senses, has found herself, and has been made whole.

Aubrey's father has also failed as a parent. While Mrs. Mopply has found herself as a result of her trauma, the Elder, claiming that he is sane in a world of lunatics, feels himself "falling into [an] abyss, down, down, down. . . . our dizzy brains can utter nothing but madness . . ." (501). Mrs. Mopply, too, is "falling through the bottomless abyss" (521), not knowing her head from her heels.

Rather than being a problem-resolving dream, this comic fantasy is a nightmare from which the dreamer cannot awake. The dreamer, appearing first as the Microbe, then as Aubrey the burglar, then as Private Meek the apparent dogsbody who actually runs the outfit, then as the Sergeant, and then as the Colonel, seeks a way to expiate the horrors committed by the monster that each had become in the nightmare that was World War I. For the Monster's alter egos to be healed, to find their way of life, society needed to heal itself lest they "surely perish" (527). But in 1932, when the play was first presented, the audience was suffering through the Great Depression. Manchuria had been invaded by the Japanese. Mussolini was consolidating his power in Italy. It was clear that Hitler would soon succeed the doddering Hindenburg and take power in Germany. Organizations such as Henri Barbusse's "World Congress to Organize Resistance to War" were attempting to hold back the tide. World War II was not far off. Another of Shaw's apocalyptic plays that began with *Heartbreak House* and reflect the despair that World War I engendered, *Too True to Be Good* was quite simply too true to be in any way good.

Notes

1. Margery Morgan, *The Shavian Playground* (London: Methuen, 1972), pp. 258–59.

2. Named after the lies and excessive exaggeration of Baron Munchausen. Persons suffering from the disease often seek drastic treatment, including surgery, for imaginary physical ailments. In some cases, sufferers of the disease, rather than professing themselves ill, claim that it is a child who is acutely ill.

3. All quotations are from *The Bodley Head Bernard Shaw: Collected Plays with Their Prefaces* (London: Max Reinhardt, 1973), 6:429–528.

4. William R. Everdell, *The First Moderns* (Chicago: University of Chicago Press, 1997), pp. 356–57. Everdell proposes that the essence of modernism, beginning in the 1870s with the discovery of the set that divided mathematical continuity, is discontinuity.

5. See Rodelle Weintraub, "Johnny's Dream: *Misalliance*," *SHAW* 7 (1987): 175–77, for a fuller discussion of the pre-Freudism in Shaw's early dream plays. See also "Bernard Shaw's Fantasy Island: *Simpleton of the Unexpected Isles*," *SHAW* 17 (1997): 97–105; " 'Oh, the dreaming, the dreaming': *Arms and the Man*," in *Shaw and Other Matters*, ed. Susan Rusinko (Selinsgrove,

Pa.: Susquehanna University Press, 1997), pp. 31–40; and "Extracting the Roots of Sorrow: *You Never Can Tell* as Dream Play," *SHAW* 18 (1998): 137–46.

6. Morgan, p. 259.

7. Robert L. Van Castle, *Our Dreaming Mind* (New York: Ballantine Books, 1994), p. 123.

8. Freud, quoted by Van de Castle, p. 123.

9. David Foulkes, "The Sources of Our Dreams Lie in What We Know," in *Dreaming: A Cognitive-Psychological Analysis* (London: Lawrence Erlbaum Associates, 1985), p. 22.

10. August Strindberg, *Dream Play* (1901). Reprinted in translation in *Dream Play and Four Chamber Plays: Stormy Weather; The House That Burned; The Ghost Sonata; The Pelican*, translated by Walter Johnson (New York: W. W. Norton, 1975).

11. Stanley Weintraub, "Lawrence of Arabia: Bernard Shaw's Other Saint Joan," in *Shaw's People: Victoria to Churchill* (University Park: Penn State University Press, 1996), pp. 175–76.

12. Foulkes, p. 18.

13. Martin Gilbert, *Winston S. Churchill: The Challenge of War 1914–1916* (Boston: Houghton Mifflin, 1971), pp. 502–3, 798.

14. *The American Heritage Dictionary of the English Language* (Boston: Houghton Mifflin, 1976), p. 145. This was also the name given by Jesus to the apostles John and James (Mark 3:17).

Michael M. O'Hara

FEDERAL THEATRE'S *ANDROCLES AND THE LION:* SHAW IN BLACK AND WHITE

Now that more than one hundred years have passed since the first production of *Widowers' Houses,* Shaw and his plays are firmly embedded in our own sense of history. In his book *Shaw's Sense of History,* J. L. Wisenthal explored the means by which Shaw manipulated both historical incidents and historical narratives to achieve Shavian ends.[1] As a part of history, both Shaw and his plays can be, and have been, subjected to manipulations similar to those that Shaw himself employed. Although interpretations of Shaw's texts can be compared with Shaw's interpretations of history, there are some important differences. History has multiple authors, is differently "authorized," and has no copyright. Plays, on the other hand, are works of art, and some interpretations are more mutilations than manipulations. The production by the Federal Theatre of Bernard Shaw's *Androcles and the Lion* was, by and large, a case of artistic manipulation that followed similar patterns to Shaw's own efforts to create relevance.

Wisenthal and others have classed *Androcles* as one of Shaw's "history plays." *Androcles,* Wisenthal argued, illustrates Shaw's use of an historical subject to point up its "contemporary relevance," an argument that Shaw himself repeated on several occasions. In a "note written for the New York production in 1915," Shaw argued that the play was equally relevant to "such people as may be found in the United States today." The play illustrates not only Shaw's "conception of organic continuity in history," but also a continuity across continents.[2] How America's Federal Theatre Project (FTP) of the 1930s performed the play yields insights that are applicable across time and geography.

The FTP's five productions of Shaw's *Androcles and the Lion* are significant in themselves for several reasons. They occurred in five widely different locations—Denver, Atlanta, Seattle, Los Angeles, and New York City—and in very different styles. Three productions were performed by what were then called Negro companies. Although scholars have examined the FTP's productions of *Androcles* by Negro companies as part of studies treating black participation within the FTP, none compares the Negro productions of *Androcles* with the white productions.[3] The records of the FTP detail nearly all aspects of five distinct productions of *Androcles,* including different theater buildings, casts, designs, directors, and administrators. The differences between text and performances seem not only to highlight Shaw's sense of history but also to undermine Shaw's arguments against changes to his texts, changes that in the case of *Androcles and the Lion* accented powerful issues not present in the text.

Although *Androcles* was not well received by critics when it was first performed, it has become one of Shaw's most popular and most often revived works. The play had offended the critics' religious sensibilities. Briefly, the play dramatizes Shaw's belief that humans "must have something worth dying for to make life worth living."[4] A recently converted Christian, Androcles, and his shrewish wife, Megaera, stumble upon a lion who has a thorn in his paw. Androcles pulls out the thorn for the grateful lion, and both continue on their way to be captured, separately, by the Romans. Among the company of captured Christians are Lavinia, a beautiful girl who struggles with her faith, and Ferrovius, a muscular Christian who struggles with turning the other cheek. All are to be thrown to the equally captured lions in the Coliseum in Rome. After Ferrovius succumbs to his militant nature and slaughters six gladiators—earning a royal pardon for all the Christians by impressing Caesar—Androcles is nevertheless put into the arena to satisfy the mob's lust for Christian blood. Inside, Androcles finds his old friend from the forest, and they are joyously reunited and earn their freedom.

The Negro Repertory Company in Seattle presented the first all-black production of a play by Shaw on 2 November 1937 in the Federal Theatre. George Hood, acting state director for the FTP, cabled Shaw to ask whether Negroes had performed his work previously. Shaw responded, "not that I know of." Apparently, the FTP produced the first all-black Shaw anywhere.[5] To accommodate the Seattle Project's small stage, director Edwin O'Connor placed much of the action among the audience and divided the last act into three scenes instead of two but made no other changes in the text, and he made no attempt to adapt Shaw's play to a Negro cast or audience.[6] Blanche Morgan's costumes and sets were designed to "produce an all-round colorful 'spectacle' effect within the general style of the period," and no attempt was made at authenticity.[7]

Advance publicity for the production highlighted "a cast of local favorites in riotous roles" that would present "a Negro cast for the first time in [the play's] history."[8] Audiences were encouraged to see "a brilliant satire by the famous English wit, George Bernard Shaw," one that was "probably the most uproarious of [his] works." The local critics agreed, and they wrote that the "colorful settings, lusty acting, and sparkling technique were popular" with "a large and appreciative audience." One critic hoped that the FTP would "continue to choose such witty plays as the Shavian satire" but noted that "the cast was amusing . . . because it had funny lines to say, felt no self-consciousness, [and] was having a good time performing for the audience. But it had no conception of anything but the surface humor of the piece." The critic felt that "better mention goes to Blanche Morgan, who design[ed] colorful, crude scenery and effective costumes."[9]

The audience survey reported mixed responses to the play. Shaw's play was "funnier than the Marx Brothers," wrote one audience member. The Negro actors were "definitely good," and had "acted splendid, but the stage was awfully small." Others wrote that the "music was too loud for the size of the theatre," that the "acting was a bit stiff and at times overdone," that the "diction could be clearer," and that "plays dealing with modern social problems are, as a whole, better." The house averaged only thirty percent capacity, according to the survey report, and the low attendance was attributable to an inconvenient location "away from the downtown district" and the "smallness of the theatre (seating capacity: 496) and poor stage facilities."[10]

Figure 12 shows the Seattle unit's small stage, the spectacle of the crude costumes and set, and Negro actors enacting Shaw's play. The actors' apparent stiffness, their unsophisticated grouping on the small stage, and the simple costumes and sets suggest that the mixed reception was justified, if not generous. Lavinia is the only exception. She stands proudly, naturally, and her costume's simplicity and elegance set her apart.

Androcles opened again in Los Angeles on 23 December 1937 at the Hollywood Playhouse and moved to the Belasco Theatre before it closed on 16 January 1938.[11] The play had been hastily chosen after a poor production of *Captain Brassbound's Conversion* convinced the FTP that it lacked the necessary talent and resources to produce the originally selected *Major Barbara*.[12] Director Max Pollack "took a great number of liberties in the treatment without in any way changing the text."[13] In order to fill out the evening bill and to create a racial context for the play, he joined forces with the Federal Music Project and added a choral prelude that included several spirituals, among them "When Gabriel Blows His Horn," "Po' Mourner's Got a Home at Las'," and "I Got a Home in Dat Rock."[14] The racial context for the production could hardly have been lost on the audience, one member of which complained that the point had been overdone: there was "too much singing in the first part" of the play.[15]

Fig. 12. *Androcles and the Lion,* Seattle. Photograph #P-23-WA-5-4d, in Production Record Book, *Androcles and the Lion,* Seattle, 1937, B 439, RG 69. Reprinted courtesy of National Archives and Records Administration.

Advance publicity focused on the "fabulous" and "well-known comedy" by Shaw. The "first joint production of the Federal Theatre and Music projects" promised audiences an "all-colored choral group [that] open[s] the program singing a group of Negro spirituals" that should prove "to be one of the highlights of [the show]."[16]

Local critics were pleased with the FTP's efforts. *Androcles* was "richly studded with the enjoyable and rib-tickling humor of [Shaw] . . . [in] an evening of superb entertainment." Max Pollack was "to be congratulated" for helping the Negro players "to keep a spirit of fun and sly wit in the farce, as Mr. Shaw intended." The acting was "fine" and "far from disagreeable." Critics noted that the "first all colored staging of *Androcles and the Lion* ever brought to [Los Angeles]" was "preceded by a concert chorus [that] introduced [the audience] to the comedy hit that followed." No explicit comment was made on the racial context created by the Negro spirituals. All press reviews focused on Shaw's play and its humor.[17]

Audience responses were equally positive. "Excellent entertainment— clever and skillful handing of a good play," wrote one member of the audience. The "Negroes are superb actors" who had "a fine sense of comedy." Several audience members complained, however, about "too much sing-

Fig. 13.   *Androcles and the Lion.* Los Angeles, Photograph #P-23-CA-LA-3d, FTP
Collection. Reprinted courtesy of Library of Congress.

ing" and wondered whether the chorus "should be put on as a separate
show." The audience survey report concluded that the play was "well-re-
ceived by the overwhelming majority of Hollywood Playhouse patrons."[18]
Like the production in Seattle, the Negro actors were praised, but no evidence suggests that the production was viewed in a racial context. The play
was a great comedy by a famous author that was enacted by Negro actors.

   Figure 13 shows the powerful Ferrovius attempting to convert the Roman
dandy, Lentulus, who cowers in Ferrovius's grasp. The Hollywood's large
stage is filled with comic spectacle. The cartoonish set is dominated by a
Coliseum decorated with a comically drawn lion and the comically anach-
ronistic "Welcome to Rome." The costumes are richly made but do not
attempt to be historic. The production photographs generally confirm the
audience's appreciation of the production's emphasis on farce. The Christian women are demurely dressed with covered heads and passively await
their turn at the lion's den. Lavinia stands with her hands folded across
her waist, serenely detached, while Androcles stands agitated and afraid.

   Nearly a year later in New York, director Samuel Rosen followed Pollack's
example in trying to fill out the evening and to create a specific context.
Although the only musical change this time was a switch to "I'm Bound

Fig. 14.   Publicity poster, *Androcles and the Lion,* New York, 1938, original in Posters File, FTP Collection. Reprinted courtesy of Library of Congress.

for the Promised Land" from "Onward Christian Soldiers," the New York production attempted to create both a specific racial and political context. The production opened on 16 December 1938 in Harlem's newly renovated Lafayette Theatre.[19]

In an effort to affix the right message to the performance, the Negro Theatre Project released an informative brochure that sought to ensure that audiences would see the play as an illustration of the oppression not only of religious minorities but also of the Negro race.[20] A publicity poster printed by the FTP also reinforces these themes. In Figure 14, an heroically posed Negro (Androcles?) restrains a proud and powerful lion that would otherwise attack the approaching Roman soldiers. The images in the poster neither match Shaw's own description of Androcles as "*a small, thin, ridiculous little man*"[21] nor reflect the lion created in the FTP's production (see Fig. 15). The image does not exactly depict Shaw's play, but it does reveal the FTP's efforts to shape the public's reception along the lines of racial oppression. Further, the image is unusual for its heroic treatment of a Negro, an image absent from most New Deal culture.

Fig. 15. *Androcles and the Lion,* New York, photograph in Production Record Book, *Androcles and the Lion,* New York, 1938, FTP Collection. Reprinted courtesy of Library of Congress.

The Negro project faced internal difficulties in mounting this play, however, and the themes focused on changed during the rehearsal process. When it was first selected, the production was intended to be "a fill-in—somewhat light, vivid and good." Hallie Flanagan, when she previewed a run-through a few weeks before the play's opening, was in "somewhat of a shock to find [the play] grown into such a mammoth, major production." Because it was "too late to change the point of view from which the whole thing has been attacked," Flanagan gave only a few suggestions on specific details to improve what she thought was a "somewhat solemn production." She asked that the "chorus of Christians" better exploit the "flamboyant quality which [Flanagan] had expected negroes to bring to this script"; that the actors' movements and singing "be much more vigorous and emotional"; that there be "as much off-stage sound as possible" to create excitement; that several scenes "be played up for comedy"; and that they seek to include more "qualit[ies] of the negro [because] to [Flanagan] this is its greatest lack."[22]

Flanagan's efforts to lighten up the production worked. Most critics found that the advance publicity had been misleading and agreed with Brooks Atkinson's observation that the play "is easier to enjoy if the mind

Fig. 16. *Androcles and the Lion,* New York. Photograph #P23-NYC-48d, FTP Collection. Reprinted courtesy of Library of Congress.

does not hunt too furiously for the intellectual significance of Shaw's [or the FTP's] symbols." Nevertheless, many critics noted the several attempts at political symbolism in the production.[23] A new Interlude, in which Roman soldiers marched a slave around the stage, was inserted before the Prologue.[24] Several reviewers noted the visual connection to Jews in Germany that this *mise en scène* created.[25]

Figure 16 shows the scene from the apocryphal Interlude in which a slave wearing the placard "I am a Christian" was ridiculed by Roman soldiers. Despite the Romanesque costumes, the photograph shows the racial signification that Negro actors inevitably brought to the play. Furthermore, the Interlude established an emphasis on religious oppression that resonated throughout the production.

Several other attempts were made in the production to reinforce political symbols. Perry Watkins, the first black man to be allowed to join the Set Designer's Union, designed the costumes for the New York production. Figures 17 and 18 show that Watkins's original sketches for the Roman Centurion include an eagle emblazoned on his chest, a twisted cross on his belt, and one on a shield. These emblems closely resemble Nazi symbols and were removed for unidentified reasons before the costumes were constructed. Notation on the plate indicates a later censorship of these emblems, and no image of these symbols appears in the production photographs. Manuel Essman's sets, however, smuggled in subtle Nazi references. One reviewer for the *New York Sun* noted "a glimpse of swastikas

ANDROCLES AND THE LION
PERRY WATKINS   #1126

Caesar

#19

This quality failure in blue shown

PURCHASE

BLUE BLUE
PURPLE
#5 WEST
LINED
WITH GOLD
SATIN

APPLIQUE
LAHME ON
SILVER
PERMABRITE

Change
Emblem

"ANDROCLES & THE LION"

— Perry Watkins —

Fig. 17.   Perry Watkins, Costume Design for *Androcles and the Lion*, New York, Plate #19, Costume Design File, FTP Collection. Reprinted courtesy of Library of Congress.

Fig. 18.   Perry Watkins, Costume Design for *Androcles and the Lion*, New York, Plate #24, Costume Design File, FTP Collection. Reprinted courtesy of Library of Congress.

Fig. 19.   *Androcles and the Lion,* New York. Photograph #P23-NYC-6d, FTP
Collection. Reprinted courtesy of Library of Congress.

on the hangings of a Coliseum box."[26] Although the symbols seen in Figure
17 are not as visually conspicuous as swastikas, the strong geometrical lines
of the set and the dramatic banners stretching up through the stage picture
here are suggestive of photographs of Nazi rallies at Nuremberg Stadium.
Political symbols were not limited to the design, for staging of some scenes
appears to reinforce visual references to the Nazis. For example, in Figure
19, Caesar's entrance in Act II prompts a stiff-armed salute and "Hail, Caesar!" Although Shaw's original text was intact, the visual salute created a
powerful link to contemporaneous images seen in newsreels and photographs of Hitler's reception in similar circumstances.

   Although no audience survey report documents the responses of audience members in New York, critics praised the play and the production
with equal enthusiasm. Atkinson wrote that the combination of Shaw and
Negro actors "may not sound ideal in prospect, but live and learn."[27] Arthur Pollock stated that Shaw's play "fit the times neatly . . . with the salute
the Fascists and the Nazis lifted from the Romans."[28] Robert Sylvester also
noted that "with religious persecution and its problems the timely theme
that it is, [the FTP] has wisely enough assigned [Shaw's play] as the current
chore for its Negro Theatre project." Other critics found the production
"enjoyable," "consistently humorous and highly interesting," and "a

friendly and engaging evening." The actors were praised for "acting that is vigorous and apparently backed by conviction. It isn't subtle acting, but it's often effective." Atkinson, along with other critics, praised Daniel Haynes's Ferrovius: "Manly in stature and voice, tortured in spirit, Mr. Haynes could represent the sorrows and strength of the Negro race quite by himself." The FTP had succeeded in blending a winning comic style, Shaw's excellent text, and political and racial symbols to create a significant and powerful piece of theater.

Of the three Negro productions of this play, Seattle's was the first all-Negro cast of a Shavian drama, Los Angeles's was the first to use Negro spirituals to reinforce the racial context, and New York's used Negro spirituals and then went one step further by adding several visual symbols of Nazism. Two of these productions consciously used theatrical mechanisms to create meanings beyond the script's textual authority but did not necessarily violate the artistic integrity of Shaw's play.

The changes by white companies in Atlanta and Denver, however, were more substantial. Albert Lovejoy, director of Atlanta's Project, placed *Androcles* in a double bill with *The Man of Destiny*, with Lovejoy himself as Napoleon. The production opened on 15 March 1939 in the apparently much better equipped Atlanta Theatre, and was "the most successful, artistically, and the best liked from an audience angle" the project had seen for many months. Although Lovejoy reported that the play could work in a simple setting, "it also len[t] itself beautifully to a lavish production bill such as ours."[29] The critics agreed and showered this production with praise. Dudley Glass reported that the play "was to my mind far and away the best thing the theatre has done." Edith Hills noted Lovejoy's introduction of jazz to the play: "the audience laughed . . . from the first entrance . . . until his triumphant exit in swing-time, when he [Androcles] gave as neat a truckin' exhibition as you are ever likely to see." Critics praised the "sterling" actors, the "imaginative and well executed" sets, and Lovejoy's "able direction."[30] Although Lovejoy had not made any overt references to racial or political symbols, he did significantly change the text.

Glass noted in his review that the program "was billed as a 'double-feature,' something G.B.S. probably would disapprove, but then there would be nothing unusual about that." Risking a greater reproach, Lovejoy added dialogue and cut several pages from the script. Both the additions and deletions seem to accommodate a presumed religious conservatism of Atlanta's audience. Additions include "God will protect me!" (I–3), "I'm not afraid, God is with us!" (I–3), "Glory to God!" (II–19), and "Hallelujah— Thank God!" (II–21). On the other hand, the entire scene between Lavinia and the Captain (I–6), in which she flirts with the Captain and he attempts to dissuade her from her faith, is cut, as is a similar scene when she is faced with death and utters "my faith has been oozing away minute by minute

Fig. 20.   *Androcles and the Lion,* Atlanta, photograph in Production Record Book, *Androcles and the Lion,* Atlanta, 1938, FTP Collection. Reprinted courtesy of Library of Congress.

whilst I've been sitting here" (II–15).[31] Lovejoy was evidently mindful of his Bible Belt constituents.

Figure 20 shows the Atlanta Theatre's large stage filled with the spectacle of a stylized Coliseum. The Christian women, looking extraordinarily demure and chaste, sit on stage right, and a defiant Ferrovius stands stage center left. The pose and attitude of the women seem mindful of what audiences might expect in the Bible Belt. They all have covered heads, including Lavinia, who stands at stage center right next to Androcles. Lavinia, in poses similar to ones by actors in Los Angeles and New York, stands with her hands clasped at her waist. Also, the twin spires of the Coliseum recall images of paddle-wheelers, perhaps suggesting an unconscious link to the production's Southern location.

The innovative Denver production opened on 30 December 1937 and closed, after ten performances, on 9 January 1938. Michael Slane, director, made his motives clear in his production report: "*Androcles* is written for an English audience . . . [and] an English audience is not as lazy as an American audience. An English audience will sit and listen. An American audience has to be shown." His goal was apparently to link religious oppression with political oppression and, perhaps obliquely, racial oppression. The program for the evening began with "A Group of Negro Spirituals" directed by Irene McWilliams "as they were sung by her mother and her grandmother with their friends." The songs were viewed as an

Fig. 21.   *Androcles and the Lion,* Denver. Photograph #P-23-CO-D-7d, FTP
Collection. Reprinted courtesy of Library of Congress.

added Christmas bonus and "drew eight curtain calls at the first performance."[32]

Advance publicity for the play included mention of the "concert of
Negro Spirituals and Christmas carols" and promised audiences, in a re-
vival of "an old stock company practice on New Year's Eve," that "the cast
will entertain at open house following the evening performance." Any
thoughts that the production would follow other stock techniques were
dispelled by Slane's plan to use the production "to develop ideas he has
long cherished to present to Denver audiences the much touted 'experimental theatre.' " Audiences were warned that "there are four sets of very
eccentric design and the [production] is unique in that no props are required to conform with the set." Critics were charmed by these experiments and uniformly praised the direction, acting, and design and noted
that the "admixture of Salvation Army and old Roman [costumes]" linked
Shaw's Christian martyrs with contemporary practitioners of "old time religion or [others] who were fanatical on some other topic such as the Com-
munistic Party."[33] The mixture of costumes is clearly visible in Figure 21.
More striking, however, was that Caesar was made to look like Hitler.
Slane's message was not limited to the costuming: the swastika on the door
to the Coliseum is unmistakable.

The actors in this photograph share similarities with other productions
despite the differences in costume and political engagement. Like actors in
other productions, the Christian women are posed in attitudes of feminine

Fig. 22. *Androcles and the Lion,* Denver. Photograph #P-23-CO-D-4, FTP Collection. Reprinted courtesy of Library of Congress.

passivity, hands clasped at the waist, and Lavinia's white purity sets her apart from the others. The men, including the plucky Androcles, stand in poses of manly purposefulness.

Slane was apparently not subtle in his message of political and religious repression and could, in fact, be said to have employed a political soap box quite literally. Figure 22 shows the Roman Captain standing on a literal "soap box" as he argues with Lavinia. Another visual joke is hidden in the set here as well: the stylized crossroads indicate that all roads lead to Rome. The mixture of costumes in this photograph, most notably the British pith helmet for the Roman Sergeant, also suggests a subtle jab at imperialism.

Both the set and staging were experimental, and critics found the innovations "a refreshing departure from tradition which ha[d] characterized many of the productions" in Denver.[34] Figure 23 shows the highly stylized forest in which Androcles, his wife, and the Lion first meet. Slane had learned how to overcome the Baker Theatre's limitations and used experimental techniques to enlarge the visual impact of his productions. He also enlarged his acting area quite literally by staging the play so that "Androcles and the Dictator [were] climbing all over the audience in the big chase sequence," and he placed Caesar/Dictator in the audience for the Arena scenes, thus involving the audience by implication with Hitler's activities.[35]

Fig. 23. *Androcles and the Lion,* Denver. Photograph #P-23-CO-D-3, FTP Collection. Reprinted courtesy of Library of Congress.

Atlanta's production made significant concessions to a perceived level of religious tolerance. Lovejoy's additions and cuts de-clawed the play with little regard for Shaw's expressed wishes. In Denver, on the other hand, no cuts or additions were made to the text, but visual references to Hitler boldly contradicted a WPA directive issued in 1936 that "no one impersonating a ruler or cabinet officer shall actually appear on the stage."[36] Other shows had been prevented from opening in New York City for this very reason.

Several factors might explain why Slane was able to circumvent this standing order. Although both the national and international press maintained a strong presence in New York City and subjected FTP's local projects to intense scrutiny, Denver was internationally and even nationally remote. No evidence suggests that the Denver productions received any significant attention from sources other than the local newspapers.

This same reasoning can be applied to Lovejoy's cutting of Shaw's text in Atlanta, which was also theatrically remote. Lovejoy was able to cut the play, whereas the New York production, which was intended to be performed at the World's Fair, could not be altered. When the FTP had inquired about cutting *Androcles* for the World's Fair, Shaw responded:

"Positively No. Either full length or another play. Suggest Blanco Posnet as simpler, shorter and cheaper. What price admission if performance free." The FTP did not, however, take advantage of Shaw's offer of free royalties if they would produce *Blanco Posnet* for the World's Fair.[37] Although Lovejoy adapted Shaw's text to conform to his audience's tolerances and the productions were uniformly praised, he clearly sabotaged Shaw's satire on religious fervor.

Three dominant factors established the contexts in which audiences received these productions: musical settings, racial acculturation, and iconographic images. Musical contexts—Negro spirituals or jazz—were established for all productions except in Seattle. Racial modifications—Negro spirituals—were manifest in productions in Los Angeles and New York, and political images—Nazi symbols—were created in productions in Denver and New York. These contexts not only changed Shaw's texts but also theatrically illustrated the sometimes conflicting historical strategies that Shaw used in his texts.

Seattle's production, at first glance, does not appear to have created any specific context. Still, the novelty of an all-Negro cast is a subtle visual expression of a simple, yet powerful, image of racial oppression. The very image of Negroes on stage was enough to add the context of racial oppression to Shaw's otherwise unchanged text. That O'Connor in Seattle chose not to emphasize racial overtones in any production element did not diminish this impact. Similarly, the Negro productions in Los Angeles and New York generated unavoidable reverberations of racial issues. The latter two productions created additional reinforcement through the use of Negro spirituals. The unmistakable mood and rhythm of this music altered the audience's perception of Shaw's original message without in any way changing the text.

Visual references to Nazism also created a context that was new to Shaw's text. The appearance of these images was controversial for two reasons. First, Shaw himself initially supported fascist groups in Europe. Second, many powerful Americans also supported Nazi doctrine, prominent among them being Henry Ford. New York's production, probably because of its high profile and its international audience, was more restrained than Denver's in its reinterpretation (and reinvigoration) of the text through performance.

These changes in the theatrical text explicitly or implicitly manipulated Shaw's written text in ways surprisingly similar to Shaw's own manipulations of historical narrative. On the one hand, these theatrical intrusions reinforce the Shavian "dramatization of cyclical recurrence or history as a level line." *Androcles* can speak to people of different colors, countries, and religions and can do so more pointedly, and perhaps more successfully, through changes or additions to the theatrical text. At the same time, however, these additions to the theatrical text seem to undermine Shaw's own text and reflect a "Macaulayite viewpoint," theatrically speaking. The modern, progressive director updates Shaw's supposedly antiquated text through theatrical means. As Shaw himself "vehemently and decisively rejected the idea of progress in history," so too did he reject changes to his texts. But Shaw also found progress in history "highly attractive."[38]

Much of his work points to a future that he hopes will be progressively better if the human race listens to Shaw and evolves beyond its current shortcomings. Perhaps such an understanding of Shaw's sense of history can thus guide progressive efforts to stage Shavian works for modern audiences. Shaw's plays should continue to evolve through theatrical transformations that seek both to reinforce Shaw's view that people have not really changed and to prompt audiences to see his messages in new ways. As Shaw implied in *The Apple Cart*, productions of his plays that simply "explain the past whilst [leaving us] to grapple with the present . . . [with] the ground before our feet in black darkness whilst [the production] lights up every corner of the landscape behind us," are of little use.[39]

Notes

1. See J. L. Wisenthal, *Shaw's Sense of History* (Oxford: Clarendon Press, 1988).

2. Ibid., pp. 106–7.

3. For a general survey of Black drama in the FTP, see Quita E. Craig, *Black Drama of the Federal Theatre* (Amherst: University of Massachusetts Press, 1972). For a detailed history of the Negro Theatre Unit of the New York City Project of the FTP, see Robert A. Adubato, "A History of the WPA's Negro Theatre Project in New York City, 1935–1939" (Ph.D. diss., New York University, 1978). For a corrective study of New York's Negro unit, see Jay Plum "Rose McClendon and the Black Units of the Federal Theatre Project: A Lost Contribution," *Theatre Survey* 33 (November 1992): 144–53. For a detailed history of Seattle's Negro Repertory Company, see Evamarii A. Johnson, "A Production History of the Seattle Federal Theatre Project Negro Repertory Company: 1935–1939" (Ph.D. diss., University of Washington, 1981).

4. Charles Purdom, *A Guide to the Plays of Bernard Shaw* (London: Methuen, 1963), p. 242.

5. See George Hood to Bernard Shaw (6 October 1937), carbon-copy telegram, in Washington—1937—Vol. 1, Oversized, Record Group 69, National Archives and Records Administration, Washington, D.C. (hereafter referred to as RG 69); and Bernard Shaw to George Hood (8 November 1937), original telegram, in Washington—1937—Vol. 1, Oversized, RG 69.

6. Edwin O'Connor, *Director's Report,* Production Record Book, *Androcles and the Lion,* Seattle, 1937, B 439, RG 69.

7. Blanche Morgan, *Costume Notes,* Production Record Book, *Androcles and the Lion,* Seattle, 1937, B 439, RG 69.

8. Unless otherwise specified, reviews in this paragraph are from press clippings in Washington—1937—Vol. 1, Oversized, RG 69.

9. "Androcles and the Lion," *The Argus* (6 November 1937), press clipping in Washington—November 1937, B 66, RG 69.

10. *Audience Survey Report* (3 January 1938), typed copy in *Androcles and the Lion*, Seattle, B 254, RG 69.

11. *Androcles and the Lion*, Production Record Book, Los Angeles, 1937, B 432, RG 69; and *Audience Survey Report, Androcles and the Lion*, 5 March 1938, typed copy in *Androcles and the Lion*—Los Angeles, B 254, RG 69.

12. Ole M. Ness to Hallie Flanagan (30 October 1937), typed original in Region V, June–December 1937, B 100, RG 69.

13. *Director's Report, Androcles and the Lion*, Production Record Book, Los Angeles, 1937, B 432, RG 69.

14. Program for *Androcles and the Lion*, Los Angeles, 1937, original in Playbills, Library of Congress Federal Theatre Project Collection, Washington, D.C. (hereafter referred to as FTP Collection).

15. *Audience Survey Report, Androcles and the Lion*, Los Angeles (5 March 1938), typed copy in *Androcles and the Lion*—Los Angeles, B 254, RG 69.

16. "Projects Unite for Shaw Comedy," *Daily News* (23 December 1937), press clipping in Southern California—December 1937 #2, B 11, RG 69; and "Federals Combine for Play," *Evening News* (24 December 1937), press clipping in Southern California—December 1937 #2, B 11, RG 69.

17. "All-Negro Cast Gives Shaw Play," *Daily News* (24 December 1937), press clipping in Souther California—December 1937 #2, B 11, RG 69; *Press Notices—Evening News* (24 December 1937), reprinted in Production Record Book, *Androcles and the Lion*, Los Angeles, 1937, B 432, RG 69; and *Press Notices—Times* (2 January 1938), reprinted in Production Record Book, *Androcles and the Lion*, Los Angeles, 1937, B 432, RG 69.

18. *Audience Survey Report*, Los Angeles.

19. *Technical Survey Report—Lafayette-NYC*, n.d., typed original in Surveys—New York City #3, B 253, RG 69.

20. Adubato, "History of the WPA's Negro Theatre," p. 191.

21. Bernard Shaw, *Androcles and the Lion* (New York: Penguin, 1989), p. 111.

22. Brooks Atkinson, "The Play," *New York Times* (17 December 1938), p. 10; and Hallie Flanagan to George Kondolf (9 December 1938), typed original in Kondolf, George—Director NYC #2, B 35, RG 69.

23. Atkinson, "The Play"; and see reviews of *Androcles and the Lion*, press clippings in New York City—December 1938 #2, B 51, RG 69.

24. *Complete Working Script*, typed copy in Production Record Book, *Androcles and the Lion*, New York, 1938, FTP Collection.

25. Adubato, "History of the WPA's Negro Theatre," pp. 191–96.

26. "Shaw in Harlem," *New York Sun* (17 December 1938), press clipping in New York City—December 1938 #2, B 51, RG 69.

27. Atkinson, "The Play."

28. Unless otherwise noted, all quotations in this paragraph are from press clipping in New York City—December 1938 #2, B 51, RG 69.

29. *Director's Report*, Production Record Book, *Androcles and the Lion*, Atlanta, April 1939, FTP Collection. No advance publicity survives for this production.

30. Dudley Glass, "Glass Pleased by Shaw Play," n.d., n.p.; Edith Hills, "Two Plays Delight Atlantians," n.d., n.p.; and " 'Androcles and the Lion' Federal Theatre Presentation," n.d., n.p., press clippings in Production Record Book, *Androcles and the Lion*, Atlanta, April 1939, FTP Collection.

31. All page references to Atlanta's production of *Androcles* are from Script #S66(22), *Androcles and the Lion*, FTP Collection.

32. *Critics' Opinion;* and *Director's Report,* Production Record Book, *Androcles and the Lion,* Denver, January 1938, FTP Collection.

33. *Copies of Press Releases,* n.d., typed original in CO—Press Releases—March 1936–March 1938, B 108, RG 69, pp. 29–31; and *Critics' Opinion,* Denver.

34. *Critics' Opinion,* Denver.

35. *Director's Report,* Denver. This is the scene in the final act where the lion chases Caesar until Androcles rescues him.

36. Hallie Flanagan, *Arena* (New York: Duell, Sloan, and Pearce, 1940), pp. 65–66.

37. Shaw quoted in George Kondolf to Hallie Flanagan, 15 March 1939, typed original in NYC—January–July 1938, B 97, RG 69.

38. Wisenthal, *Shaw's Sense of History,* pp. 126, 129.

39. Bernard Shaw, *The Apple Cart,* in *Plays Political,* ed. Dan H. Laurence (London: Penguin, 1986), p. 86.

Gale K. Larson

"IN GOOD KING CHARLES'S GOLDEN DAYS": AN IMAGINATIVE AND TRUTHFUL HISTORY

The Theatre Programme for the 1939 Malvern Festival, dedicated to Bernard Shaw, contains a two-page preface by Shaw entitled "An Author's Apology." He begins by noting the differences between history plays or "chronicles dramatized" and the historical romance. In this latter category he places his play *"In Good King Charles's Golden Days"*, and he notes that the "stage Charles" never had any resemblance to the "real Charles." But, says Shaw, when we turn away from the "sordid facts of Charles's reign" and from his "Solomonic polygamy," we enter into a situation that becomes "interesting and fresh." In other words, it becomes a situation in which Charles is viewed from perspectives other than that of the oft-repeated historical views, whether from the Whig Macaulay or the Jacobite Hilaire Belloc or the "stage Charles" view popularized in "intolerable stale" romances. Implicit in these words is Shaw's belief that another perspective on Charles will not only be "interesting and fresh" but will reveal the "real" Charles. The argument is reminiscent of Shaw's characterization of Caesar in *Caesar and Cleopatra* and his view that Shakespeare's Caesar is an "admitted failure" because the Bard "never knew human strength of the Caesarian type."[1] Just as Shaw believed that in *Saint Joan* he had gotten into "Joan's skin" and had rendered her alive dramatically, so too he believed that he had captured the "real Charles" by going a different way to work, first by ignoring the Macaulay and Belloc historical views, popularized in historical romances, and second by imposing his own views on the facts of Charles's life, but views, I will argue, well corroborated by other writers on Charles II and his times.[2]

What is Shaw's dramatic strategy of rescuing Charles II from the grips of

Theatre Programme

WHAT SAY THEY?	James Bridie
THE PROFESSOR FROM PEKING	S. I. Hsiung
DEAD HEAT	Robert Vansittart
OLD MASTER	Alexander Knox
BIG BEN	Evadne Price and Ruby Miller
IN GOOD KING CHARLES'S GOLDEN DAYS ..	Bernard Shaw

●

ROY LIMBERT
(for English Festivals Ltd.)

PRESENTS THE ELEVENTH

MALVERN FESTIVAL

IN ASSOCIATION WITH

CEDRIC HARDWICKE

DEDICATED TO

BERNARD SHAW

●

All the Plays produced by **H. K. AYLIFF**.
PAUL SHELVING has designed Settings and Costumes.
Stage Manager: **HAROLD CHAPIN**.

Fig. 24.   "Theatre Programme," from *1939 Malvern Festival* booklet.

the conventional historians and the "stale romances" in order for Shaw, as chronicler/playwright, to put "novelty" on the stage and still claim historical authenticity? I believe that Shaw, always skeptical of those writers who make eroticism the be all and end all of public interest, wished to show the "other side" of Charles in order to demonstrate the complexity rather than the simplicity of his character. There is more to Charles than just his libertine side. What better way to present a novel dramatization of Stuart history than to conceive of something that never happened but should have? Shaw, the creative dramatist and thinker, knew that there were more ways of presenting a vision of the truth of Charles's life than merely perpetuating the reduction of his life to that of a charming libertine, "the Merry Monarch." Shaw speculates on what might have happened had Charles actually met "the human prodigy Isaac Newton" together with the founder of the Quakers or Society of Friends, the leather-breeched George Fox. This imaginary meeting embodies the intellectual tension between science and religion, relieved with humor and good fun by the arrival of Charles's paramours: Nell Gwyn, "the player woman"; Lady Castemaine, Barbara Villiers; and the Frenchwoman, Louise de Kéroualle, or Madame Carwell. Added to the tension between science and religion is the "eternal clash between the artist and the physicist," represented by the arrival of Godfrey Kneller, portrait artist. Shaw would have liked to have had William Hogarth available as his representative artist, but, unfortunately, he was not around in 1680, Shaw's chosen date for this dramatized meeting. Kneller, Shaw asserts, did not have the brains of Hogarth, whose famous dictum, "the line of beauty is a curve" Shaw treats as antithetical to Newton's view of the universe as, in principle, rectilinear. While the meeting of these representatives of a broad cultural spectrum of seventeenth-century England is imaginary, Shaw still wished to impose the law of probability on his dramatic structure within the limitations of "what might have happened." Shaw subtitled his play "A True History That Never Happened," a paradoxical utterance that gives credence to something and nothing simultaneously.

In dramatizing a conversational piece among these well-known personalities of the seventeenth century, Shaw showcases Charles and his times. Shaw further delineates Charles in a clash with his impulsive brother James, later King James II, and in Act II Shaw presents another side of Charles, a domesticated Charles, in a charming boudoir scene with his Portuguese wife, Catherine of Braganza. Shaw thus presents more than just the intellectual history of Charles's reign. The initial scientific, religious, and artistic tension of the play eventually gives way to politics in the form of a debate over kingship between Charles and his younger brother James. That debate, which focuses on the issue of who is in control of the kingdom and ends with Charles's prediction that James will be overthrown and replaced with his Protestant daughter and her Dutch husband, gives way to Shaw's more personal view of Charles as husband. Shaw's intention here, as clearly stated in the 1939 Malvern Festival Theatre Programme, is to underscore Charles's "political ability" and his role as "the best of husbands." This revisionist's view of the historical Charles is a shocker, as it is meant to be, and yet Shaw had utter confidence in portraying Charles in this manner because he was well acquainted with historical views that gave support to such a characterization of Charles. One such view known to Shaw was that of Sir Arthur Bryant.[3] His biography, *King Charles the Second*, published in 1931, may have come to Shaw's attention from his Fabian associate and friend, Beatrice Webb. In a letter to her, Shaw wrote on 17 January 1939,

> I have Bryant on Charles.
> I will look him up on Pepys; but I want to keep Pepys out of it, as he is in it anyhow by strong association, and I have no new light to throw on him.
> Charles I have to invent all over again. Newton and Fox I have only to put on the stage, as they are strangers there, and are far too little known.[4]

Bryant was one of the early biographers who challenged the Whig historians' assessment of Charles II. While he does not ignore the many sexual liaisons of the King, he makes it clear that Charles was not a political slave to his mistresses, a view with which Shaw concurred. "If there was one insinuation Charles hated more than another," writes Bryant, "it was that, in political affairs, he could be swayed by his mistresses" (248). Although Bryant characterizes Charles as an "unfaithful husband," he does not consider him an "inconsiderate one" (200n). Bryant shifts much of the focus away from the amorous side of Charles and concentrates more on his easy manners and gentle nature, his wit and humor, his personal popularity, his imperturbable temper, his walks, his interest in the physical sciences, his taste for architecture, his love of ships and shipbuilding, and his love of drama, especially the works of his favorite, John Dryden. He was an accomplished conversationalist, "discussing freely and without restraint on every subject under heaven and telling stories so well that, not out of flattery, but for mere joy of listening to them again, his ministers would pretend they had not heard them" (350). Bryant believes that James never realized how the "inexplicable triumph of the monarchial principle over its once all-powerful enemies . . . was due to his brother's skill and patience" (351). Unlike Charles, it was beyond James's "comprehension that a victory over his enemies could be pressed too far, or that old enmities might be wisely appeased" (351). Charles, writes Bryant, "had small liking for his brother's political philosophy—'la sottise de mon frère,' as he called it" (354). James wanted "to increase the royal authority, [while] Charles was averse to

Fig. 25. "G.B.S. and Plans for a New Theatre" (photograph by the *Picture Post*) in *1939 Malvern Festival* booklet.

changing the form of Government or to making himself any more absolute than he was; his real aim was to preserve the prerogative and secure peace and an adequate revenue" (354).

The political difference depicted here between the two brothers is the substance of Shaw's debate between the two in his play. In that particular scene, Shaw has Charles ruminate what will become of James after Charles's death. Bryant, quoting Charles, writes, " 'But when I am dead and gone, I know not what my brother will do; I am much afraid that when he comes to wear the crown he will be obliged to travel again. And yet I will take care to leave my kingdoms to him in peace, wishing he may long keep them so. But this hath all of my fears, little of my hopes and less of my reason.' Time was to prove the truth of this shrewd, melancholy prophecy" (351–52). All these sentiments that Bryant puts into Charles's mouth Shaw lifts for his play.

A similar borrowing can be seen in Bryant's treatment of Charles's Queen, Catherine of Braganza. He quotes a letter that the Queen wrote to her brother Pedro II in Portugal:

> "There is nothing," wrote Catherine to her brother, "that concerns me more than to tell you how completely the King releases me from all trouble . . . by the care which he takes to defend my innocence and truth. Every day he shows more clearly his purpose and goodwill towards me, and thus baffles the hate of my enemies. . . . I cannot cease telling you what I owe to his benevolence, of which each day gives better proofs, either from generosity or from compassion, for the little happiness in which he sees I live." (291)

This letter was written in 1679, the year preceding the time of Shaw's play. The letter reveals a Catherine who responds warmly to her husband's deep concern for her and her concomitant appreciation. Bryant, writing about Charles's life a year before his death, refers to his "two walks a day, working in his laboratory with his chemist, Dr. Williams, and showing his age a little by the regularity of his post-prandial slumbers. He was living very simply now . . . [and] twice daily [he was] in the Queen's withdrawing-room . . ." (353).

Shaw's reading of Bryant's biography may have suggested the final act of the play where Charles and Catherine engage in a touching domestic conversation, but I believe that this domestic scene was suggested to Shaw by his reading of Lillias Campbell Davidson's biography, *Catherine of Braganza: Infanta of Portugal and Queen-Consort of England*.[5] This work was published by John Murray in London in 1908, and, more importantly, is part of the Shaw collection of books at Shaw's Corner, Ayot St. Lawrence, where I discovered the book in the rotating bookshelf located in the drawing-room. It is also a source from which Bryant drew much of his material.

Bryant quotes Catherine's letter to her brother, noted above, from Davidson's biography.

Davidson may well be the source that induced Shaw to ignore for the most part the "Solomonic polygamy" side of Charles's character. She writes, "One age can no more be judged by the standard of another than a savage can be criticized by the standard of the civilized. What in one period is praised and approved, in another is condemned and outcast. Morality is morality all the world through, but till the Victorian age in England what were called affairs of gallantry were not only condoned but lauded" (22). Davidson, like Shaw, takes Macaulay to task for his "misleading accounts which go far to distort real history. He does Charles, in these descriptions, a great deal of injustice" (31). She continues,

> To unwind this web, and disentangle the threads of truth from those of fiction, is not an easy task. One must depend a great deal on unbiased records, written by those who were not partisans. To impute every evil to the other side was the general practice, and to laud one's own party was as common. This is one reason why, for centuries, the character of Charles II has stunk in the nostrils of his countrymen, when men a hundred times worse than he, without the whit of his good parts, have come down to us with glowing tints in the pictures painted of them. (33–34)

She describes Charles as "the most popular monarch, perhaps, that ever filled the English throne. The people adored him. He was gracious to them, friendly in talk, allowed them to mob him in his walks, and at his table, and his wit and good nature made him an idol amongst them" (43).

Describing the relationship between Charles and Catherine, Davidson writes that Charles treated her with "respect and kindness, and insisted that respect be shown her by others. She was able to testify of him, with utter truth, that she had never received anything but goodness from his hands. He never again said a word of anger or authority to her, and never again did he ask her to receive his mistresses" (163). Late in their marriage, Davidson records that Charles's respect and attention he had always paid her now turned into tenderness and that "he lavished upon her kindness and affectionate intimacy which amazed the court, and filled her with bliss" (361). Davidson quotes from one of her letters to her brother: "I have everything that can give me complete satisfaction in this life, nor do I now wish to think I have reason to complain" (362). Davidson summarizes Charles's reign as

> an Augustan age of science, literature, architecture, and the arts in England. He came to the throne with a nation groaning under taxa-

tion, and denuded of art, science, and learning, society in a state of barbarism, religion a tyrannical oppression of half the community. In twenty-four years of his reign the country found peace. Taxes were abated, religious differences healed, and he abolished the statute for the burning of heretics. People worshiped God in their own way. He helped Penn with all his might in establishing a colony in the New World, where freedom of religion and thought might flourish. He provided for naval veterans at Chelsea; . . . he helped to soften and civilize life throughout the kingdom. (363)

This picture of Charles as an enlightened ruler who had to balance so many political and religious matters to stay in power, who was kind to and considerate of his Queen, and who carried on in good humor with his mistresses, closely resembles that of Shaw's Charles and his court in *"In Good King Charles's Golden Days"*.

It is certain that Shaw used other sources to get the right slant on the other principals in the play. It is known that he perhaps based his depiction of Isaac Newton on his reading of Sir D. Brewster's *Memoirs of the Life, Writings, and Discoveries of Sir Isaac Newton,* first published in 1885, with a new issue in 1893. However, he may also have consulted William Stukeley's *Isaac Newton: Memoirs of Sir Isaac Newton's Life,* published in 1936.[6] That book is also in the library at Shaw's Corner. Stukeley writes about his presence at the portrait sitting of Newton with Sir Godfrey Kneller: "Both Sir Isaac and Sir Godfry [*sic*] desired me to be present all the times of sitting, and it was no little entertainment to me, to hear all the discourse that passed between these two great men" (12). He goes on to say that "Tho' it was Sir Isaac's temper to say little, yet it was Sir Godfry's art to keep up a perpetual discourse, to preserve the lines and spirit of a face. I was delighted to observe Sir Godfry who was not famous for sentiments of religion, sifting Sir Isaac to find out his notions on that head, who answered him with his usual modesty and caution" (12–13). He refers to Newton's "absence of mind, from common things of life" (61), and adds that he would often "sit down to paper and forget his friends" (61). These references may indeed suggest that Shaw read Stukeley's *Memoirs of Sir Isaac Newton's Life* and was under his influence while writing his play.

T.F. Evans, in his splendid article, " *'In Good King Charles's Golden Days':* The Dramatist as Historian," refers to two possible sources that may have influenced Shaw in his characterization of George Fox: Fox's own *Journal* and William Penn's "A Character Sketch."[7] I would suggest another possibility. In Shaw's library at Ayot St. Lawrence there is a copy of William C. Braithwaite's *The Beginnings of Quakerism,* published in London in 1912.[8] Chapter II of that book, entitled "The Founder of Quakerism," covers

George Fox. Many of the incidents recorded there as well as the character description of Fox himself are not at all in variance with Shaw's treatment.

Another source that was possibly used for many of the details in *"In Good King Charles's Golden Days"* is Clive Bigham's *The Kings of England 1066–1901*, published in London in 1929.[9] That rather large tome is also in Shaw's library at Ayot St. Lawrence. When I pulled it off its shelf and put it on Shaw's desk, it opened to the section on Charles II as if it had previously been lying open on Shaw's desk for some period of time. This source, similar to Bryant and Davidson, also mentions Charles's need "to keep a balance between royalist and republican, Puritan and Papists, Churchmen and Nonconformists—a none too easy task" (357). Such information as Charles's use of the expression "oddsfish," his dancing and tennis playing, his numerous walks accompanied by his spaniels, his perfect manners, his good humor and sociability, his taste for music and the arts, and especially his "good knowledge of the drama" are all covered here; however, it also contains a depiction of Charles that Shaw pointedly ignores, namely the assessment of the King as "bad" and "immoral." He does mitigate that harsh judgment by stating that his "engaging personality and his romantic history appealed to a nation which was tired of psalm singing and penitence" (363). Bigham makes reference to James's popularity over Charles, listing as factors his military successes and the fact that he had children and his brother had not. Readers will recall that in the play the Queen makes reference to James's popularity with the Court because Charles spends more time talking to gardeners and the like than attending to members of the Court. Bigham, like Bryant and Davidson, delineates a sharp contrast between the brothers, favoring, of course, Charles over James.

We know that Shaw started writing *"In Good King Charles's Golden Days"* in November 1938 and finished it in April 1939 in time for its production at the Malvern Festival on 12 August 1939, where it ran for six performances. During those composing months, Shaw divided his time, almost equally, between Ayot St. Lawrence and his Whitehall residence in London. He consulted with others to get certain aspects of the play right, checking logarithms with Sir James Jeans, astronomer and physicist, and conferring with Sir Arthur Eddington, who, Shaw says, "gasped at the perihelion of Mercury."[10] Shaw kept the anachronism just for the "stage laugh" he knew that it would evoke, but he also believed that it was not without some plausibility. In a "First Rehearsal Copy" of *"In Good King Charles's Golden Days"* in the library at Ayot St. Lawrence, Shaw wrote in that "Fully Corrected Copy," "This is an appalling anachronism, but I contend that it is not impossible that Newton may have put a coin into his telescope to produce an artificial eclipse, and found that Mercury was not in his calculated position." He also consulted the historian G. M. Trevelyan, who corrected Shaw's Calvin blunder (wrong century). But for the most part, I believe Shaw consulted various ready-reckoners, encyclopedias, and biographies to fill in many of the historical details. For example, Sotheby's sale catalogue of Shaw's possessions at 4 Whitehall, London, dated 25 July 1949, lists the fourteenth edition of the *Encyclopaedia Britannica* for sale. At Shaw's Corner there are a number of such sources that Shaw could have used for quick references, such as *Chamber's Encyclopaedia, Dictionary of National Biography,* the ninth and tenth editions of *Encyclopaedia Britannica* (thirty-six volumes), and *Nelson's Encyclopaedia* (twenty-four volumes).

Shaw's play gives readers and audiences alike a view of Charles that is rarely heard or seen these days, but it is one that, like his portraits of Caesar and Saint Joan, has a definite claim of "assisting at an act of historical justice."[11] Shaw boasted to Beatrice Webb that "Charles I have to invent all over again," and he did so in a novel and fresh manner, providing history that never happened but should have, resulting in a depiction of the "real Charles." The historians and biographers that I have mentioned as reference sources would recognize Shaw's appropriation of their treatment of and perspectives on Charles II and his times.[12]

Notes

1. Cf. Bernard Shaw, "Better than Shakespear?" in *Three Plays for Puritans* (London: Constable, 1931), pp. xxvii–xxxvi.

2. I wish to express my gratitude to Rosemary Jury, custodian in 1988 of Shaw's Corner for the National Trust, who invited me to come to Ayot St. Lawrence to check Shaw's library holdings while I was doing research on *"In Good King Charles's Golden Days",* even though the house was closed for the season.

3. Arthur Bryant, *King Charles the Second* (London: Longmans, Green, 1931). Subsequent references to Bryant will appear parenthetically in the text.

4. Bernard Shaw, *Collected Letters 1926–1950,* ed. Dan H. Laurence (New York: Viking, 1988), p. 524.

5. Lillias Campbell Davidson, *Catherine of Bragança: Infanta of Portugal and Queen-Consort of England* (London: John Murray, 1908). Subsequent references to Davidson will appear parenthetically in the text.

6. William Stukely, M.D., F.R.S., *Memoirs of Sir Isaac Newton's Life, 1752: Being Some Account of His Family and Chiefly of the Junior Part of His Life,* ed. A. Hastings White, Consulting Librarian to the Royal Society (London: Taylor & Frances, 1936). Subsequent references to Stukeley will appear parenthetically in the text.

7. T. F. Evans, "'*In Good King Charles's Golden Days*': The Dramatist as Historian," *SHAW* 7 (1987): 269–77.

8. William C. Braithwaite, *The Beginnings of Quakerism* (London: Macmillan, 1912).

9. Clive Bigham, "Charles II: 1630–1685," in *The Kings of England 1066–1901* (London: John Murray, 1929), pp. 352–63.

10. *Collected Letters 1926–1950,* p. 545.

11. Malvern Festival Theatre Programme, p. 9.

12. I wish to thank Jonathan Wisenthal for reading this article, for his generous remarks, and for his extremely helpful suggestions for revision.

Sidney P. Albert

BALLYCORUS AND THE FOLLY: IN SEARCH OF PERIVALE ST. ANDREWS

> If Lawrence likes travelling let him fly to Dublin. There he must take the Harcourt St train to Shankill. Thence he must walk or drive (if he can get a conveyance) to Ballycorus smelting works, where he will see the chimney up the hill and the tower on the top, unless their ruins have totally disappeared, which suggested my scene.
>
> At Faringdon in Oxfordshire Lord Berners has built a campanile with a view of the white horse which is much more English than desolate Irish Ballycorus.

This passage, in a 1939 letter from Bernard Shaw to Gabriel Pascal, then unpublished, was generously shown to me by Dan H. Laurence around 1981.[1] It posed an irresistible challenge and prompted a decision on my part to attempt to follow its directions to the sites identified as scenic sources for the envisioned town of Perivale St. Andrews in *Major Barbara.* Opportunity to pursue such inviting Shavian field research came in the summer of 1982, when the venture dovetailed neatly with prior plans to engage in more conventional-style research in England and Ireland.

The Irish quest benefited uniquely from the enthusiastically proffered assistance of the late John O'Donovan—assistance that proved indispensable. As prologue, he had me engage a taxicab for a drive around Dublin, with stops at various locations associated either with Shaw's life in that city or with Irish literary history. Drawing upon his encyclopedic knowledge of Ireland, Dublin, and matters Shavian, he conducted a guided lecture tour, replete with lively anecdotes—all delivered with his characteristic wit and flair. The experience converted the cab fare into a relatively inexpensive tuition fee (even though not paid to the worthier renderer of service).

The prospect of the adventurous expedition to Ballycorus excited

Fig. 26.   John O'Donovan on the stairway near the base of the hilltop tower at the Ballycorus works.

O'Donovan. The train was long gone, he pointed out, but he knew the exact locality in question and could readily drive us there, which he did. Arriving at our destination, we discovered that the Ballycorus works was not in ruins, but, as memory serves, there was visible evidence of the depredations wrought by the passage of time. Lines of pipe, for example, lay exposed on the surface of the terrain. The chimney had vanished, but the hilltop tower had survived, more or less intact. I scurried up the incline, followed by O'Donovan, and upon reaching that giant structure, took numerous snapshots of it.

Also on the premises was a house, occupied by a family named Dunne: a couple and their two grown sons. They welcomed us warmly, especially when they realized that John O'Donovan was in their midst, for by virtue of his popular radio program on the National Broadcasting Service (R.T.E.), he was an admired celebrity. Mrs. Dunne invited us into her home and served us scones and tea. As we chatted and explained our mission, she remarked, "I do believe we have a photo album with pictures of the smelting works as it was in the nineteenth century." Naturally, we were

Fig. 27.   The base of the hilltop tower at the Ballycorus works in 1982.

more than eager to see the album, which she fetched for us. To our delight it contained, as she had indicated, photographs of the place as it would have looked during Shaw's Dublin years. I asked if they were willing to have copies made for me at my expense. Happily, Larry Dunne, one of the sons, agreed to do so. Months later—in December—a package arrived from " 'The Nook,' Lead Mines, Ballycorus, Kiltiernan Co., Dublin, Republic of Ireland," containing six $8'' \times 10''$ glossy prints from the album, along with a Larry Dunne letter message on a Christmas card. The letter concluded with the greeting: "Go n'eirigh an ho thair libh (May the road rise with you)." On the verso of each of the prints he had added holograph explanatory comment in ink, which fortunately does not bleed through when copied.

In January 1985, John O'Donovan wrote to me that in looking through the photograph collection that Shaw had bequeathed to the British Library of Political and Economic Science at the London School of Economics, he had discovered several photographs that G.B.S. himself had taken of Ballycorus and its various towers. T. F. Evans subsequently hunted for these

Fig. 28. Larry Dunne's caption: "The tower to foreground is long demolished. The other tower is still standing and indeed has recently been cleaned in conjunction with the renovation of the adjoining building: formerly a 'smelting house' for lead ore. Indeed the purpose of the towers (chimneys really) was to handle the lead fumes."

pictures at the London School of Economics but was able to report only that Shaw's photographs were in boxes, mostly with unlisted contents, none of them identifiable as being of Ballycorus. Recently, however, Librarian Mrs. C. Mays of the British Library of Political and Economic Science discovered Shaw's Ballycorus photographs in an undated album. These consist of six black-and-white deteriorated pictures, five of them of the hilltop tower shown in Figure 30. Shaw's concentration on the tower with the spiraling stairway appears to support the connection between Ballycorus and Perivale St. Andrews. The sixth photograph, rather fuzzy, shows a building and the surrounding landscape, resembling parts of Figure 31. Pictured are also several slender chimneys, suggestive of the *"chimneys sprouting like huge skittles into the middle distance"* described in the play's stage directions.

Ballycorus did not end this exploratory journey. Still to be found was the campanile at Faringdon in England, advanced as an alternative in the second paragraph of Shaw's letter to Pascal. Setting out from Oxford, I enlisted the service of a taxicab driver, who, although he had never heard of the campanile, nevertheless fancied the search and willingly took me to Faringdon.

Fig. 29. Larry Dunne's caption: "The tower in photo 1 [Fig. 28] at closer angle."

Fig. 30. Larry Dunne's caption: "The large chimney shown here stands at the highest local point (800 ft.). It was connected to the main smelting works shown in photo 4 [Fig. 31] by a mile-long stone "flue," section of which may be seen behind cottage in photo 1 [Fig. 28]. The idea was that at this height the deadly un-refined lead fumes would disperse into the air. This was fine until the wind blew the fumes back into the valley (again photo 1) with disastrous effects on livestock and indeed humans."

Fig. 31.   Larry Dunne's caption: "Smelting works with manager's house on left. Chimney on right no longer standing. The rather ornate tower shown in photo 2 [Fig. 29] is barely visible just left of and above house."

In plain sight during the drive to that town was White Horse Hill, on which the famous gigantic ancient figure of a horse (374 feet long) is carved into the chalk hillside—the white horse alluded to in G.B.S.'s letter, and sketched in verse by Henry James Pye (1745–1813):

> Carved rudely in the pendant sod is seen
> The snow white courser stretching o'er the green.[2]

The White Horse is also the central image in a long epic poem, *The Ballad of the White Horse*, penned by Shaw's friend G. K. Chesterton. It begins with these lines:

> Before the gods that made the gods
>   Had seen their sunrise pass,
> The White Horse of the White Horse Vale
>   Was cut out of the grass.[3]

At Faringdon, the driver parked the taxicab in a neighborhood that he suspected would be a promising vicinity in which to search. We knocked

Fig. 32. Larry Dunne's caption: "Entrance to smelting works. Completely unchanged today except for railing in foreground."

Fig. 33. Larry Dunne's caption: "Other view of Valley. House still extant."

Fig. 34.   The White Horse, Uffington (postcard). Reproduced with kind
permission of Dennis Print, Scarborough, United Kingdom.

on the doors of several houses close by and made inquiries about the campanile—to no avail. None of these people had any knowledge of it, and its whereabouts began to take on the aspect of an unsolvable mystery. Perhaps it had become a forgotten ruin. Or had I committed some topographical error? Finally, however, we came to a house where what we were seeking suddenly dawned on the woman queried. "Oh," she exclaimed, "you mean the Folly!" and straightaway gave directions to the nearby park in which it was located. Thence we went, and, climbing through a heavily wooded area, we soon beheld the high tower. Once more I held my camera up to a dwarfing edifice for picture-taking, but this time with scant success, owing to the sylvan shadows that darkened the area. Then, just before departing from Faringdon we visited a local shop, where, unexpectedly, a conspicuous rack featured picture postcards in color of "The Folly, Faringdon," and "The White Horse, Uffington"!

Unaware at the time of the specific architectural meaning of a folly, I presumed that the local residents had attached the name to the tower in order to ridicule its erection as an act of folly on the part of Lord Berners. That is not too far off the mark, for "folly" is, loosely, a general term for a costly ornamental building that serves no useful purpose. At the same time such a simple definition fails to do justice to the complexity and broad scope of the term's denotation. In fact, follies constitute a variegated architectural genre. In a work devoted to the subject, Jeffery W. Whitelaw explains,

Fig. 35.   The Folly, Faringdon (postcard). Reproduced with kind permission of Dennis Print, Scarborough,
United Kingdom.

It is impossible to find a universal definition of a folly: structures as
diverse as grottoes, wellheads, houses, pyramids, prospect towers,
cottages, bridges and pagodas have been called follies, but no characteristic can be singled out as common to all of them, other than,
perhaps, a departure from a very general norm—unlike other buildings which have an accepted usefulness, most follies require further
explanation. . . . But one common factor is that folly builders intended their creations to be looked at and enjoyed. . . .

More specifically, "the most familiar type of folly is a tower, sham castle or
other substantial building set in a prominent position where it can be seen
from afar and in particular from the house or garden of the builder. . . .
They will almost always draw attention and indeed were usually designed
to impress, amaze or delight."[4]

Sir Gerald Hugh Tyrwhitt-Wilson (1893–1950) became the fourteenth
Lord Berners in 1918.[5] A composer, writer, and painter, his career included
service as an honorary attaché in the British embassies in Constantinople
(1900–1911) and Rome (1911–19), in the latter city coming to know com-
posers Igor Stravinsky and Alfredo Casella. As an author, he produced five
humorous novels and two volumes of autobiography. In the main a self-
taught musician and a gifted dilettante, he first wrote small ironic songs

and piano pieces, then later found his forte in music for ballets, among them three scores for the Sadler's Wells Ballet: *The Triumph of Neptune* (1926), *Luna Park* (1930), and *A Wedding Bouquet* (1936). He died at Faringdon House on 19 April 1950, a little more than six months prior to G.B.S.'s death.

Obviously Shaw was aware of Lord Berners's Folly, even though he referred to it inaccurately as a campanile. (It was not a bell tower.) Moreover, he knew where it was and what could be seen from it. Nor was Lord Berners a stranger to him. Dan H. Laurence includes Lord Berners's autobiographical *First Childhood* among the many books that G.B.S. and his wife read during their voyages in the early 1930s, and Michael Holroyd lists the baron as one of a number of personages for whom Charlotte Shaw gave lunches. David Huckvale has reported that Shaw "acquired an almost complete collection of compositions by Lord Berners in all their original editions, including piano reductions of the ballets *A Wedding Bouquet* and *Luna Park* and the opera, *La Carosse du Saint Sacrement*."[6]

It would indeed have been surprising if Shaw had not heard of Lord Berners's Folly at Faringdon, for not only was it historically famous, but its planned construction proved controversial and, in consequence, garnered considerable publicity. Completed in 1935, barely four years before its mention in the letter to Pascal, it was the last major folly tower to have been built in Britain. Lord Berners had found a hill just outside Faringdon already crested with a *feuillée*, a stand of beech and pine trees. These had been planted in the eighteenth century, on the ruins of a long chain of fortifications, by Henry James Pye, who had been named Poet Laureate in 1790 and whose verse about the White Horse was quoted above. He also wrote a poem titled "Faringdon Hill" about this site, which had been called Faringdon Folly for more than 200 years.

On this hill Lord Berners proposed to place his tower.[7] That proposal sparked vehement local opposition, and the furor provided lively copy for the newspapers all through 1935. Before even seeing the plans, the local Council denied permission for the project, responding to a rumor that Lord Berners intended to install a powerful siren on the building. However, the Ministry of Health did examine the plans, after which it conducted a particularly contentious inquiry. Some admirals and generals who resided in the region found objectionable the fact that Lord Berners was too patently unmarried. One fulminating admiral complained that the structure would spoil the view from his house. When Lord Berners's architect pointed out that it would be impossible for him even to see it without a telescope, the old mariner replied that, as an admiral, the only way he ever looked at the view was through a telescope. In another exchange between the two, when the architect remarked how magnificent the scenery from the tower would be, the admiral demanded to know how to get there, to which the architect retorted, "By the stairs." The Ministry approved the plans, and Lord Berners, emerging victorious from the fray, was at last free to build his folly, which one of the defeated opponents, a disgruntled old soldier, spoke of as "Lord Berners's monstrous erection."

The architects engaged to build the Folly were Lord Gerald Wellesley, later the seventh Duke of Wellington, and Trenwith Wills. On 5 November 1935, Guy Fawkes Day, Lord Berners celebrated the completion of the tower with a grand party, a fireworks display, and the setting free of hundreds of doves dyed red, white, and blue. The event was reported in the *Tatler,* highlighted with a whole page of photographs.

The basic structure of the Folly is square and 140 feet high. Made of brick, it was originally cream-colored, but the coloring was eventually effaced. According to one description, "A staircase goes up inside to a belvedere room, with nine large georgian round-headed windows for appreciation of the splendid view (six counties claimed). Above is an octagonal tower, slightly castellated, with eight pinnacles, and in Lord Berners' time a flag."[8] At the top a note from Lord Berners bore this warning: "Members of the public committing suicide from this tower do so at their own risk." A victim of neglect over the years, by five decades after its creation, the Folly had become derelict and was devolving into a moldering ruin.

Shaw, we saw, wrote of Ballycorus as having suggested his scene for the last act of *Major Barbara* and of Lord Berners's campanile as a more English substitute. How much of what these two sites reveal is to be found in the description of Perivale St. Andrews in the stage directions of the play? Here is the pertinent portion of that description:

> *Perivale St Andrews lies between two Middlesex hills, half climbing the northern one. It is an almost smokeless town of white walls, roofs of narrow green slates or red tiles, tall trees, domes, campaniles, and slender chimney shafts, beautifully situated and beautiful in itself. The best view of it is obtained from the crest of the slope about half a mile to the east, where the high explosives are dealt with. The foundry lies hidden in the depths between, the tops of its chimneys sprouting like huge skittles into the middle distance. Across the crest runs an emplacement platform of concrete, with a firestep, and parapet which suggests a fortification, because there is a huge cannon of the obsolete Woolwich Infant pattern peering across it at the town.*

Separately noted is a *"path down the hill through the foundry to the town,"* the path by which Cusins arrives to open the scene.[9]

Since Lord Berners's Folly did not exist before 1935, it could have had no bearing on this depiction, written for the play in 1905. In fact, it was in connection with the motion picture production of *Major Barbara* that Shaw wrote his 1939 letter calling attention to the Folly. Hence the altered portrayal of the scene in the published screen version needs to be taken into account as well. The initial description reads, "*A road skirting a green hill, up the opposite slopes of which, parallel to the road, runs what appears to be a white wall ending at the top in a tower with steps winding up it spirally. In enormous black letters on the white wall are the names UNDERSHAFT up one side and LAZARUS down the other.*" Ensuing dialogue adds to the picture:

> BARBARA. . . . This is the whited wall in the Bible. How could you spoil that hill with it merely to flaunt your name on it?
> LADY BRITOMART. . . . You must have all that knocked down and taken away instantly, Andrew. I will not have our name daubed all over the home counties.
> UNDERSHAFT. . . . They are not walls my love. They are the chimneys of my smelting works. When they are swept twice a year we get some tons of silver out of the soot, which is quite clean and white. The name of the firm can be read for ten miles with a good glass: it is one of the sights of the county. People feel as Sarah does that they must photograph it. For twenty square miles you cannot escape from it. . . .[10]

Surprisingly, no recognizable earmarks of the Folly are apparent in these lines, with the possible exception of the white wall, which could conceivably have been suggested by Lord Berners's structure while it was still cream-colored. But even that link is unlikely since white walls were already included in the original word portrait of the town. Nor does this Perivale tower betray any similarity to the one at Faringdon. Oddly enough, it does bear some resemblance to an entirely different folly, that at Castle Howard (in North Yorkshire), long the home of the Earl and Countess of Carlisle, parents-in-law of G.B.S.'s friend Gilbert Murray. As is well known, Murray and his mother-in-law were intricately involved in the story of *Major Barbara*.[11] Castle Howard was designed early in the eighteenth century by the playwright Sir John Vanbrough. "In 1709," Whitelaw tells us, "he rounded off his grand design with a great wall which incorporated the first sham fortifications, complete with turrets and towers. This has remained the biggest folly in England."[12] Is not the "*white wall ending at the top in a tower*" at Undershaft's factory designed along similar lines?

In the ostensible absence of any distinctive attributes of Lord Berners's Folly in the cinematic text of *Major Barbara,* one might well wonder what Shaw had in mind in proposing it as an English alternate for the Irish smelting works. He certainly could not have regarded it as in any sense a close counterpart. But judgments about its possible relevance are best deferred until after assessing the more basic role of Ballycorus, which is, after all, the primary locus to explore for stimuli capable of evoking the dramatist's images of Perivale St. Andrews.

The most explicit linkages to Ballycorus, it turns out, are to be found in the printed screen version. There the "*tower with steps winding up it spirally*" exactly matches the perduring Irish tower of Figure 30. Clearly discernible only at close range, those really are steps that snake up its exterior. The later photograph of John O'Donovan standing on one of its lower treads is visible confirmation of that fact. An equally manifest reminder of Ballycorus is Undershaft's designation of his plant as a smelting works, with chimneys as purported cleansing agents.

Two other delineated scenes in the film edition warrant consideration in relation to Ballycorus. In one of them Undershaft has his visitors go to a window to look at the homes of his older workpeople: "*The view from the window is of a green valley dotted with bungalows of various design: each with its verandah and garden.*" Later, a long variant of the play's gun emplacement setting includes "*a very unimposing old brick edifice at the west end of the emplacement, with the word MANAGER over the door. . . .*"[13] It would appear, however, that neither of these passages exhibits items particularly suggestive of a Ballycorus lineage, let alone of the Folly.

Returning to focus on the stage play, it is now pertinent to ask what impress Ballycorus could have made on the Perivale St. Andrews scene back in 1905. Certainly it could have imparted a subtle Irish aura. In the previous year Shaw had written *John Bull's Other Island,* all about Ireland, and the second half of *Major Barbara* was composed at Derry in that country (although substantially revised in England).[14] That he might have relished transplanting a plant with Irish roots to English soil should occasion no surprise.[15]

The creative process is inevitably selective, obviating anything approaching a precise replication of originals. Instead, an artist will be inclined to utilize only those aspects of observed phenomena that serve or fulfill his larger design and purpose. In another letter to Pascal anent *Major Barbara* dated 5 September 1939, G.B.S. himself avers that "the artist can always improve on nature."[16] Accordingly, nowhere in sight in the pictures of Ballycorus are there any reminders of Perivale St. Andrews's domes, campaniles, "*roofs of narrow green slates or red tiles,*" or simulations of fortifications. At the same time, identifiable are equivalent white walls, tall trees, slender chimney shafts, and possibly the vaguer beauty of situation, although that may be ruled out by the characterization of the works as desolate.

Yet, there is more to be gleaned from the photographs than just constituent particulars. For these are all comprehended in a total landscape in which the smelting works is community matrix. In his prefatory note to the screen edition of *Major Barbara,* Shaw refers to "the great Undershaft factory and industrial colony." Does not the panoramic expanse of countryside in Figures 28 and 33 provide more than a modicum of the desiderated components for such a factory and industrial colony scene? Spread out before us is a verdant vista in which nestle workers' homes and, overlooking them, "the chimney up the hill and the tower on the top" that Shaw remembered.

The artist is also as free to add as to subtract. In the original Derry manuscript of the drama, Shaw set the scene simply as "a platform with a sham rampart & a cannon pointing over it: . . . Also a flagstaff. From the rampart the model village can be seen on a hillside in the distance."[17] Despite being supplanted later, this capsule stage direction does express some of the playwright's initial ideas (formulated in Ireland) about the location of the town. (A sham rampart, interestingly, would qualify as a folly.) A distant hillside is in plain view in Figure 33, but it is open, unpopulated land. One could imagine a complete model village superimposed on that hillside, giving it "a local habitation and a name," even a name such as Perivale St. Andrews. Whether Shaw ever entertained such a notion matters not. The point is that he could have, that he could also have rearranged what he saw there in ways unbeknownst to us. In this manner Ballycorus could have furnished matter, ambience, and conceptual building blocks for assembling his more exemplary fictional townscape.

In recommending on-site viewing of the two locales, Shaw must have expected that seeing them would provide something inaccessible from the printed words alone. What? Closer scrutiny and analysis of the adduced evidence does disclose certain recurrent integral features: the persistent landmark presence of an imposing *tower* (or campanile or chimney) on a *hill* (or slope) commanding a spacious *view* (generally of a valley below). A hill and tower with a view are conspicuously present in Ballycorus and its environs and are the sum total of what Lord Berners's Folly had to offer. They are also perceivable in the textual scenic details of both the stage and screen editions.

Hills and towers are lofty vantage points from which to survey the countryside below and the sky above. By their very height they dominate their surroundings, and in doing so can serve as symbols of dominance, an important theme in *Major Barbara*. At this point the drama rises to high ground, literally and figuratively. The stage itself is the summit of a hill, with the foundry at the middle level and the town at the bottom, although "*half climbing*" another hill. Cusins's entrance comes at the end of a climb from the town. Of critical significance is the compositional placement of Barbara, who, according to the stage directions, "*is standing on the firestep, looking over the parapet towards the town,*" with the huge Woolwich Infant cannon mounted symbolically close by. At the apex of the *mise en scène* she remains, perched above the other characters, silently observing and listening to them for a very long spell. As the late Dame Sybil Thorndike (who had enacted the role under Shaw's rehearsal guidance) once told me, Barbara, even when silent, held a dominant position on stage, above guns and armaments.[18]

An emphasis on verticality, magnitude, and scope singularly befits a drama that unfolds on multiple levels, with heaven as the figurative zenith, culminating in a "transfigured" Barbara's commitment to "the raising of hell to heaven and of man to God." [19] What better visual metaphor could there be for such a challenging ascension than the massive Ballycorus tower with its spiral steps winding precariously skyward? The incorporation of an elevating vision and perspective of this sort may well have been at the heart of the intimated intent of Shaw's invitation to evocative site-seeing.

In retrospect, this odd odyssey of search and research was attended by good fortune in virtually every respect: in being able to reach its territorial targets, in finding them reasonably intact, and in capturing camera likenesses of the sights at these sites. Best of all was the reward of being vouchsafed glimpses of architectural and landscape models that once caught Bernard Shaw's artistic eye, whence filtered facets eventually made their way to his virtuosic pen.

Notes

1. The letter, dated 12 September 1939, has since been printed in *Bernard Shaw and Gabriel Pascal*, ed. Bernard F. Dukore (Toronto: University of Toronto Press, 1996), pp. 64–65. "Lawrence" is Laurence Irving (grandson of Sir Henry Irving), the scene-designer for the motion picture *Pygmalion*, acting at the time in the same capacity for the filming of *Major Barbara*. He subsequently resigned, and the film credits the settings to his successors, Vincent Korda and John Bryan.

2. Quoted in Martin Tingle, *The Vale of the White Horse Survey* (n.p.: Tempus Repartum, Bar British Series 218, 1991), p. 120.

3. Chesterton, *The Ballad of the White Horse* (New York: John Lane, 1911), p. 3.

4. Jeffery W. Whitelaw, *Follies* (n.p.: Shire Publications, n.d.), pp. 3–4.

5. Tyrwhitt-Wilson's name is misspelled as Wyrwhitt-Wilson in *Bernard Shaw and Gabriel Pascal*, p. 65.

6. Bernard Shaw, *Collected Letters 1926–1950*, ed. Dan H. Laurence (New York: Viking, 1988), p. 223; Michael Holroyd, *Bernard Shaw, Volume III, 1918–1950, The Lure of Fantasy* (New York: Random House, 1991), p. 98; David Huckvale, "Music and the Man: Bernard Shaw and the Music Collection at Shaw's Corner," *SHAW* 10 (1990): 111. Huckvale remarks that Lord Berners's artistic achievements were so bewildering that in 1939 *The New Statesman* satirized him in this fashion:

> "Lord Berners
> Told a crowd of learners
> That if they wished to compose
> They should paint or write prose."

7. The recounting of the story of Lord Berners's Folly that follows draws principally on the accounts in Barbara Jones, *Follies and Grottoes* (London: Constable, 1953), pp. 147–48; Gwyn Headley and Wim Meulenkamp, *Follies, A National Trust Guide* (London: Jonathan Cape, 1986), pp. 262–63; and Whitelaw, p. 15.

8. Jones, *Follies and Grottoes,* p. 148.

9. Bernard Shaw, *Collected Plays with Their Prefaces,* ed. Dan H. Laurence (London: Max Reinhardt, 1971), 3:157–58. This part of the stage directions is identical in the 1907 Constable first edition.

10. Bernard Shaw, *Major Barbara: A Screen Version* (New York: Penguin, 1945), pp. 133–34. Undershaft's pride in the salubrity of his silver product stands in sharp contrast to Larry Dunne's ironic comment (on Fig. 28) about the lead fumes at Ballycorus.

11. For details, see my " 'In More Ways Than One': *Major Barbara*'s Debt to Gilbert Murray" (1968) in *Bernard Shaw's Plays,* ed. Warren Sylvester Smith (New York: W. W. Norton, 1970), pp. 375–97.

12. Whitelaw, p. 8; Jones, pp. 18–19. Another folly of possible passing interest to Shavians, because of its place name, is the sham Gothic temple at Shotover, a few miles southeast of Oxford near Wheatley. The temple, built around 1720, was the first false façade, having nothing behind it save a few trees (like a stage set?). Whitelaw, pp. 9, 11, 27; Headley and Meulenkamp, p. 265.

13. *Major Barbara: A Screen Version,* pp. 145, 147.

14. "In More Ways," p. 376.

15. An instance of Shaw importing a bit of Ireland into England is in Undershaft's biographical sketch of the offstage distiller, Sir Horace Bodger, in *Major Barbara,* whose career in large part resembles that of the Irish Guinnesses. See my " 'Letters of Fire against the Sky': Bodger's Soul and Shaw's Pub," *Shaw Review* 11:3 (September 1968): 87–88.

16. *Bernard Shaw and Gabriel Pascal,* p. 61.

17. Bernard Shaw, *Major Barbara: A Facsimile of the Holograph Manuscript,* ed. Bernard F. Dukore (New York: Garland, 1981), p. 185. British Library Add. MS. 50616D, fol. 53.

18. For this and additional testimony about Barbara's positioning and long silence, see my "More Shaw Advice to the Players of *Major Barbara,*" *Theatre Survey: The American Journal of Theatre History* 11:1 (May 1970): 75–77. The original typescript of *Major Barbara* adds, after "towards the town," the subsequently deleted phrase, "*her back turned to the foreground.*"

19. *Collected Plays with Their Prefaces,* 3: 184.

REVIEWS

The Burgunder Shaw Collection

"The Instinct of an Artist" / Shaw and the Theatre. An Exhibition from the Bernard F. Burgunder Collection of George Bernard Shaw. Edited by Ann L. Ferguson. Ithaca: Cornell University Library, 1997. iv + 56 pp. Unpriced.

"The Instinct of an Artist" is a valuable yet deeply flawed publication. Shaw scholars and theater people will be indebted to it for making available significant Shaw writings and theater-related pieces from programs to associated production documents. Since the exhibition it samples closed on 13 June 1997, the assemblage is now dispersed—but available physically, with many more of the riches of the Burgunder Collection, at Cornell itself. Even in capsule form the revelations are often striking and may tempt Shavians to Ithaca.

Perhaps the most eye-catching items are shrewdly reserved for the front and back covers, inside and outside. In May 1911 Shaw, as he did on other occasions, sent a series of related postcards to a member of the cast of one of his plays in rehearsal. Eight of the ten are reproduced, both back and front. The comedy was *Arms and the Man;* the actress was playing Raina. Each postcard, a revelation of Shaw's vanity at the acme of his fame—or perhaps of his intention to furnish Margaret Halstan with a complete set—had a different portrait of Shaw, and on the text side, advice about some aspect of her acting in the role. *"Dont* hurry," he warns on one card. "Raina never hurries." The unhurried Shaw in the picture wears a soft felt hat and raincoat—in a studio.

Postmarked 18 May 1911, the series is *not* in the *Collected Letters,* nor are letters quoted or reproduced to Tighe Hopkins, Stella Campbell, and others. Nor is the letter to Mrs. Campbell in the Alan Dent edition—but it does turn up in the Laurence *Bernard Shaw Theatrics.* However we learn none of that from the catalogue copy. A letter to Viola Tree assigned in the *Collected Letters* to 5 February 1920 (and we do not learn that) is dated *ca.* February 1920. Documents are treated with equal spareness. "The Principles That Govern the Dramatist," an autograph manuscript dated 1 May 1912, and written at the request of the (U.S.) Modern Historical Records Association, is reproduced in part from the original. Yet nowhere do we learn that it was prepared for an American organization, published in the *New York Times* under another title on 2 June, and reprinted under still another title in the *Daily Express* on 13 June. The Shaw *Bibliography* cites it as C1828, B73, and A275 (a posthumous appearance in *Shaw on Theatre*). Lacking such knowledge, the reader or viewer may jump to the conclusion that it is an unpublished "find."

Similarly, Shaw's letter of 18 November 1912 to Lady Gregory confessing that rather than paying attention to his professional business he was paying court to Mrs. Campbell, with whom he was "violently in love," would be less attention-getting if we realized that it has already appeared in *Shaw, Lady Gregory and the Abbey,* a correspondence published in 1993.

Perhaps the most interesting matters are the afterthoughts to Shaw's plays and his tinkering, almost all his long life, with his texts—to get them right *in performance.* The length of Shaw's play texts—he insisted on giving audiences their money's worth, but later playgoers were more impatient— often tempted directors to cut. Shaw sometimes gave in, but never to shorten a play merely to meet suburban train schedules, as he famously thundered by cable to Lawrence Langner about the first New York *Saint Joan* (". . . RUN LATER TRAINS"). Even earlier, it turns out, he had cautioned James B. Fagan about the London production of *Heartbreak House* in 1921 not to hurry the ending, "for if you make an actor speak faster than he can think, his part will be like nothing at all, and you will lose the play to save the last train." The entire letter is in print, but the reader of the catalogue will not find that information there.

Although other such instances can be cited, most readers can do their own homework and find some of the material without venturing to the shores of Lake Cayuga. The catalogue samples Shaw's rehearsal notes, prompt books, textual annotations and revisions, photographs, posters, Shaw's own poster and costume designs and ideas, receipts, and even the official license for the 1895 copyright performance of *Candida.* Despite its pamphlet-sized form, limited in this printing to a thousand copies, one gains an understanding of the biographical, literary, and theatrical research opportunities of the Burgunder Collection—which is still growing. I hope the next catalogue will be more scholar-friendly.

Stanley Weintraub

Two by Shaw

Bernard Shaw on Cinema. Edited by Bernard F. Dukore. Carbondale and Edwardsville: Southern Illinois University Press, 1997 [1998]. xxx + 189 pp. Index. $39.95 (cloth); $19.95 (paper).

Not Bloody Likely! And Other Quotations from Bernard Shaw. Edited by Bernard F. Dukore. New York: Columbia University Press, 1997. xviii + 214 pp. $19.95.

Along with Dan Laurence and Stanley Weintraub, Bernard Dukore publishes so prolifically that Shavians can scarcely blink before another book or edition or article by one or another appears. In many ways each is distinctive, with Laurence focusing on Shaw editions, Weintraub venturing abroad through biographies and historical events of the past 150 years, and Dukore exploring other playwrights, dramatic criticism, and dramatic theory. Yet in common all have great energy and immense value as Shavian editors and scholars.

These two volumes add to signs that this energy still has a head of steam. Since Shaw's late-life efforts to film his plays have long been among Dukore's most distinctive interests, *Bernard Shaw on Cinema* may catch our attention first. Following Donald Costello's pioneering critical survey, *The Serpent's Eye: Shaw and the Cinema* (1965), Dukore has dominated the field with *Saint Joan: A Screenplay by Bernard Shaw* (1968), *The Collected Screenplays of Bernard Shaw* (1980), and *Selected Correspondence of Bernard Shaw and Gabriel Pascal* (1996). These would be important just as editions of many previously unpublished materials relating to Shaw's creative life, but enhancing their importance are long, carefully wrought introductions. Most impressive is *The Collected Screenplays,* a standard edition whose 177-page introduction alone eclipses Costello's good book.

Complementing these editions, *Bernard Shaw on Cinema* provides 107 articles, letters, notes, fragments, interviews, and speeches by Shaw that illuminate his engagement with films. Nearly half collected for the first time, these include sources cited in the screenplay volumes, previously unpublished materials, and selections from correspondence, especially to Pascal. The result is an editorial coup—the first book to collect a good portion of Shaw's many words about cinema, an autobiographical, critical, and theoretical counterpart of *The Collected Screenplays.*

Given the heterogeneous, sporadic, often informal and piecemeal nature of these utterances, the medium's infancy, and its rapid evolution during his lifetime, Shaw's views on cinema lack the critical orchestration and

sophistication of his music and theater reviews in the 1890s. Hardly competing with anthologies of those, this collection fits more aptly into the
"Shaw on . . ." genre, a posthumous sage-of-the-age series including *Shaw
on Theatre, Shaw on Shakespeare, on Language, on Religion, on Dickens*. As a
solid addition to these, it has careful, thorough footnotes (although some
only touch on complex contexts), and a useful index.

Dukore's introduction to the volume is shorter than those that so fully
serve the screenplays and the Pascal correspondence, but it compensates
in part by being remarkably compact. Both descriptive and analytical, it
adroitly sketches backgrounds and highlights Shaw's views on cinema
through a telling fabric of quotations, mostly from the following collection,
relating them to the film industry then and now. Dukore takes a Shavian
tack on most professional and aesthetic issues, not lingering on possible
points of contention. Perhaps assuming certain truths to be self-evident, or
perhaps sensing that some issues, fully argued, might propel him into a
hundred more pages, he leaves most arguments up to Shaw or the
reader—a sound editorial option.

Films fascinated Shaw from the early days of the silents, and entries reveal his foresight in pointing up their potential as a huge entertainment
business (1908) and medium of widespread, inexpensive education (1914).
He speculates that films and the phonograph could be far more revolutionary than writing and printing since they can even communicate to the illiterate. Yet he also observes their dangerous underside: exploitative
capitalist trusts, a "serpent's eye" that mesmerizes, a worldwide dissemina-
tion of romantic sentimentality, stultifying morality, mediocrity, and vulgar-
ity. Anticipating the great societal influence of films and television in the
twentieth century, he declares that "the cinema is going to form the mind
of England. The national conscience, the national ideals and terms of conduct, will be those of the films" (1914).

Stirred up by cinema's immense monetary potential, Shaw's business instincts surface often and variously here. In the very first entry, a letter to
Arthur Wing Pinero in 1908, he writes about "this delirious field," "a pro-
moter," and "a bloated trust," convinced that the Society of Authors must
take these in hand to protect the interests of authors. In the book's last
entry (1950), he corresponds with an Italian lawyer about producing *Androcles and the Lion*, explaining, "I never sell my rights: I retain them all
intact, and proceed by licensing their exploitation," whereupon he suggests an ingenious maneuver to dodge a legal obstruction. Elsewhere, he
urges young actors to join an organization that protects their interests, and
comments that film producers are fools if they do not join employers' fed-
erations.

Shaw's early interest in cinema became professional when American producers pursued him with lucrative offers for film rights to his plays. Color-

ful and explicit about this is an unpublished letter, probably unknown to
Dukore, that Shaw sent to Arthur Brentano, his American publisher, in
October 1920:

> My dear Brentano,
>
>   I am greatly concerned to find that the film people are worrying
> you about me. They are worrying everyone they can lay their hands
> on. The principle of American business is that if you want to get
> anything from A you must go to B, C, D and so on to Z for it, but
> never, under any circumstances go to A himself. I believe that if they
> wanted to read my plays (the last thing they would ever think of
> doing) they would pay a literary agent a large commission to induce
> Arthur Brentano to sell them one, instead of sending down the of-
> fice boy to buy it across the counter.
>
>   The result is that I am inundated with golden offers from all sorts
> of people . . . promising me proposals which I already have in my
> desk at first hand. This game gets madder and madder as my refus-
> als make the film people more eager and desperate. But it is all pure
> waste of time. You tell me I can get £200,000 spread over ten years.
> But I have long since had a direct offer of £200,000 down on the
> nail; and I have neither refused nor accepted it: I have simply noted
> it, and said what I say to all of them, that I will go into this business
> in my own way and at my own time.

Six years later, Shaw reports a visit from Samuel Goldwyn. Asking for a
scenario, Goldwyn declared he did not really care about money, but
wanted to raise the level of art in the world. Shaw replied famously that he
feared they could not do business together because "youre an artist, and
care only about art, while I'm only a tradesman and care only about
money." In this one-upping vein he advises William Archer, who had recently written a popular melodrama: "Do not let your film rights go too
cheap; and do not, as the silly American authors do, give the managers
half." Urging playwrights to collect royalties on a percentage of gross receipts, not net receipts he coolly dodges the sort of "creative accounting"
that often makes great profits vanish in Hollywood: "There may be no
profit but there are always receipts and sometimes it may take ten lawsuits
to determine what the profits are but you can always determine the receipts."
Such canniness goes hand in hand with Shaw's visionary views, dramatizing his coming to grips with the new medium in many ways. His tabling of
lucrative film offers mixed pragmatism and artistic integrity: filming could
compromise his plays' stage life; income taxes would be huge; producers
were after his name more than his art; films were not attracting the best

actors; and, most telling of all, what could silents do with his drama or any great drama? Without speech, what could distinguish his plays or Shakespeare's from melodrama? His jest with Goldwyn called Goldwyn's bluff with another: he would not sell out artistically, even for a fortune.

But then came the talkies. And their advent in 1927 presaged a Shavian rebirth. In fact, at seventy-one the prospective newborn had already given a 1926 holiday interview in Italy that synchronized filming with a phonograph, and the next summer Sybil Thorndike performed *Saint Joan*'s cathedral scene on phonofilm, two months before *The Jazz Singer* premiered in America. Shaw had one-upped Hollywood again.

As with life, however, birth brought problems as well as promise. First came a flash of Shavian enthusiasm anticipating modern politics. Upon witnessing Mussolini speaking impressively in *Movietone Voice of Italy*, Shaw urged Ramsay MacDonald to "go and hear it. . . . It is of e n o r m o u s political importance. . . . The political party that wakes up to the possibilities of this method of lecturing will, if it has money enough, sweep the floor with its opponents. Order the whole Labor Cabinet to go."

Cinema magnified, intensified, and multiplied Mussolini and his audience much as it magnified and intensified legitimate actors. Beyond this, entries reveal Shaw aspiring to the permanence that films could give to the finest performances of his plays, performances that could move free of boxed-in stages, with the finest actors, with re-takes until each scene was just right, with his own oversight, his dramatic values, his character contrasts, his eloquence, verbal music, rhythms, moods, timing, nuances of meaning, all finely realized. And within the time he had left. By 1930 he declared, "The poor old theatre is done for! All of my plays will be made into 'talkie' films before long. What other course is open for me? The theatre may survive as a place where people are taught to act, but apart from that there will be nothing but 'talkies' soon."

Ironically, other entries show that this exuberance came just as his film pursuits were about to be bombarded by years of problems, most of which reflected an old bone of contention in legitimate theater: how much control should a playwright have over productions of his work? Well known in his prime for assuming great control, Shaw still hung on to a fair amount through his self-drafted contracts. But films involved more money, larger organizations, and a more complex medium; in short, many more persons and interests between a script and its production. For all his acumen, Shaw underestimated these. Entries show him undaunted, indeed stimulated by the challenge, reviving his old assertiveness while relishing how film's freedoms, realism, and perspectives could complement dialogue and story lines—obviously his forte and, he thought, the *sine qua non* distinguishing "talkies" from the silent action of mere move-ies.

Shaw perceived that "a new kind of artist exclusively devoted to this type of entertainment has to be discovered." Specifically, stage actions are too exaggerated for cinema: "One only has to move slightly. Even one's thoughts are turned by the camera into movements." Then, too, the microphone accentuates accents and vocal pitch and "makes audible a number of tones and peculiarities in the voice which we do not hear if we are listening to the person speaking." Clearly learning, he evolved from declaring in 1929 that "I see no reason why *The Apple Cart,* for instance, should not be [filmed] exactly as it stands," to extensive revisions in adapting *Saint Joan* and *Pygmalion* for filming five years later, to commenting in 1946 that his texts "must always be adapted intelligently to the studio, the screen, the stage, or whatever the physical conditions of performance may be."

Such flexibility, however, was only one side of his coin. For Shaw, "adapted *intelligently*" left out many people, especially in Hollywood: "Scenically, histrionically, photographically, and wastefully, Hollywood is the wonder of the world, but it has no dramatic technique and no literary taste. . . . When it gets a good bit of stuff it takes infinite pains to drag it down to its own level, firmly believing, of course, that it is improving it all the time." While it lavishes money on films, he often observes, Hollywood will hire an "office boy" to adapt (ruin) scripts. Its film language resembles the curt subtitles of silent films. It would have Michelangelo painting Felix the Cat, art by Augustus John repainted by a local sign-painter, the Virgin Mary played by Mae West. And most vacuous of all, it emphasizes the pictorial above dialogue and storytelling, the very stuff of dramatic art.

Sparking many entries that make these points is Shaw's dismay at Hollywood's attempt to adapt *The Devil's Disciple,* an ineptitude causing him to abort the project in 1935. He felt similar disgust upon seeing German and Dutch film versions of *Pygmalion* in 1936 and 1937, but Catholic objections to his screenplay for *Saint Joan* in 1935 were a greater blow because they scotched its American financing. Shaw's responses to this and other censorship resemble his eloquence about play censorship in 1909: pedantic bureaucrats, powerful beyond their taste or intelligence, mindlessly exercise rules that suppress worthy art and let devious trash slip by.

Although the 1938 triumph of the Pascal-Asquith *Pygmalion* and Shaw's Academy Award–winning screenplay for it argue for his theories of cinema, the subsequent shortcomings of Pascal's films of *Major Barbara* and *Caesar and Cleopatra* seem to argue against them. Touches of Shaw's parallel decline occur in these selections: he remains vigorous, but becomes increasingly repetitive and inconsistent. For example, contradicting his distinctions between stage and screen acting, he comments that George Arliss proved good acting was good acting "on the screen exactly as on the stage." Similarly, "the talkie does not ape the theatre any more than a Rolls Royce apes a Victorian four-wheeled cab"; then, "the art is exactly the same." In an interview he says it is important for an actor to understand what he is saying, but soon declares rhythm and melody are more important than understanding. He advises director Cecil Lewis, "Get drama and picture making separate in your mind, or you may make ruinous mistakes," and later seeks a dramatic effect in a setting as "a really beautiful picture."

Of course, Shaw uses total-stage pictures and pictures in his plays' settings again and again. The opening description that descends into the Morell parsonage in *Candida* is cinematic, as are settings in *Caesar and Cleopatra*. In *Arms and the Man* a picture becomes a character; in *Saint Joan* a pennon does, with a dramatic action that speaks louder than words. In many contexts, pictures may be worth a thousand words much for Shaw as for Stanley Kubrick. But then, a word like "irony" may be worth a thousand pictures.

What one may conjecture fragmentarily from this volume, melding it a bit with *The Collected Screenplays*, is that Shaw was largely right in his general principle that a good playwright should have primary control over the interpretation of his plays or films, partly because it is easier for a weak director to sink a good play than for a strong director to float a poor one. Cecil Lewis, Shaw's first film director, was inexperienced while Pascal, his second, was erratic, slipping in non-Shavian effects, offending actors, bumbling camera work, and squandering money much like Hollywood. Having befriended them, however, Shaw was faithful to each in turn. He should have been less so. Having begun in cinema when, as he often observed, his capacities were diminishing, he was remarkably resilient, but his creative grip, like his handwriting, had become less steady and, struck by frustrations, his heady dreams of filming many of his plays faded into resignation.

Bernard Shaw and Cinema serves such conjectures.

On the other hand, *Not Bloody Likely! And Other Quotations from Bernard Shaw* serves us more broadly and narrowly: broadly in terms of subject matter and wit; narrowly in its epigrammatic focus on specific topics. This is also a type of "Shaw on . . ." book: a *Shaw on a Whole Lot of Things*, for which *Not Bloody Likely!*, although catchy, may not be the best title. A good predecessor is Caroline Harnsberger's *Bernard Shaw: Selections of His Wit and Wisdom* (1965), whose selections are more epigrammatic than her title suggests.

As part of a press series including Wilde, Lincoln, Twain, Emerson, and Thoreau, various standards of length, format, and editorial details may have constricted Dukore, limiting his freedoms and compromising the volume. For example, it is too long and too short: too long for the average non-academic who wants to hop from witty quote to quote, too short for scholars, journalists, and sophisticates, given the immense quantity of Shavian wit on all sorts of subjects it could contain. It is about half the length of Harnsberger's book. Were its topical entries less widely spaced it could include more material; topics in Harnsberger's index are extensively cross-referenced, these are not; sources for her entries can be vague, but some include page numbers, which all of these lack; a random comparison of numbers of entries (Harnsberger/Dukore) runs: Criticism 28/16, Marriage 32/17, Money 22/7, Religion 29/12, Sex 16/9, Socialism 15/12.

Quotations of one to three lines tend to be most effective, since they catch attention more pointedly and memorably than longer selections. This is particularly clear in Dukore's introduction, where the quotations he selects, most of them scintillatingly short, seem to be among the cream of the crop. The volume itself has very good selections but poses a fair number of puzzlements, such as these: entries on *Hedda Gabler* and *A Doll's House* but none on other plays; one entry on dipsomania and two on Zola but none on Dickens and just one on the devil. Might not the quotation— "that most horrible form of dipsomania, the craving for afternoon tea"—be more useful under "tea"? How specifically Shavian are many quotations of Shaw's varied dramatic characters, without their contexts?

Still, Shavians can delight in this volume as the spicy selections of an eminent colleague, and a worthy resource in addition to Harnsberger. Some may also enjoy conjuring up entries they might add, such as "I dont believe in morality. I'm a disciple of Bernard Shaw," and "Morality can go to its father the devil," and "It is immorality, not morality that needs protection: it is morality, not immorality, that needs restraint." So much for the Moral Majority.

Charles A. Berst

Writings for "The Dreaded Weintraub"

Shaw and Other Matters: A Festschrift for Stanley Weintraub on the Occasion of His Forty-Second Anniversary at the Pennsylvania State University. Edited by Susan Rusinko. Selinsgrove, Pa.: Susquehanna University Press, 1998. 222 pp. Index. $37.50.

As the volume title announces, this collection celebrates Stanley Weintraub's long and distinguished career as scholar and teacher. The editor, Susan Rusinko, wrote her dissertation under the direction of Stanley Weintraub, and all the contributions to the volume are from his students, advisees, or collaborators.

Although the essays are wide-ranging and without a central theme or

approach, they are offered as extensions of the interests of Stanley Weintraub. An introductory biographical essay by Fred D. Crawford identifies
these interests; it also recounts his own relationship with the "Dreaded
Weintraub" he first came to know as a student in Weintraub's Victorian
literature seminar. The collection includes separate essays in sections "On
Shaw," "On Shaw's Contemporaries," "On Speculative Fiction," "On
Modern Drama," and "On Military History," followed by a Select Bibliography of Weintraub's many books and articles.

The Shaw matter comprises five essays. It is fitting that the first essay
in the collection be by Rodelle Weintraub. In " 'Oh, the dreaming, the
dreaming': *Arms and the Man*," she applies Freudian dream theory to *Arms
and the Man*. She calls it Shaw's earliest dream play, that is, "a wish fulfillment play" in which "the underlying fantasy reflects upon and illuminates
the manifest surface of the play in much the same way as the latent dream
represents the thoughts and feelings of the manifest dream." In the second
essay, Michel W. Pharand looks at another of the Plays Pleasant as he considers Shaw's historical and artistic sources for *The Man of Destiny*. In "Bernard Shaw's Bonaparte: Life Force or Death Wish?" Pharand examines
Shaw's lifelong fascination with the soldier he called that "vile, vulgar Cor-
sican adventurer," concluding that Napoleon "formed an integral part of
Shaw's worldview."

Kinley Roby's "Arnold Bennett: Shaw's Ten O'Clock Scholar," a reprint
of an article that appeared in the *Shaw Review* in 1970, details the ex-
changes between Shaw and the novelist as they clashed on politics and
on playwriting. Shaw's playwriting lesson to Bennett in 1925 was to study
Beethoven: "A play should go on like a symphony; its themes should be
introduced . . . again and again until they are red hot, the pace and inten-
sity increasing to the end with every possible device of unexpected modula-
tions and changes, and sudden pianisimos. . . ."

In *Sixteen Self Sketches,* Shaw stoutly declares, "Creative Evolution can re-
place us; but meanwhile we must work for our survival and development as
if we were Creation's last word. Defeatism is the wretchedest of policies."
It is this "obstinately optimistic" interest in Creative Evolution that occupies Julie Sparks. In "The Evolution of Human Virtue: Precedents for
Shaw's 'World Betterer' in the Utopias of Bellamy, Morris, and Bulwer-
Lytton," she looks at literary precedents for *Back to Methuselah,* considers
Creative Evolution in *Man and Superman,* and traces Shaw's treatment of
the subject to the end of his life. From metabiological myth, the collection
moves to Greek myth. The final Shaw piece, Kay Li's "*Heartbreak House* and
the Trojan War," expands on the oft-remarked link between the play and
the myth, fleshing out both positive and negative dimensions of Shaw's
modern version of Troy.

The Shaw material totals just sixty pages, so the "other matters" of the

title actually form the bulk of the volume. They include pieces by two Shavi-
ans writing on speculative fiction: Milton T. Wolf offers "The Golem-Robot
Intersection" and John R. Pfeiffer offers "Octavia Butler Writes the Bible."
There are various essays on Shaw's contemporaries: George Gissing's nov-
els, the first Western woman to reach Mecca, and some (possibly) pre-
viously unpublished verse by Hilaire Belloc. There are also essays on
Marsha Norman, on Frederick Knott, and on military history. The editor,
Susan Rusinko, is represented by a piece on Joe Orton.

In a collection of this kind, it is perhaps to be expected that the quality
of the essays is not entirely consistent. Nevertheless, the intent of the contributors is completely praiseworthy: to honor their teacher, mentor, colleague, and friend. Indeed, everyone in Shaw studies is indebted to the
untiring efforts of Stanley Weintraub.

Sally Peters

John R. Pfeiffer*

A CONTINUING CHECKLIST
OF SHAVIANA

I. Works by Shaw

Shaw, Bernard. *Bernard Shaw on Cinema*. Ed. Bernard F. Dukore. Carbondale: Southern Illinois University Press, 1997 [1998]. Presents more than 100 pieces by G.B.S. Dukore's fifteen-page "Introduction" presents a cogent agenda of the principal information and generalizations about Shaw and movies necessary for more study of this very important subject. Reviewed in this volume.

———. "George Bernard Shaw," a check, undated [circa 1885], endorsed "G. B. Shaw" on the back, "The London & South, Western Bank, Limited," signed by Annie Besant. She paid "G. B. Shaw Esq . . . Two pounds 15 S[hillings] for the Free Though[t] Publishing Co." *Scott J. Winslow Associates*, Mail and Phone Auction catalogue (8 July 1998), item 544, $400–up.

———. "George Bernard Shaw," a letter in Shaw's hand of 15 September 1918 to Hugo Vallentin on "Great Southern Hotel" letterhead. The text: "Behold me settled here until the end of the month. No news whatever. Receipt annexed. Methuselah play unfinished and in incoherent fragments at Ayot St. Lawrence. Love to your ladies. . . ." *Scott J. Winslow Associates*, Mail and Phone Auction catalogue (8 July 1998), item 543, $900–1,200.

———. "George Bernard Shaw on *Socialism*." *The Treasury of the Encyclopaedia Britannica*. Ed. Clifton Fadiman. New York: Viking, 1992: pp. 612–21.

*Thanks to Richard E. Winslow III for discovering and supplying page copies for a number of entries in this list. Professor Pfeiffer, *SHAW* Bibliographer, welcomes information about new or forthcoming Shaviana: books, articles, pamphlets, monographs, dissertations, films, videos, reprints, and the like, citations of which may be sent to him at the Department of English, Central Michigan University, Mt. Pleasant, MI 48859.

Reprint of Shaw's 1926 essay for the thirteenth edition of the *Encyclopaedia*. The headnote reads in part, "We reproduce the whole of this piece by G.B.S. (1856–1950) for two reasons: First, it is a superb piece of writing. Second, in view of socialism's contemporary disarray, it is alive with an accidental irony Shaw could not possibly have foreseen." Thanks to Michel W. Pharand.

———. *John Bull's Other Island* [an extract from the play]. *The Oxford Book of Ireland*. Ed. Patricia Craig. Oxford: Oxford University Press, 1998. Not seen. Information from a review in *TLS* (24 July 1998), p. 8.

———. Letter to Letitia Fairfield of 31 July 1930. *Lion Heart Autographs, Catalogue Thirty-Six* (1997), item 104. Apparently an answer to a request that Shaw participate as a patron to a Fairfield undertaking.

———. Letter written 18 July 1949 as part of Sotheby auction sale. See "**Shaw (G. B.)** Shaw's Clavichord" in "Other Media," below.

———. "Lettre au Times." *Notre Amie la Femme* [Our Friend Woman]. Trans. Elisabeth Gille. Lausanne: Editions L'Age d'Homme, 1992: 95–98. This Shaw letter to *The Times* (3 July 1905), "Sumptuary Regulations at the Opera," is included in a compendium of quotations on (more specifically "against"!) women. Thanks to Michel W. Pharand.

———. *Not Bloody Likely! And Other Quotations from Bernard Shaw*. Ed. Bernard F. Dukore. New York: Columbia University Press, 1997. Shaw on hundreds of subjects from "Abortion" to "Zola, Emile." Quotations are drawn from every form of discourse in which Shaw wrote and are provided with precise descriptions of their sources. Reviewed in this volume.

———. "On *A Doll House*." *Literature and Its Writers: An Introduction to Fiction, Poetry, and Drama*. Ed. Ann Charters and Samuel Charters. Boston: Bedford Books, 1997; pp. 2022–24. An excerpt from *The Quintessence of Ibsenism* (1891), from the Brentano edition (1913).

———. *Selected Plays: Mrs. Warren's Profession, Caesar and Cleopatra, Man and Superman, Major Barbara, Pygmalion, Heartbreak House*. New York and Avenel: Gramercy Books/Random House, 1996. The editions from which these texts are drawn are not given. No Prefaces or excerpts from Prefaces are provided.

———. "**Shaw (G. B.)** *Saint Joan*." Author's inscribed presentation copy, "to W. Duncan Little G. Bernard Shaw 30th Oct. 1924." *Sotheby's* LN8412 (15 July 1998), item 356, £350–350 [*sic*].

———. "**Shaw (G. B.)** Two autograph letters and two cards signed ('G.B.S.'), to Gabriel Pascal." Written from Ayot St. Lawrence, 28 February to 31 December 1940, during Pascal's work on the film of *Major Barbara*. *Sotheby's* LN7755 (11 December 1997), item 370. £1,200–1,500.

———. "**Shaw (George Bernard)** Amusing autograph postcard signed." "In shorthand to a prospective secretary, explaining that 'you must be a very unwise young lady if you would exchange a permanent employer like the Manchester Public Libraries Department, for an old gentleman in his 80th year and no expectation of life.' " Ayot St. Lawrence, 6 February 1944 [the age and date are as given in the catalogue; Shaw was actually in his eighty-eighth year]. *Sotheby's* LN8412 (15 July 1998), item 357, £250–350.

———. "**Shaw (George Bernard)** Typed letter signed," 10 Adelphi Terrace, 28 November 1908. To Mrs. Bandmann Palmer, about the granting of rights of performance to his plays in India ("I had rather not make any arrangements . . . just at present"). *Sotheby"s* LN8412 (15 July 1998), item 358, £400–600.

———. *Shaw on Theatre: A Half Century of Advices* [*sic*]. Ed. Mary Chenoweth Stratton. Introduction by Stanley Weintraub. Lewisburg, Pa.: Ellen Clarke Bertrand Library, Bucknell University and The Press of Appletree Alley, 1998. A collection of fourteen pieces of correspondence by G.B.S. to T. T. Watson, R. G. Bright, C. M. S. McLellan, A. Bishop, *The World*, D. Dix, A. S. Bourchier, S. Luther, and J. N. Doley. The material comes from the LaFayette Butler George Bernard Shaw Collection at Bucknell. Only the letters to McLellan, Bishop, and Doley are previously unpublished.

———. "Shaw's Advice to Irishmen." *SHAW: The Annual of Bernard Shaw Studies*. Volume Eighteen. University Park: Penn State University Press, 1998; pp. 63–66.

———. "Shaw's *Saint Joan*, Inscribed and Signed First Edition." 1924, inscription: "To Doris Littell / from Bernard Shaw / 25th June 1926." *Bauman Rare Books, A Late Summer Selection of Rare Books and Autographs* [1998]. "August," item 289, $950.

———. "Social Criticism in *Hard Times*." *Readings on Charles Dickens*. Ed. Clarice Swisher. San Diego: Greenhaven Press, 1998. Not seen. This probably reprints the 1913 "Introduction to *Hard Times*" in the Waverley Book Co. thirty-volume complete works of Dickens.

II. Books and Pamphlets

Anderlini-D'Onofrio, Serena. *The "Weak" Subject: On Modernity, Eros, and Women's Playwriting*. Madison, N.J.: Fairleigh Dickinson University Press, 1998. Takes up the Eliza character in *Pygmalion* as a reusable touchstone for her account of how far male playwrights such as Shaw (and Ibsen) brought an authentic representation of women to the stage. "But these plays were realistic only in a sociohistorical sense: . . . the family exploited women just as the factory exploited workers. . . . A more accurate picture of women's situatedness was provided by American female writers."

Appleyard, Bryan. *Brave New Worlds: Staying Human in the Genetic Future*. New York: Viking, 1998. This conservative approach to genetic manipulation wants to realign technological advances with human values, noting un-

easily that Wells, Russell, Churchill, and Shaw were convinced that eugenics was desirable. Shaw: "Being cowards, we defeat natural selection
under cover of philanthropy; being sluggards, we neglect artificial selection under cover of delicacy and morality." Appleyard extracts from such
declarations that eugenics in the early years of this century allowed the
elites to sound both tough-minded and socially concerned. It also required open and frank discussion of sexual behavior, and this gave men
like Shaw the opportunity to shock the older generation.

Basalla, Susan. *Register of the George Bernard Shaw Collection.* Lewisburg, Pa:
Ellen Clarke Bertrand Library, Bucknell University, 1998. No. 14 in the
Special Collections series. Not seen. The collection was a gift of Dr. La-
Fayette Butler and includes more than 400 items, dating from 1882 to
1950.

Bauschatz, Paul. "The Uneasy Evolution of *My Fair Lady* from *Pygmalion.*"
SHAW: The Annual of Bernard Shaw Studies. Volume Eighteen. University
Park: Penn State University Press, 1998; 181–98.

Beerbohm, Max. *Max Beerbohm Caricatures.* Presented by N. John Hall. New
Haven: Yale University Press, 1997. Not seen. Beerbohm's caricature of
Shaw is included.

Berg, Fredric. "Structure and Philosophy in *Man and Superman* and *Major
Barbara.*" *The Cambridge Companion to George Bernard Shaw.* Ed. Christopher Innes. Cambridge: Cambridge University Press, 1998; pp. 144–61.
"While he utilized many of the structures of the nineteenth-century theatre, the basic structure most often found in Shavian drama is the trian-
gle, with its strong character conflicts allowing him to present his
theories in a form that could both amuse and educate on stage."

Berlin, Isaiah. *The Proper Study of Mankind: An Anthology of Essays.* Ed. Henry
Hardy and Roger Hausheer. New York: Farrar, Straus & Giroux, 1997/
1998. Berlin includes Shaw in his list of "benevolent humanitarian
prophets" with Jules Verne, H. G. Wells, and Anatole France.

Berst, Charles A. "New Theatres for Old." *The Cambridge Companion to
George Bernard Shaw.* Ed. Christopher Innes. Cambridge: Cambridge University Press, 1998; pp. 55–75. "Shaw the critic-artist sets out as a Pro-
methean culture hero to replace stale, mediocre theatre with drama at
the cutting edge of consciousness, because drama and life cross-circu-
late: 'Public and private life become daily more theatrical: the modern
[leader] is nothing if not an effective actor; all newspapers are now edited histrionically; and the records of our law courts shew that the stage
is affecting personal conduct to an unprecedented extent. . . . The truth
is that dramatic invention is the first effort of man to become intellectually conscious.' "

Bertolini, John A. "Film-Plays by the Devil and His Director" (review of
Bernard Shaw and Gabriel Pascal, edited by Bernard F. Dukore). *SHAW:*

The Annual of Bernard Shaw Studies. Volume Eighteen. University Park: Penn State University Press, 1998; pp. 199–204.

Blockbuster Entertainment Guide to Movies and Videos 1998. New York: Dell Publishing Co., 1997. Lists with summaries, directors, major actors/actresses, and ratings on a five-star scale, the following twelve Shaw works on video and/or film: *Androcles* (1952; film/video; 4 stars); *Caesar and Cleopatra* (1945; film/video; 4 stars); *Devil's Disciple* (1959; film/video; 4 stars); *Doctor's Dilemma* (1958; film; 4 stars); *Great Catherine* (1968; film; 2 stars); *Heartbreak House* (1986; video; 3 stars); *Major Barbara* (1941; film/video; 5 stars); *Man of Destiny* (1973; video; 3 stars); *Millionairess* (1960; film; 3 stars); *My Fair Lady* (1964; film/video; 5 stars); *Pygmalion* (1938; film/video; 5 stars); and *Saint Joan* (1957; film/video; 3 1/2 stars).

Bryden, Ronald. "The Roads to *Heartbreak House.*" *The Cambridge Companion to George Bernard Shaw.* Ed. Christopher Innes. Cambridge: Cambridge University Press, 1998; pp. 180–94. An examination of the initial influences and sources Shaw employed in the writing of *Heartbreak House.*

———. See *Major Barbara,* below.

Carpenter, Charles A. "Shaw, George Bernard." *Modern Drama Scholarship and Criticism 1981–1990: An International Bibliography.* Toronto: University of Toronto Press, 1997. Before his long tenure as compiler of the annual international drama bibliography for the journal *Modern Drama,* Carpenter was the Bibliographer for *Shaw Review.* His listings in *Modern Drama* have always contained items on G.B.S. that appeared in no other annual bibliography. Here are listings of more than 320 pieces on Shaw.

———. "Shaw's Dramatic Reactions to the Birth of the Atomic Age." *SHAW: The Annual of Bernard Shaw Studies.* Volume Eighteen. University Park: Penn State University Press, 1998; pp. 173–79.

Collins, L. J. *Theatre at War, 1914–18.* London: Macmillan, 1998. Not seen. The *TLS* review (15 May 1998, p. 11) notes its reference to Shaw's *Common Sense about the War* and his playlets *Augustus Does His Bit* and *O'Flaherty, V.C.*

Crawford, Fred D. "The Dreaded Weintraub." *Shaw and Other Matters: A Festschrift for Stanley Weintraub.* Ed. Susan Rusinko. Selinsgrove, Pa.: Susquehanna University Press, 1998; pp. 15–28. A sketch of the academic life and work of Stanley Weintraub, a great deal of which has been devoted to teaching, research, and criticism on Bernard Shaw.

Davis, Tracy C. "Shaw's Interstices of Empire: Colonizing at Home and Abroad." *The Cambridge Companion to George Bernard Shaw.* Ed. Christopher Innes. Cambridge: Cambridge University Press, 1998; pp. 218–39. For a new colonialism Shaw might be suggesting, "New hybridities, certainly. A generous helping of social reductionism. A culture that redistributes the idea of gender assignments, respecting biology but regarding the origins and keepers of wealth as broadmindedly as the definition of wealth itself. A society that knows the relatedness of behavior at home to behavior abroad, and the attitudes of the private citizen to the conduct of governments. An enlightened politics that is performed, not just espoused, and which reaches into the most fundamental aspects of private life." Davis finds these propositions in *Simpleton, Too True, Captain Brassbound, Heartbreak, Misalliance, Pygmalion, Candida,* and *Getting Married,* as well as in *Caesar, John Bull,* and *Saint Joan.*

Douglas-Home, Jessica. *Violet: The Life and Loves of Violet Gordon Woodhouse.* London: Harvill Press, 1996. Provides an account of Shaw's visit to Violet in November 1943, during which she played the piano for him. Letters by both Violet (to her sister Dorothy) and Shaw (to her husband, Gordon, after Violet's death) describing the occasion are reprinted here.

Drew, Anne Marie. "Embracing Ambiguity: Shaw's Women." *Staging the Rage: The Web of Misogyny in Modern Drama.* Ed. Katherine H. Burkman and Judith Roof. Madison, N.J.: Fairleigh Dickinson University Press, 1998; pp. 158–70. "Shaw grew increasingly adept at resisting his tendency to provide answers to the 'woman question.' " In *Arms and the Man* he says women must be free but provides no space for freedom. The same is true for *Mrs Warren.* He begins to allow women more space in *Devil's Disciple, Heartbreak House,* and *Saint Joan.* Remarkably, in the character of the Patient in *Too True to Be Good,* "the mature playwright gives . . . [her] room to roam" and be free with a fullness of prerogative that Shaw himself has relinquished to her.

Dukore, Bernard F. "Evidence and Inference: *The Philanderer.*" *SHAW: The Annual of Bernard Shaw Studies.* Volume Eighteen. University Park: Penn State University Press, 1998; pp. 131–36.

———. See *Bernard Shaw on Cinema* and *Not Bloody Likely!* in "Works by Shaw," above.

Easterbrook, Gregg. *Beside Still Waters: Searching for Meaning in an Age of Doubt.* New York: William Morrow, 1998. Easterbrook admires and likes G.B.S. and enlists his pronouncements three times: "Suppose the world were only one of God's jokes. Would you work any the less to make it a good joke instead of a bad one?" "The nearer the church, the farther from God." "The problem with Christianity is that it's never been tried."

Eltis, Sos. "Bernard Shaw (1856–1950)." *Dictionary of Literary Biography, Volume 190: British Reform Writers, 1832–1914.* Ed. Gary Kelly and Edd Applegate. Detroit: Gale Research, 1998; pp. 273–88. "Bernard Shaw was one of the most important, and certainly the most prolific, reform writers of the twentieth century. In provocative, trenchant, and humorous style he tried to formulate a constructive alternative to the sham ideals of the Victorian age. His ideal vision was of a classless society based on equality of income and opportunity regardless of sex, creed, race, or birth, and he attempted to combine this vision with a realistic assessment of the facts of social and political life."

Evans, T. F. "The Later Shaw." *The Cambridge Companion to George Bernard Shaw.* Ed. Christopher Innes. Cambridge: Cambridge University Press, 1998; pp. 240–58. "The plays of the 1930s were marked by a greater and certainly more obvious concern with politics than any series of plays at earlier periods in Shaw's career as a playwright."

Everding, Robert G. "Planting Mulberry: A History of Shaw Festivals." *SHAW: The Annual of Bernard Shaw Studies.* Volume Eighteen. University Park: Penn State University Press, 1998; pp. 67–91.

———. "Shaw and the Popular Context." *The Cambridge Companion to George Bernard Shaw.* Ed. Christopher Innes. Cambridge: Cambridge University Press, 1998; pp. 309–33. "This chapter examines Shaw's post-1950 reception with a focus on the multiple ways in which performers and producers used Shaw's characters as actor vehicles. The essay explores not only stage productions but also the film and broadcast media as it charts the evolution of Shaw's growing popularity with the general public." A valuable representation of the career of Shaw's works and reputation after his death, including a discussion of the editorial liberties taken with scripts.

Galens, David, ed. *Drama For Students: Presenting Analysis, Context and Criticism on Commonly Studied Drama.* Detroit: Gale Research, 1998. Not seen. Includes an entry on *Major Barbara.*

Gänzel, Kurt. "Shaw, George Bernard." *The Encyclopedia of the Musical Theatre.* New York: Schirmer Books, 1994; p. 1306. This is a belated listing of a useful information-filled entry on Shaw's "musicalized" works: *Arms, Caesar, Pygmalion, Bashville, Androcles, You Never Can Tell, Great Catherine,* and *Mrs Warren.*

Goldsworthy, Vesna. *Inventing Ruritania: The Imperialism of the Imagination.* New Haven: Yale University Press, 1998. Not seen. Includes a treatment of "Bernard Shaw's Bulgaria."

Gordon, David J. "Shavian Comedy and the Shadow of Wilde." *The Cambridge Companion to George Bernard Shaw.* Ed. Christopher Innes. Cambridge: Cambridge University Press, 1998; pp. 124–43. "The difference between the artistic goals of these two masters of dramatic comedy should not, I think, be expressed in terms of aesthetic evaluation but in psychological and historical terms. Shavian comedy seeks to resolve the will and firm up ego boundaries, Wildean comedy to dissolve the will and loosen ego boundaries—and both goals, although entailing different comic effects, can give audiences pleasure."

Gregory, Augusta, Lady. *Lady Gregory's Diaries, 1892–1902.* Ed. James Pethica. New York: Oxford University Press, 1996. The entry for 25 March 1898 includes her report of hearing G.B.S. at the Irish Literary Society:

"The afternoon was redeemed by Bernard Shaw, who spoke very wittily— extinguished poor Whyte who he said, truly enough, had enumerated the best actors & actresses—& then said they were not Irish—but yet had proceeded to hold forth about them—As to what an Irishman is, he said, is a complex question—for wherever he may have been born, if he has been brought up in Ireland, that is quite sufficient to make him an Irishman—It is a mistake to think an Irishman has not common sense—it is the Englishman who is devoid of common sense—or at least has so small a portion of it that he can only apply it to the work immediately before him to do—that is why he is obliged to fill the rest of his horizon with the humbug & hypocrisy that fill so large a part of English life—The Irishman has a better grasp of facts & sees them more clearly—only, he fails in putting them into practise & has a great objection to doing anything that will lead to any practical result—It is also a mistake to think the Irishman has feeling he has not—but the Englishman is full of feeling—What the Irishman has is imagination, he can imagine himself in the situation of others—But the Irish language is an effete language—& the Irish nature is effete, & as to saying there are good Irish actors, there are not—& there won't be until the conditions in Ireland are favourable for the production of drama—'& when that day comes I hope I may be dead'—." Pethica believes that this was the first meeting between Lady Gregory and G.B.S.

Hall, N. John. See Beerbohm, Max, above.

Harper, Sue. " 'Thinking Forward and Up': The British Films of Conrad Veidt." *The Unknown 1930s: An Alternative History of the British Cinema 1929–39*. Ed. Jeffrey Richards. London and New York: I. B. Tauris, 1998. In analyzing Veidt's choices of characters to represent, Harper refers to the teaching of F. M. Alexander, founder of the Alexander technique. It is based on the principle that the individual's life can be transformed by the correct alignment of head, neck, and back; "think forward and up" was the key principle of the technique. Alexander's book, *The Use of the Self* (1932), prompted Huxley, Stafford Cripps, Archbishop William Temple, and Shaw to become Veidt's pupils.

Herrmann, Dorothy. *Helen Keller: A Life*. New York: Alfred A. Knopf, 1998. Includes a description of the meeting between Shaw and Keller. When Lady Astor introduced the two, saying that Miss Keller was deaf and blind, Shaw responded, "Why, of course, . . . all Americans are blind and deaf." Shaw did not escape unshamed in this instance. Keller did not think Shaw "one of the kindest men that ever lived." She said that she believed him to be one of the greatest of men, not one of the kindest, and that he had not been "particularly gracious" that afternoon.

Hogben, Lancelot. *Lancelot Hogben, Scientific Humanist: An Unauthorized Autobiography*. Ed. Adrian Hogben and Anne Hogben. Rendlesham: Merlin

Press, 1997. Not seen. The *TLS* review (30 January 1998, p. 27) retells a Hogben story: when he and a research student were caught at sea in a small boat in a storm, the two "joined in prayers to Darwin, Marx, and Bernard Shaw."

Holroyd, Michael. *Bernard Shaw: The One-Volume Definitive Edition.* New York: Random House, 1998. A U.S. issue of the 1997 Chatto & Windus British edition.

"Holroyd, Michael (de Courcy Fraser) 1935–." *Contemporary Authors: New Revision Series.* Volume 63. Detroit: Gale Research, 1998; pp. 191–94. A complimentary summary of Holroyd's major writing, noting that with *Bernard Shaw* "the biographer has firmly established his reputation in the field."

Hugo, Leon. "The Quest for Shaw: An Interview with Michael Holroyd." *SHAW: The Annual of Bernard Shaw Studies.* Volume Eighteen. University Park: Penn State University Press, 1998; pp. 101–12.

———. "Shaw Reviews His World" (review of *Bernard Shaw's Book Reviews, Vol. 2: 1884–1950,* edited by Brian Tyson). *SHAW: The Annual of Bernard Shaw Studies.* Volume Eighteen. University Park: Penn State University Press, 1998; pp. 208–12.

Hutchinson, Dennis J. *The Man Who Once Was Whizzer White: A Portrait of Justice Byron R. White.* New York: The Free Press, 1998. White was a great scholar-athlete and one of the longest surviving Supreme Court Justices in American history. Shaw met him at a Lady Astor party in the late 1930s and found him at first an intriguing curiosity, but too ironic a conversationalist for sustained repartee.

Innes, Christopher, ed. *The Cambridge Companion to George Bernard Shaw.* Cambridge: Cambridge University Press, 1998. This volume consists of fifteen essays on Shaw and is not a "Companion" in the handbook sense. See entries for individual authors: Berg, Frederic; Berst, Charles A.; Bryden, Ronald; Davis, Tracy C.; Evans, T. F.; Everding, Robert G.; and Gordon, David J., above; Innes, Christopher J., following entry; and Kelly, Katherine E.; Marker, Frederick J.; McDonald, Jan; Peters, Sally; Powell, Kerry; Wikander, Matthew H.; and Wisenthal, J. L., below.

———. " 'Nothing but talk, talk, talk—Shaw talk': Discussion Plays and the Making of Modern Drama." *The Cambridge Companion to George Bernard Shaw.* Ed. Christopher Innes. Cambridge: Cambridge University Press, 1998; pp. 162–79. Shaw's "preference for dialogue over plot leads to the one unique theatrical form that Shaw evolved: the Discussion Play." The first play with this subtitle was *Getting Married* (1908). "By inventing the 'play of ideas' Shaw created a prototype that set the conditions for a whole line in modern theatre, in England as well as abroad, from Bertolt Brecht and Edward Bond . . . to Joe Orton. In extending the logic of

argument to deconstructing and theatricalizing self-reference, he anticipated the principles that have become associated with postmodernism."

Isherwood, Christopher. *Christopher Isherwood: The Diaries. Volume One: 1939–1960.* Ed. Katherine Buckness. London: Methuen, 1996. Isher-wood liked Shaw. Includes a reference to seeing *Major Barbara* in the January 1957 New York production.

Jameson, Fredric. "Longevity as Class Struggle." *Immortal Engines: Life Extension and Immortality in Science Fiction and Fantasy.* Ed. George Slusser, Gary Westfahl, and Eric S. Rabkin. Athens and London: University of Georgia Press, 1996; pp. 24–42. Jameson determines that in *Back to Methuselah,* the explicit longevity topic of the play conceals its true topic, "History itself," or "historical change, radical mutations in society and collective life itself," or "revolution": "The motif of longevity or immortality" with "a second set of consequences that flows from the choice of the cover motif itself . . . has to do with the coexistence of long-living characters with the older, short-lived kind, so that the new, semiautonomous, independent story the coexistence begins to tell . . . becomes a story that can only be identified as that of class struggle."

John Bull's Other Island: Shaw Festival 1998 (Shaw Festival production program, 1998). Includes "Director's Notes" by Jim Mezon and "Shaw's Irish Inferno" by Michael J. Sidnell, which reviews the circumstances of the first performance of the play in Ireland in 1916 and discusses its meaning, that "in the emergent Ireland of Shaw's play, everything of real value is . . . unrealizable. Therefore, in an extract from Father Keegan's lines, "This earth of ours must be hell. . . .""

Kelly, Katherine E. "Imprinting the Stage: Shaw and the Publishing Trade, 1883–1903." *The Cambridge Companion to George Bernard Shaw.* Ed. Christopher Innes. Cambridge: Cambridge University Press, 1998; pp. 25–54. "Shaw aimed to fashion his plays as 'high' art by giving his published scripts the material look and poetic weight of fiction and poetry. Shaw promoted play publication not to devalue stage production but to reclaim for the playwright from the actor-manager both legal ownership and primary authorship of the written script. Determined to strengthen playwrights' economic and cultural leverage by establishing their status as authors, Shaw argued for the literary merits of drama and for the author's exclusive right to the script as a property."

Kohl, Norbert H. *Bernard Shaws viktorianisches Erbe.* Heidelberg: Winter, 1992. Not seen. Listed in *Victorian Studies* 1996 annual bibliography, noted as reviewed by "B. Goerke in *ZAA* 44: 274–77."

Lambert, Gavin. *Nazimova: A Biography.* New York: Alfred A. Knopf, 1997. The actress Alla Nazimova was considered by Lawrence Langner for the lead in a 1925 Theatre Guild production of *Saint Joan* at Shaw's suggestion. Parts of Langner's letters explaining why he did not choose Nazimova are included here. Later, she played Prola in *Simpleton*. Sent production stills of the play by the Guild, Shaw wrote to Mrs. Patrick Campbell, "Nazimova, in *your* part, appears a slinking sinuous odalisque. She should have been straight as a ramrod: an Egyptian goddess. When I am not on the spot, the harder they try, the wronger they go."

Laurence, Dan H. "The Shaws and the Gurlys: A Genealogical Study." *SHAW: The Annual of Bernard Shaw Studies*. Volume Eighteen. University Park: Penn State University Press, 1998; pp. 1–31.

Leider, Emily Wortis. *Becoming Mae West*. New York: Farrar Straus Giroux, 1997. The furor over the 1907 production of *Mrs Warren's Profession* is noticed as an example of the increase of "sexual expressiveness" in advertising and, especially, entertainment, wherein West would have an impact. The text notes a 1930s cartoon by James Montgomery Flagg in the *Los Angeles Times* showing Mae West yanking Shaw's beard.

Li, Kay. "*Heartbreak House* and the Trojan War." *Shaw and Other Matters: A Festschrift for Stanley Weintraub*. Ed. Susan Rusinko. Selinsgrove, Pa.: Susquehanna University Press, 1988; pp. 83–92. "Although *Heartbreak House* . . . contains references to the Trojan War and other Greek myths, most obviously in the use of names such as Hector, Hesione, and Ariadne, the play does not merely mirror an ancient myth. There are various Shavian distortions as Shaw manipulates the interplay between ancient myth and modern reality for his own purposes."

Major Barbara: Shaw Festival 1998 (Shaw Festival production program, 1998). Includes "Director's Notes" by Helena Kaut-Howson and "A Play with Dynamite" by Ronald Bryden that notes that in *Major Barbara*, "Shaw himself was not preaching revolution, but he wished to remind middle-class liberals like the Fabians that power need not be a monopoly of tyrants and exploiters." This was the line that H. G. Wells supported in his efforts to reform the Fabians into a group that would believe in the use of force. The Fabians did not comply.

Mann, Heinrich. *Letters of Heinrich and Thomas Mann, 1900–1949*. Ed. Hans Wysling. Trans. Don Reneau, Richard Winston, and Clara Winston. Berkeley: University of California Press, 1998. Shaw is named three times, insubstantially.

Mann, Thomas. See Mann, Heinrich, above.

Mann, William J. *Wisecracker: The Life and Times of William Haines, Hollywood's First Openly Gay Star*. New York: Viking, 1998. At a San Simeon Hollywood party for Shaw in the 1930s, Haines encountered the dramatist and was unimpressed: "I thought he was a horrible-looking old man; . . . he needed a shave."

Marker, Frederick J. "Shaw's Early Plays." *The Cambridge Companion to George Bernard Shaw*. Ed. Christopher Innes. Cambridge: Cambridge University Press, 1998; pp. 103–23. "*Mrs. Warren's Profession* clearly foreshadows the future direction of Shavian drama—yet it also marks the end of a distinct phase in the playwright's development. The publication of *Plays Unpleasant* and *Plays Pleasant* as companion volumes in 1898 served to highlight the contrast between his earlier preoccupation with specific social problems in his first three plays and the broader concern with human folly in general that takes over in the 'pleasanter' plays which follow. With the subsequent publication two years later of the anti-romantic *Plays for Puritans*, the shift away from the earlier social realism became still more pronounced, as the scope of Shaw's subject matter broadened and the grip of Ibsenism on his writing relaxed."

McBrien, William. *Cole Porter: A Biography.* New York: Alfred A. Knopf, 1998. At Yale in 1881, Porter read plays in a course taught by William Lyon Phelps—the most legendary of Yale's faculty in Porter's day—reading Ibsen, Hauptmann, Maeterlinck, Wilde, Pinero, and Shaw.

McDonald, Jan. "Shaw and the Court Theatre." *The Cambridge Companion to George Bernard Shaw.* Ed. Christopher Innes. Cambridge: Cambridge University Press, 1998; pp. 261–82. Provides a summary of the history and influence of the Court Theatre venture, which, between 1904 and 1907, mounted 988 productions, 701 of which were Shaw plays.

McGrath, Charles, ed. *Books of the Century: A Hundred Years of Authors, Ideas and Literature.* New York: Random House, 1998. All entries were reviewed in the *New York Times Book Review.* Holroyd's *Bernard Shaw, Volume One, 1856–1898, The Search for Love* (with reference as well to the subsequent volumes) is among the works selected.

Mitford, Jessica. *The American Way of Death Revisited.* New York: Alfred A. Knopf, 1998. Shaw, "Thorny old critic of the status quo," is quoted in support of cremations: "Dead bodies can be cremated. All of them ought to be, for earth burial, a horrible practice, will someday be prohibited by law, not only because it is hideously unaesthetic, but because the dead would crowd the living off the earth if it could be carried out to its end of preserving our bodies for their resurrection on an imaginary day of judgment (in sober fact, every day is a day of judgment)."

Murray, Christopher. *Twentieth-Century Irish Drama: Mirror Up to a Nation.* Manchester and New York: Manchester University Press, 1997. Numerous references to Shaw, including mentions of *Methuselah, Doctor's Dilemma, Heartbreak, John Bull, Matter with Ireland, Blanco Posnet,* and *Widowers' Houses.*

Murray, Paul. "Lafcadio Hearn and the Irish Tradition." *Irish Writing on Lafcadio Hearn and Japan.* Ed. Sean G. Ronan. Folkestone, Kent: Global Oriental, 1997. Murray finds Hearn one of four extraordinary Irish writers born near the midpoint of the nineteenth century, including Bram Stoker, Oscar Wilde, and Shaw, and explains how especially similar were the early lives of Hearn and Shaw. Both also became socialists.

Nathan, Rhoda. "Arguments, Asides, Addenda: The Last Words" (review of *The Complete Prefaces, Vol. 3: 1930–1950*, edited by Dan H. Laurence and Daniel J. Leary). *SHAW: The Annual of Bernard Shaw Studies*. Volume Eighteen. University Park: Penn State University Press, 1998; pp. 204–8.

Nicholson, Helen. "Writing Plays: Taking Note of Genre." *On the Subject of Drama*. Ed. David Hornbrook. London and New York: Routledge, 1998. Discussing "the hierarchy of dramatic forms" within "the literary tradition," Nicholson offers as examples Shakespeare, Marlowe, and Shaw. In a note, she refers readers to the UK National Curriculum "Order for English," *The National Curriculum* (London: HMSO, 1995), which lists Marlowe, Sheridan, and Shaw among "great literary playwrights . . . thought suitable for children."

Paine, Jeffery. *Father India: How Encounters with the Ancient Culture Transformed the Modern West*. New York: HarperCollins, 1998. Includes a chapter on Annie Besant, advocate of appreciation for India, with a number of references to G.B.S. Shaw would be "Mahatma Minor" next to Gandhi's Mahatma Major when they met in London in 1931. Later Shaw would be among those who would damn the imperial adventure that humiliated India. Besant, herself, was not wise. She wanted a narrow European model for India's "home rule."

Palmer, Richard H. *The Contemporary British History Play*. Westport, Conn.: Greenwood Press, 1998. Shaw history plays like *Man of Destiny, Caesar, Disciple*, and *Joan* reflected one of the two principal moods of such plays, the didactic, the other being romantic. Shaw was one of the moderns to resurrect the medieval practice of depicting history in terms of the present. Pointedly, Shaw did not "originate this practice."

Passion, Poison and Petrifaction, in *Lunchtime Theatre: Shaw Festival 1998* (Shaw Festival production program, 1998). Includes program and production commentary for *Passion, Poison, and Petrifaction: or, The Fatal Gazogene* and "Director's Notes" by Gyllian Raby.

Pearson, Hesketh. "Shaw, George Bernard (1856–1950)." *Collier's Encyclopedia*. Volume 20. New York: Colliers, 1997. Collier's retains this Pearson-authored entry from its numerous prior editions.

Peters, Sally. "Shaw's Life: A Feminist in Spite of Himself." *The Cambridge Companion to George Bernard Shaw*. Ed. Christopher Innes. Cambridge: Cambridge University Press, 1998; pp. 3–24. "Far more enigmatic and complex than the fabricated G.B.S. image, the real Shaw was a man whose relation to the feminine—in himself and others—hailed from a highly extravagant inner life. As he struggled heroically against his own ambivalences, the artist emerged triumphant. Nurtured too in such rich soil was Shaw the feminist, not only by the standards of the nineteenth century but also by today's criteria as we approach the twenty-first century." Concerning gender relations, "There is a pattern of evidence in

Shaw's life, including his preoccupation with questions of heredity, genius, and 'inversion,' that suggests that he secretly viewed himself as a
'noble invert'—an ascetic artist whose gifts were linked to a homoerotic
source." Shaw further believed that "the fates of artists, homosexuals,
and women are intertwined."

Pharand, Michel W. " 'Almost Wholly Cerebral': Richard Aldington on
Bernard Shaw." *SHAW: The Annual of Bernard Shaw Studies.* Volume Eighteen. University Park: Penn State University Press, 1998; 93–100.

———. "Bernard Shaw's Bonaparte: Life Force or Death Wish?" *Shaw and
Other Matters: A Festschrift for Stanley Weintraub.* Ed. Susan Rusinko. Selinsgrove, Pa.: Susquehanna University Press, 1998; pp. 41–52. "If we examine briefly what Shaw's Bonaparte owes to biography and art, compare
him with one famous contemporary French stage Napoleon, and analyze
how Shaw's estimate of the historical Bonaparte varied with the times,
we will better understand why the very idea of a Napoleon in the world
remained essential to Shaw's worldview, and why this Great Man continued to fascinate Shaw to the end of his life," even though "in the after-
math of two world wars, Shaw's Bonaparte had degenerated from Life
Force to Death Wish."

———. "The Siren on the Rock: Bernard Shaw vs. Sarah Bernhardt."
SHAW: The Annual of Bernard Shaw Studies. Volume Eighteen. University
Park: Penn State University Press, 1998; pp. 33–44.

Porter, Roy. *The Greatest Benefit to Mankind: A Medical History of Humanity.*
New York and London: W. W. Norton, 1997. Three mentions of *Doctor's
Dilemma* by the "health crank" Shaw. "Scientific medicine may be the
knight in shining armour or a new body-snatcher. What Shaw called *The
Doctor's Dilemma* is humanity's."

Powell, Kerry. "New Women, New Plays, and Shaw in the 1890s." *The Cambridge Companion to George Bernard Shaw.* Ed. Christopher Innes. Cambridge: Cambridge University Press, 1988; pp. 76–100. "What is striking
here is Shaw's recognition as a male commentator that the theatre was
on the threshold of apocalypse, one that would be wrought by the efforts
of newly assertive women of the stage. It would be the manifestation in
the London theatre of the changes being wrought by the New Woman.
But Shaw's enthusiasm for those changes was not nearly as unqualified
as his remarks about a 'struggle between the sexes' would suggest. . . .
For many, including Shaw himself at times, the New Woman created intellectual panic in her function as what Carroll Smith-Rosenberg has
called 'a condensed symbol of disorder and rebellion.' "

Roby, Kinley. "Arnold Bennett: Shaw's Ten O'Clock Scholar." *Shaw and
Other Matters: A Festschrift for Stanley Weintraub.* Ed. Susan Rusinko. Selinsgrove, Pa.: Susquehanna University Press, 1998; pp. 53–61. Shaw was em-
phatic in denying any interest in teaching playwriting, but in the case of

Arnold Bennett, Shaw broke this rule, and over a period of ten years he tried without success to teach Bennett what a play should be.

Rusinko, Susan, ed. *Shaw and Other Matters: A Festschrift for Stanley Weintraub on the Occasion of His Forty-Second Anniversary at the Pennsylvania State University.* Selinsgrove, Pa.: Susquehanna University Press, 1998. Reviewed in this volume. See entries for individual authors: Crawford, Fred D.; Li, Kay; Pharand, Michel W., and Roby, Kinley, above; Sparks, Julie A.; and Weintraub, Rodelle, below. The volume contains nine additional essays on non-Shavian topics.

"Shaw, George Bernard 1856–1950." *Chambers Biographical Dictionary.* Sixth edition. Ed. Melanie Parry. New York: Chambers, 1997; p. 1684. Shaw is summarized in an eight-inch column of six-point font.

Sidnell, Michael J. See *John Bull's Other Island*, above.

Snodgrass, Mary Ellen. "Shaw, George Bernard." *Encyclopedia of Utopian Literature.* Santa Barbara: ABC-CLIO, 1995; pp. 469–71. This entry is remarkable for its failure to name or discuss Shaw's utopian plays (*Simpleton* and *Farfetched Fables*, for example) or his utopian thought. The volume also provides an entry on *Back to Methuselah*.

de Sola Rodstein, Susan. "John Bull and Paddy's Pig: Shaw and the Stage Irishman." *Beyond Pug's Tour: National and Ethnic Stereotyping in Theory and Literary Practice.* Ed. C. C. Barfoot. Amsterdam and Atlanta: Rodopi, 1997; pp. 295–312. "Shaw's inevitable use of national stereotypes in his construction of personality accords with his often expressed conviction that nationalism itself is a curse and a disease from which 'healthy' nations are happily free." In *John Bull*, a quest for a "convincing basis for nationality, "Shaw argues himself in and out of various determinisms ranging from genetics to economics to climate. . . . A satisfactory formula for the Irishness that seems to confront Shaw in such inescapable, contradictory, but essential terms ('so Irish! so Irish!') eludes him. . . . Shaw could envision Ireland's romantic ruin and infuse it with a clear sense of its economic ruin, combining both of these elements in his most memorable Irishmen of the stage—those that were intended to 'make ruins' of the Stage Irishman of old."

Solway, Diane. *Nureyev: His Life.* New York: William Morrow, 1998. Nureyev indirectly had an intense experience associated with a 1960 Russian production of *My Fair Lady*. He saw the show at least twice and struck up a friendship with Lola Fisher, the American actress who played Eliza. On this Russian production itself, many Russians knew *Pygmalion*, but could not understand *My Fair Lady*'s dialogue. Even so, their response was ecstatic. "Get Me to the Church on Time" was the showstopper.

Sparks, Julie A. "The Evolution of Human Virtue: Precedents for Shaw's 'World Betterer' in the Utopias of Bellamy, Morris, and Bulwer-Lytton." *Shaw and Other Matters: A Festschrift for Stanley Weintraub.* Ed. Susan

Rusinko. Selinsgrove, Pa.: Susquehanna University Press, 1998; pp. 63–82. Shaw agreed with Bellamy and Morris on some points, but he rejected the "simplistic environmental determinism on which their conception of human nature rested." Bulwer-Lytton was also influential, but his belief that human nature is immutable "disqualified him for the work of the world-betterer as Shaw defined it." Shaw's ultimate proposition is that we must not yield to despair.

———. "An Overlooked Source for Eliza? W. E. Henley's *London Types.*" *SHAW: The Annual of Bernard Shaw Studies.* Volume Eighteen. University Park: Penn State University Press, 1998; pp. 161–71.

Sterner, Mark H. "Shaw's Superwoman and the Borders of Feminism: One Step over the Line?" *SHAW: The Annual of Bernard Shaw Studies.* Volume Eighteen. University Park: Penn State University Press, 1998; pp. 147–60.

Sternlicht, Sanford. *A Reader's Guide to Modern Irish Drama.* Syracuse, N.Y.: Syracuse University Press, 1998. Provides a superficial four-page entry on Shaw, featuring a summary discussion of *John Bull's Other Island* (Sternlicht believes that it is as relevant today as when it was written in 1904). No attempt is made to discuss other Shavian Irish matters.

Tate, Mary Jo. *F. Scott Fitzgerald A to Z: The Essential Reference to His Life and Work.* New York: Facts on File, 1998. A few references transmit the high regard in which Fitzgerald held G.B.S.: "Shaw's aloof clarity and brilliant consistency."

Taverner, Emma. *Shaw Business Papers: The Business and Financial Papers of George Bernard Shaw* [an unpublished handlist]. London: British Library of Political and Economic Science, 1997. Not Seen. Enumerates the Library's collection of Shaw's Business Papers, consisting of Shaw's personal diaries (1885–97), engagement diaries (1877–1950), correspondence with printers, publishers, translators and literary agents, and numerous financial records, including bank statements, income-tax returns, and details of the royalties received from theatrical companies, publishers, and film companies. For the near future, photocopies are available to the public on request for £86.75. Address: c/o Emma Taverner, Archives Department, British Library of Political and Economic Science, 10 Portugal Street, London, WC2A 2HD. The handlist can be sent as an attachment to e-mail at no charge. Address: document@lse.ac.uk On floppy disc for £5.00 plus postage. Requests for searches of the collection at no charge to web pages at: http://www.blpes.lse.ac.uk/blpes/archives/

The Trial of Joan of Arc. Ed. Monica Furlong. Berkhamsted: Arthur James, 1998. Not seen. *TLS* review (24 July 1998, p. 27) notes that the Shavian view and the super-nationalist view of the far Right in France can now be assessed with this translation of all fifteen sessions of her trial.

Turco, Alfred, Jr. "Shaw as Spin Doctor" (review of *Pygmalion: Shaw's Spin on Myth and Cinderella* by Charles A. Berst). *SHAW: The Annual of Bernard Shaw Studies.* Volume Eighteen. University Park: Penn State University Press, 1998; pp. 217–19.

Turner, Tramble T. "George Bernard Shaw (1856–1950)." *Irish Playwrights, 1860–1995: A Research and Production Sourcebook.* Ed. Bernice Schrank and William W. Demastes. Westport, Conn.: Greenwood Press, 1997; pp. 322–40. This entry updates the Turner entry in the *SHAW* 18 Checklist. Turner provides synopses and facts for thirty-six of the plays, an overview of Shaw's career, and an extended bibliography which, while it lists *G. B. Shaw: An Annotated Bibliography*, omits mention of the Dan H. Laurence Soho Shaw bibliographical volumes and the *SHAW Annual.*

Tyson, Brian. "Maturity: Shaw's Novels Revisited" (review of *Bernard Shaw's Novels: Portraits of the Artist as Man and Superman* by Richard Farr Dietrich). *SHAW: The Annual of Bernard Shaw Studies.* Volume Eighteen. University Park: Penn State University Press, 1998; pp. 212–17.

Vonnegut, Kurt. *Timequake.* New York: Putnam, 1997. In this, his latest novel, Vonnegut refers to "my hero George Bernard Shaw," the most recent repetition of a statement of Vonnegut's high regard for G.B.S.

Wainscott, Ronald H. *The Emergence of the Modern American Theater: 1914–1929.* New Haven and London: Yale University Press, 1997. Three significant mentions of G.B.S.: The first notes the production of *Arms and the Man* and *Major Barbara* shortly before the U.S. entered World War I in 1917. The second is the closing by the police of Arnold Daly's production of *Mrs Warren's Profession,* starring Mary Shaw. The third is to note the advance in the technique and craft of *Back to Methuselah*'s stage-set production, which "virtually painted with light, projecting . . . images onto a translucent gauze backdrop . . ." and influenced the stage designs of *The Ancient Mariner, Beyond, Adding Machine,* and *From Morn to Midnight.*

Wallmann, Jeffrey M. "See No Evil, Hear No Evil, Speak No Evil: The Alienation Factors in Shaw's Dramas." *SHAW: The Annual of Bernard Shaw Studies.* Volume Eighteen. University Park: Penn State University Press, 1998; pp. 113–29.

Weintraub, Rodelle. "Extracting the Roots of Sorrow: *You Never Can Tell* as Dream Play." *SHAW: The Annual of Bernard Shaw Studies.* Volume Eighteen. University Park: Penn State University Press, 1998; pp. 137–46.

———. " 'Oh, the dreaming, the dreaming': *Arms and the Man.*" *Shaw and Other Matters: A Festschrift for Stanley Weintraub.* Ed. Susan Rusinko. Selinsgrove, Pa.: Susquehanna University Press, 1998; pp. 31–40. There is in *Arms,* once called forth, an obvious subtext of symbols that elementary Freudian psychoanalytical theory of dreams will identify as reinforcing the farce romance plot wherein the Sergius-Louka and Bluntschli-Raina couples are happily together in the end. Shaw is not known to have read Freud by the time *Arms* was written, but in it he "intuitively made use of a wish fulfillment dream to write his first fantasy play."

Weintraub, Stanley. "Eugene O'Neill: The Shavian Dimension." *SHAW: The Annual of Bernard Shaw Studies*. Volume Eighteen. University Park: Penn State University Press, 1998; pp. 45–61.

Wells, H. G. *The Correspondence of H. G. Wells, Volume 4, 1935–1946*. Ed. David C. Smith. London: Pickering & Chatto, 1998. This volume provides an index to the four volumes with dozens of references to Shaw and Charlotte and to Shaw's works, including *Arms, Great Catherine, John Bull*, and *Major Barbara*.

Wikander, Matthew H. "Reinventing the History Play: *Caesar and Cleopatra, Saint Joan, 'In Good King Charles's Golden Days'*." *The Cambridge Companion to George Bernard Shaw*. Ed. Christopher Innes. Cambridge: Cambridge University Press, 1998; pp. 195–217. "Shaw's reinvention of the history play takes place most importantly in a context of English theatrical practice." Other relevant plays in this discussion are *Man of Destiny, Devil's Disciple, Dark Lady of the Sonnets, Great Catherine, Arms and the Man, Heartbreak House, Major Barbara, John Bull's Other Island*, and *Back to Methuselah*. Shaw's "delight in the staggering anachronism, his assault as a kind of intellectual 'terrorist' . . . upon preconceived, heroic, pictorial notions of appropriate representation of the past, his bumptious arrogation to himself of total authority over history—all these constitute a serious challenge to the high prestige enjoyed by narrative history in the late nineteenth century. . . . Shaw's reinvention of the history play restores to lying its full fictive dignity and gives to anachronism and factual error the status of alternative truth. In their glorification of paradox, the history plays figure importantly in Shaw's larger project of the constant reinvention of himself."

Williams, William H. A. *H. L. Mencken Revisited*. New York: Twayne, 1998. Mencken's early strong respect for Shaw and the Shavian polemic, a motive for writing *George Bernard Shaw: His Plays* (1905), diminished as he lost his belief that art could be a means for intellectual and social change. By 1916 Mencken dismissed Shaw as "an orthodox Scotch Presbyterian of the most cock-sure and bilious sort" and as "the Ulster Polonius."

Wisenthal, J. L. " 'Please remember, this is Italian opera': Shaw's Plays as Music-Drama." *The Cambridge Companion to George Bernard Shaw*. Ed. Christopher Innes. Cambridge: Cambridge University Press, 1998; pp. 283–308. "In *Man and Superman* and *Major Barbara*, much of the music is operatic, but music of all sorts pervades Shaw's plays. To note just a few conspicuous examples, we hear two pianos in *The Music Cure*; a saxophone in *Buoyant Billions*; a bucina in *Caesar and Cleopatra*; two competing onstage bands in *The Devil's Disciple*; a trumpet in *The Simpleton of the Unexpected Isles*; whistling and singing in *John Bull's Other Island*; singing in *Pygmalion*, . . . and songs in *Saint Joan, On the Rocks, and Passion, Poison and Petrifaction* . . . ; a vocal 'antiphonal quartet' in *The Simpleton of the Unexpected Isles*; and a carillon, and organ, and flutes in *Back to Methuselah*. And there is Randall Utterword's flute-playing that forms part of the sound-pattern in *Heartbreak House*." The music in the plays is not merely decorative but "part of their very fabric. . . . There has been too little emphasis on the formal qualities of his plays—on their melody, their harmony, their rhythm, their movements, their changes of key."

III. Periodicals

Bemrose, John. "Anonymous Artistry." *Maclean's* (8 June 1998), pp. 52–53. Includes an account of Kelli Fox, sister of Michael J. Fox, who played the lead in the 1998 Shaw Festival *Major Barbara* production.

Berry, Kevin. "All Dolled up for the Part" (review of the Michael Friend production of *Pygmalion). Times Educational Supplement* (19 June 1998), p. SS31.

Bertolini, John A. "Shaw's Book Reviews" (review of *Bernard Shaw's Book Reviews, Vol. 2: 1884–1950*, edited by Brian Tyson). *ELT* 41:1 (1998): 68–72.

"A Better Way to Highlight Text." *Levenger, Tools for Serious Readers* (Spring 1998), p. 55. P. O. Box 1256, Delray Beach, FL 33447–1256. This catalogue of reading and writing supplies advertises "Textliners" in this listing with an illustration in which the marker is used to highlight "George Bernard Shaw" in a book text.

Blowen, Michael. "The ART's New 'Super' Man" (review of the American Repertory Theatre production of *Man and Superman). Boston Globe* (22 May 1997), Section E, p. 1.

"Book World: Nonfiction" (review of Michael Holroyd's one-volume definitive edition of *Bernard Shaw). Washington Post* (20 September 1998), p. 13.

Brandes, Philip. "Theater Review: Shaw's School for Standards: Classy *Mrs. Warren's Profession* Upends Victorian Morals" (review of the Pacific Resident Theatre Ensemble production). *Los Angeles Times* (13 February 1997), Section CAL, p. 31.

Brooks-Dillard, Sandra. "Wordy *Misalliance* Benefits from First-Class Staging" (review of the Denver Center Theatre production). *Denver Post* (20 October 1997), Section F, p. 8.

Burlin, Robert. "Shaw, Women, and Opera: Determining the Voice." *Cahiers Victoriens & Édouardiens* 45 (April 1997): 73–81. Shaw's "voice" demands careful attention. "He speaks from 'behind' the text, deconstructing, consciously or subconsciously, what appears to be expressed." Burlin concentrates on *Man and Superman* and *Heartbreak House* in which he "at least severely complicates the expressed attitude toward women." The two plays "fluctuate wildly between Germanic misogyny and doting and even identification." The "masks" of Shaw's discourse "obscure the kind of earnest sincerity" that many critics find in Shaw's works. Shaw took this rhetorical strategy from Wagner and especially from Mozart, in whose work he "recognized the power of music to make something more of the words it was setting than the libretto supplied."

Canby, Vincent. Review of Laura Pels Theater production of *You Never Can Tell. New York Times* (5 July 1998), Section AR, p. 16.

———. Review of the Roundabout Theatre production of *Misalliance. New York Times*, late NY edition (5 October 1997), p. 5.

Chen, Wendi. "G. B. Shaw's Plays on the Chinese Stage: The 1991 Production of *Major Barbara*." *Comparative Literature Studies* 35 (1998): 25–48. Because of his sometimes socialist meanings Shaw has been acceptable in China. "The 1991 production of . . . [*Major Barbara*] was a peculiar as well as highly significant event. It was peculiar because the political, social and cultural climate of the time was not in favor of staging such a play, and it was significant because the production was charged with a serious social and professional mission." The director Ying Ruocheng wanted "to further the cause of Spoken Drama" and to satisfy an audience starved for "intellectual nourishment." *Major Barbara* was chosen because its message is politically ambiguous and because Shaw has a good reputation in China. The play was successful critically and at the box office.

Christiansen, Richard. "Not Always a Shaw Thing: Canada's No. 2 Not-for-Profit Presents a Refreshing Mix." *Chicago Tribune* (3 August 1997), Section 7, p. 12. A feature account of the Shaw Festival from its founding in 1962.

Claflin, Jill. "Myths and Truths." *Habitat World* 14 (February/March 1998): 4–7. Shaw is quoted in text superimposed on an illustration of people building a house: "We are all dependent on one another, every soul of us on earth."

Clute, John. "Back to the Drawing Board" (review of *Shaw and Science Fiction* [*SHAW* 17], edited by Milton T. Wolf). *Science Fiction Studies* 25 (July 1998): 381–83.

Coakley, James. Review of *Shaw's People* by Stanley Weintraub, *Bernard Shaw: The Ascent of the Superman* by Sally Peters, and *George Bernard Shaw and the Socialist Theatre* by Tracy C. Davis. *Comparative Drama* 32 (Summer 1998): 297–98.

Cohen, Edward H. "Shaw." In "Victorian Bibliography for 1996." *Victorian Studies* 40:4 (Summer 1997): 897. Sixteen entries retrospective to 1992.

Cotes, Peter. "Obituary: Ellen Pollock: Shavian Lisp Service." *Guardian* (14 April 1997), Section l, p. 19. Not seen. Pollock died at ninety-four on 29 March 1997. She is perhaps best known for her association with G.B.S. She played the nurse, Sweetie, in the first production of *Too True*—at the Malvern Festival.

Crowley, Tony. "Uniform, Excellent, Common: Reflections on Standards in Language." *Language Sciences* 19:1 (1997): 15–21. " 'Standard English' both reflected and projected social conflict, and it helped in the process of constructing all sorts of social identities upon the precarious matter of speech patterns." Shaw's pronouncements on the connection of language and social class, especially in *Pygmalion*, are appropriated in the discussion of this proposition.

Cunningham, John. "Arts: Authors at the Bottom of the Garden so George Bernard Shaw Wrote in a Rotating Garden Shack. He Wasn't the Only Literary Great to Make Use of the Potting Shed." *Guardian* (27 August 1998), Section l2, p. 12. Not seen. A feature piece on Shaw's rotating writing hut at Ayot St. Lawrence.

Daniels, Robert L. "*Major Barbara*" (review of the Irish Repertory Theatre production). *Variety* (1–7 December 1997), p. 82.

Evans, Greg. "*Misalliance*" (review of the Roundabout Theatre production). *Variety* (11–17 August 1997), p. 64.

F[allon], B[rian]. "Paperback Choice" (review of *Bernard Shaw: The Ascent of the Superman* by Sally Peters). *Irish Times* (1 August 1998).

Faulkner, Peter. Review of *Bernard Shaw: The Ascent of the Superman* by Sally Peters. *Journal of the William Morris Society* 13:1 (Autumn 1998): 78–80.

Feingold, Michael. "The Family Business" (includes review of the Roundabout Theater production of *You Never Can Tell*). *Village Voice* (14 July 1998), p. 157.

———. "Irish (Contra) Dictions" (includes a review of the Irish Repertory Theatre production of *Major Barbara*). *Village Voice* (9 December 1997), p. 107.

Freedland, Jonathan. "Intellectuals for Racial Purity." *World Press Review* 44 (November 1997): 47. Not seen. Leading socialists, including Shaw, hoped that through the science of eugenics the strong parts of society could be strengthened and the weak ones eliminated. The Nazi genocide program, however, deflected eugenics study in post-war science.

Fricker, Karen. "*Saint Joan*" (review of the Abbey Theater production). *Variety* (20–26 July 1998), p. 54.

Friedlander, Mira. "*John Bull's Other Island*" (review of the Shaw Festival production). *Variety* (27 July–2 August 1998), p. 63.

———. "Unshaven Shaw Show" (includes a review of the Shaw Festival production of *Major Barbara*). *Variety* 371:4 (1–7 June 1998): 43–44.

Gibson, Melissa. Review of *British Playwrights, 1880–1956: A Research and Production Sourcebook*, edited by William W. Demastes and Katherine Kelly. *Theatre Survey* 39 (May 1998): 99–102.

Glaister, Dan. "By George They've Got It: Shaw's Lost $2M Royalties." *Guardian* (6 February 1997), Section 1, p. 2. A feature newspiece on a two-million-dollar settlement paid by CBS to Shaw's beneficiaries—the Royal Academy of Dramatic Art, the British Museum, and the National Gallery of Ireland—as part of the proceeds from *My Fair Lady*. The Shaw Estate issued its writ in 1993.

Graham, Brad L. "Fine Arts: Theater Playwright Puts a New Twist on a Classic Theater Theme" (review of the St. Marcus Theatre production of *Pygmalion*). *St. Louis Post-Dispatch* (29 January 1998), Section GO, p. 24.

Guthrie, J. Brenna. Review of the Pacific Resident Theatre production of *Candida*. *Back Stage West* 5 (30 April 1998): 10.

Hall, Peter. "Shaw on Robin Cook" (review of the Piccadilly Theatre production of *Major Barbara*). *Spectator* (16 May 1998), pp. 21–22.

Hampton, Wilborn. "Shaw, in Gentle Mood, Relaxes at the Beach" (review of the Roundabout Theater production of *You Never Can Tell*). *New York Times* (23 June 1998), Section E, p. 3.

Harris, Karen. "*Pygmalion*" (review of the Los Angeles Theatre Works and Chicago Court Theatre production). *Booklist* (15 December 1997), p. 711.

Hartigan, Patti. "Even with Raquel, It's a Poor Imitation" (review of the Orpheum Theatre production of *Millionairess*). *Boston Globe* (5 June 1998), Section D, p. 4.

———. "Raquel Welch Gets Serious about Acting." *Boston Globe* (24 May 1998), Section N, pp. 1, 6. A feature story on Welch's rehearsal experience for the Orpheum Theatre production of *Millionairess*.

Horwitz, Simi. "Designs on Directing: Tony Walton Takes on *Major Barbara*" (review of the Irish Arts Theatre production). *Back Stage* 38:49 (5 December 1997): 6.

Hughes, Leonard. "*Misalliance* Not the Usual Shaw" (review of the Mount Vernon Players production). *Washington Post* (15 May 1997), Section DC, p. 4.

Isherwood, Charles. "*You Never Can Tell*" (review of the Roundabout Theater production). *Variety* (13–19 July 1998), p. 64.

Istel, John. "Shaw's Talking Cure" (preview notice of Seattle Repertory Theatre production of *Pygmalion*). *Atlantic Monthly* 282:6 (December 1998): n.p. (in "Special Advertising Section").

Jones, Chris. "Greasy Joan Troupe Enfolds 'Arms' in Funny Embrace" (review of the Greasy Joan & Co. production of *Arms and the Man*). *Chicago Tribune* (28 October 1997), Section 5, p. 2.

———. "He's a Fan." *American Theatre* 15 (January 1998): 12. A mural in the lobby of the Cincinnati Playhouse in the Park, newly renovated, features G.B.S. wearing a Cincinnati Reds baseball cap.

K., B. Review of *Bernard Shaw and Gabriel Pascal*, edited by Bernard F. Dukore. *TLS* (20 March 1998), p. 31.

Kanfer, Stefan. "Brandy of the Damned" (includes review of the Laura Pels Theater production of *You Never Can Tell*). *New Leader* (10–24 August 1998), pp. 21–22.

———. "Women Behaving Badly" (includes a review of the Roundabout Theatre production of *Misalliance*). *New Leader* (8 September 1998), pp. 22–23.

Kemp, Peter. "Bandages before Badinage" (review of the Piccadilly Theatre production of *Major Barbara* and the Almeida Theatre production of *Doctor's Dilemma*). *TLS* (12 June 1998), p. 20.

Kennedy, Maev. "Light Shed on Shaw's Spinning Shelter: Maev Kennedy on a Revolving Retreat." *Guardian* (27 August 1998), Section 1, p. 7. Not seen. A news feature on the completed repair of Shaw's rotating writing hut.

Klein, Alvin. "Brilliant Talk, Visceral Ideas." *New York Times* (11 May 1997), Section CN, p. 15. Not seen. A reflection on the dramatic potential of the *Don Juan in Hell* dream sequence.

Kosok, Heinz. "Shaw in Germany." *Shavian* 8:4 (Summer 1998): 14–17. Shaw was very successful in Germany. Every single Shaw play was produced in Germany, and Shaw plays were in both the metropolitan *and* the provincial playhouses. Second, the state-subsidized stage in Germany allowed the companies to keep Shaw's plays in their repertory, even when they were not "popular" although the German theatre-goer was weaned to appreciate the "play of ideas." Third, there was no censorship for the German stage. Fourth, Shaw had an active and enthusiastic translator in Siegfried Trebitsch, who also had the connections to have the plays performed.

Kugler-Euerle, Gabriele. "Educating Eliza, Rita and Frank! Rezeptionsorientierte Vorschläge zur Behandlung von Bernard Shaws *Pygmalion* und Willy Russells *Educating Rita* im Englischunterricht der Sekundarstufe II" [Reader-response-oriented proposals for the treatment of Bernard Shaw's *Pygmalion* and Willy Russell's *Educating Rita* in English instruction at secondary school, level II]. *Fremdsprachenunterricht: Zeitschrift fur das Lehren und Lernen Fremder Sprachen* 2 (1997): 91–98. A translation of the abstract: This essay will demonstrate that the success of two popular plays for English instruction [in German schools] can be even greater when both texts [by Shaw and Russell] are presented together. At the essay's center are reader-response-oriented approaches that prove that creative

approaches to a text are highly productive, even in the demanding literature instruction of the secondary school level II.

Leapman, Michael. "Diary" (includes reviews of current productions of
Pygmalion, Heartbreak, and *Misalliance*). *New Statesman* 10 (12 September
1997): 6.

Leary, Daniel. "An Approach toward Shavian Autobiography." *Independent
Shavian* 35:2–3 (1997): 27–48. "It was only in absorbing Sally Peters's
book that I began to think about how Shaw's love/hate of Irishness reflected in this passage [the two-page soliloquy Larry Doyle delivers
toward the end of the first act, ostensibly lecturing the smugly insulated
Broadbent in *John Bull's Other Island (JBOI)*, but actually haranguing him-
self] offered an emotional spectrum of Shaw at the moment of writing,
offered as satisfactory an explanation of the creative act which is GBS as
did Michael Holroyd's or Sally Peter's Freudian templates." As Leary
reads this "seminal passage in *JBOI* I find each of the play's four major
characters is an analogue of Shaw, a reflector of one of his vital options:
Larry Doyle as speaker, Tom Broadbent as audience, and the Irish priest
Peter Keegan and Irish heiress Nora Reilly as subjects of the soliloquy."

Lyons, Donald. Review of Pearl Theatre production of *Candida. Wall Street
Journal* (16 September 1998), Section A, p. 20.

———. Review of the Shaw Festival production of *John Bull's Other Island.
Wall Street Journal* (29 July 1998), Section A, p. 13.

———. "Theater: Toothache; Headache" (review of the Roundabout Theater production of *You Never Can Tell*). *Wall Street Journal* (24 June 1998),
Section A, p. 16.

Mannion, Kristina. Review of the Long Beach Playhouse production of *Misalliance. Back Stage West* (1 January 1998), p. 11.

Marks, Peter. "Country House Chatter So Rudely Interrupted" (review of
the Roundabout Theater production of *Misalliance*). *New York Times* (8
August 1997), Section C, p. 1.

———. "Reconstructing a Bygone Elite and Its Follies." *New York Times* (13
August 1998), Section E, p. 1. A feature story on the 1998 Shaw Festival
at Niagara-on-the-Lake.

Marx, Bill. "American *'Arms and Man'* Loses Needed Charm" (review of
the Peabody House Theatre production). *Boston Globe* (16 December
1997), p. D7.

———. "*Candida* a Satisfying Portrayal of a Queen Bee with Some Sting"
(review of the Yale Repertory Theatre production). *Boston Globe* (9 December 1997), Section D, p. 5.

———. "Trinity Outmuscles Shaw's *Saint Joan*" (review of the Trinity Repertory Company production). *Boston Globe* (18 December 1998), Section
D, p. 14.

McCarthy, Frances. "Shaw in Synge Street." *Shavian* 8:3 (Winter 1997–98): 13–14. The current curator of the Shaw Birthplace museum, 33 Synge Street in Dublin (where Shaw was born and spent his childhood), reports its present condition and plans for its continuing restoration and elaboration.

McDougall, Kathleen. Review of *Bernard Shaw's Book Reviews, Vol. 2: 1884–1950*, edited by Brian Tyson. *University of Toronto Quarterly* 67 (Winter 1997/1998): 270–72.

McDowell, Frederick P. W. "Shaw-Pascal Collaboration" (review of *Bernard Shaw and Gabriel Pascal*, edited by Bernard F. Dukore). *ELT* 41:2 (1998): 223–26.

Michaels, James W. "Salvation Found" (review of the film *Major Barbara*). *Forbes* 16 (20 April 1998): 502.

Minzesheimer, Bob. "A Definitive Edition of *Bernard Shaw*" (review of Michael Holroyd's one-volume definitive edition of *Bernard Shaw*). *USA Today* (27 August 1998), Section D, p. 5.

Monji, Jana J. "Theatre Review: A *Misalliance* of Talents in Long Beach." *Los Angeles Times* (2 January 1998), Section F, p. 8.

Morley, Sheridan. "Look Back in Anger" (includes a review of the Almeida Theatre production of *Heartbreak*). *Spectator* (13 September 1997), pp. 48–49.

———. "Man and the Arms" (includes a review of *Major Barbara*). *Spectator* (23 May 1998), pp. 49–50.

Nassaar, Christopher. "Wilde's *Lady Windermere's Fan* and Shaw's *Mrs. Warren's Profession*." *Explicator* 56 (Spring 1998): 137–38. "Shaw's play is a Shavian reworking of Wilde's, an attempt to squarely face the issues that Wilde sidestepped. In a nutshell, it is *Lady Windermere's Fan* intellectualized."

Nathan, Rhoda. "From Shaw to Beckett: The Road to Absurdity." *Independent Shavian* 36:1–2 (1998): 3–10. "Even though Shaw was to write a few more minor plays in the 20 remaining years of his life, *Too True to Be Good* was, in effect, the end, both in his major creative efforts, and certainly in the theme the play encapsulated, which Shaw put into the mouth of Aubrey Bagot at the conclusion: 'I have no creed, no Bible: we have outgrown our religion, outgrown our political system, outgrown our strength of mind and character.' From that despairing outcry wrenched from a wandering lost soul, it is but a step to Beckett's stripped landscape where two clowns do nothing but wait."

———. "Shaw's Nobel." *New Yorker* (9 November 1998), p. 10. This letter to the editor adds a comment about Shaw to an earlier *New Yorker* article on Nobel winners. Shaw won the prize in 1925, but it was not awarded to him until 1926, leading Shaw to inform the newspapers that "I wrote nothing in 1925, and that is probably why they gave it to me."

Neill, Heather. "Art Beat" (review of the Piccadilly Theatre production of *Major Barbara* and the Almeida Theatre production of *Doctor's Dilemma*). *Times Educational Supplement* (19 June 1998), p. SS13.

Paulin, Tom. "The Unholy One?" *London Review of Books* 19:24 (11 December 1997): 30. A prose poem—with idiosyncratic capitals and punctuation—of more than 200 lines wherein on one level the "One" is G.B.S. Sample: "so I imagine a caption in the *News Chronicle* / GBS Travels P&O / 'I always work on holiday' / says the world's most famous author / 'especially if some kind cruise liner pays me' / so there you are in a deckchair / a kind of rational tautology."

Pharand, Michel W. "Works by and about Bernard Shaw in French, and on Shaw and French Culture and Literature: A Chronological Bibliography." *Cahiers Victoriens & Édouardiens* 45 (April 1997): 83–114. "Lists as many appreciations of Shaw by French critics as are available in existing biographical, bibliographical, and archival sources." Also included "are some of Shaw's own writings (articles, excerpts from prefaces, letters to the press, etc.) published in French newspapers or journals, and translated by Augustin and Henriette Hamon, Shaw's designated official translators" for French language issues of his work.

Pottie, Lisa M. "Shaw, George Bernard." In "Modern Drama Studies: An Annual Bibliography." *Modern Drama* 41:2 (Summer 1998): 230–31. Seventeen items from 1996 to 1997.

Review of *Unpublished Shaw* (*SHAW* 16), edited by Dan H. Laurence and Margot Peters. *Nineteenth-Century Literature* 51 (March 1997): 559.

Rose, Lloyd. "*Arms and the Man*: Shaw's Bonbons Mots" (review of the Olney Theatre production). *Washington Post* (11 March 1997), Section B, p. 1.

Russo, Francine. "Close Shavians" (review of the Theatre Row Theatre production of *The Philanderer*). *Village Voice* (23 December 1997), p. 107.

Salmon, Eric. "Bernard Shaw—Poet or Propagandist?" *Shavian* 8:3 (Winter 1997–98): 9–12. "Unless one is prepared to assert that his prose pamphleteering is really more important than his plays, then one's conclusion seems to me to be inescapable—namely, that Bernard Shaw's ultimate importance to us is as an artist, not as a propagandist, and his pro-socialist stance is no more important in the long run than, say, Richard Wagner's anti-semitic stance."

Schmidgall, Gary. "Arcibravo, GBS!" *Opera Quarterly* 14:4 (Summer 1998): 5-15. Not seen. Feature account of G.B.S. as an opera critic, as "Corno di Bassetto."

Scott, Kevin. " '*Corpus Christi*': Listen to Shaw." *New York Times* (11 October 1998), p. 4. Scott comments on the controversy over the Manhattan Theater Club's decision to produce Terrence McNally's *Corpus Christi* in a letter to the editor, including a substantial excerpt from Shaw's Preface to *Androcles*.

"Shaw, George Bernard," in "IASAIL Bibliographic Bulletin for 1996." *Irish University Review* 27:2 (Autumn/Winter 1997): 351–52. Fifteen items, a few of which have not appeared in this Checklist.

"Shaw, George Bernard (1856–1950). *1997–1998 MLA International Bibliography of Books and Articles on the Modern Languages and Literatures*. On-line. October 1998. Lists ten items, all of which appear in this Checklist.

Sheward, David. Review of the Irish Repertory Theatre production of *Major Barbara*. *Back Stage* 39:3 (16 January 1998): 26.

Shirley, Don. "Theater: Resurrecting *Methuselah*: Most Theater Troupes Would Be Daunted by George Bernard Shaw's Five-Part Play. Not Los Angeles Repertory" (review). *Los Angeles Times* (2 March 1997), Section CAL, p. 49.

Shloss, Carol. Review of *Shaw and Joyce: "The Last Word in Stolentelling"* by Martha Fodaski Black. *James Joyce Quarterly* 34:1–2 (Fall 1996/Winter 1997): 192–96.

Siegel, Ed. " 'Connection' Is Reconnected to Boston." *Boston Globe* (20 June 1997), Section D, p. 3. Siegel compliments the Public Radio (WBUR-FM 90.9) program on the American Repertory Theatre's production of Shaw's *Man and Superman*.

———. "The Pleasures of *Indecency*." *Boston Globe* (18 September 1998), Section D, p. 1. A review of the Huntington Theatre production of *Gross Indecency: The Three Trials of Oscar Wilde* by Moises Kaufman. The play includes a G.B.S. among its minor characters.

Simon, John. "David as Goliath" (review of the Irish Repertory Theatre production of *Major Barbara*). *New York* 30:47 (8 December 1997): 69–70.

———. "Hit or *Misalliance*" (review of the Roundabout Theatre production). *New York* 30:31 (18 August 1997): 52–53.

———. Review of the Roundabout Theatre production of *You Never Can Tell*. *New York* 31:26 (13 July 1998): 45.

Smith, Pam. Review of *Bernard Shaw's Book Reviews, Vol. 2: 1884–1950*, edited by Brian Tyson. *Victorian Periodicals Review* 30:4 (Winter 1997): 411–12.

Starks, Lisa S. "Educating Eliza: Fashioning the Model Woman in the 'Pygmalion Film.' " *Post Script* 15:3 (Winter/Spring 1997): 44–55. "In its screen incarnation, Pascal's film [*Pygmalion*] combined the Pygmalion myth as transformed by Shaw with the intertext of 'Cinderella' to set the pattern for a string of Pygmalion-themed Hollywood romances, namely the film of the musical stage play based on Shaw's *Pygmalion*, Lerner and Lowe's *My Fair Lady* (1964), as well as others ranging from Billy Wilder's *Sabrina* (1954) to Garry Marshall's *Pretty Woman* (1990) and the recent remake of *Sabrina* by Sydney Pollack. All of the Pygmalion heroines of these films excel in the required skills of the model woman: how to shop, dress, and accessorize. More importantly, Eliza, Vivian, and Sabrina all learn how to embody the signs of consumerism themselves, how to manipulate signs of gender and class identity, and how to be seen from the Other's gaze as they desire to be seen—as classy, white 'pretty women.' "

Stokes, John. Review of *Bernard Shaw and H. G. Wells*, edited by J. Percy Smith. *Modern Language Review* 92:4 (October 1997): 960–61.

———. Review of *Shaw's People* by Stanley Weintraub. *Modern Language Review* 93:1 (1998): 203–4.

Triplett, William. "Vocal Hero: Shaw's Talky 'Superman' " (review of the Washington Stage Guild production of *Man and Superman*). *Washington Post* (3 March 1998), Section B, p. 1.

Udko, Zach. Review of the Pasadena Shakespeare Company production of *Arms and the Man. Back Stage West* (25 June 1998), p. 15.

Vanderslice, John. Review of *Bernard Shaw: A Guide to Research* by Stanley Weintraub. *Bulletin of Bibliography* 54:3 (September 1997): 281.

Walshe, Eibhear. "Erratum." *Irish University Review* 27 (Autumn/Winter 1997): v. Corrections to Walshe's article, " 'Angels of Death': Wilde's *Salomé* and Shaw's *Saint Joan*" in *Irish University Review* 27 (Spring/Summer 1997): 24–32.

Waxman, Howard. "*My Astonishing Self*" (review of the Irish Repertory Theatre production). *Variety* (3–9 February 1997): 56–57.

Weiss, Rudolf. "Harley Granville Barker: The First English Chekhovian?" *New Theatre Quarterly* 14:53 (February 1998): 53–62. Weiss concludes that the answer to his question is yes. His discussion launches itself with reflection that recent re-evaluation of Barker's drama has raised his status from second-rate Shavian to playwright of much higher achievement, with greater affinities with Chekhov than with Shaw.

" 'Why I Became a Vegetarian: Readers Share Their Stories about Parakeets, Pork Chop Bones and George Bernard Shaw." *Vegetarian Times* 248 (1 April 1998): 82–84. One of the testimonials by Leo Corrigan of London, Ontario, credits his reading of G.B.S. and awareness that G.B.S. lived to be ninety-four with Corrigan's 1956 decision to become a vegetarian.

Wingate, Phillip J. "Mencken, Shaw and Ebonics." *Menckeniana* 141 (Spring 1997): 11–12. Mencken would reject Ebonics as adding neither color nor clarity to what is said. Shaw would reject Ebonics as a signifier of lower-class membership.

Winn, Steven. "Shaw's Wit on Intimate Display in Aurora's *Widowers' Houses*" (review of the Aurora Theatre Company production). *San Francisco Chronicle* (18 October 1997), Section E, p. 1.

————. "Waiting for 'Mrs. Warren' / ACT's [*sic*] Shaw Starts Slow but Pays Off in Final Act" (review of the Geary Theatre production). *San Francisco Chronicle* (20 June 1997), Section C, p. 13.

Wolf, Matt. "*Major Barbara*" (review of Piccadilly Theater production). *Variety* (10–16 August 1998), p. 48.

Independent Shavian 35:2–3 (1997). Journal of the Bernard Shaw Society. Includes "An Approach toward Shavian Autobiography" by Daniel Leary, "Another Nobel Prize Playwright" by Richard Nickson, "Letter from England, November 1997" by T. F. Evans, "A Shavian Effect on Opera: von Hoffmannsthal on Shaw," "Book Review" (of Shaw's *Complete Prefaces, Vol. 3: 1930–1950*, edited by Dan H. Laurence and Daniel J. Leary) by John A. Bertolini, "Book Review" (of *Shaw and Science Fiction* [*SHAW* 17], edited by Milton T. Wolf) by Ben P. Indick, "Book Review" (of "*The Instinct of an Artist*": *Shaw and the Theatre*, edited by Ann L. Ferguson) by Richard Nickson, "Again: Shaw and William Carlos Williams," "Emma Goldman Extols Shaw," "Shaw On-Screen," "Milwaukee Shaw Festival," "News about Our Members," "Society Activities," and "Our Cover." See also entry for Leary, Daniel, above.

Independent Shavian 36:1–2 (1998). Journal of the Bernard Shaw Society. Includes "From Shaw to Beckett: The Road to Absurdity" by Rhoda Nathan, "FYI: Shaw in the OED," "Shaw, A Playwright Before His Time" by Damien Jaques, "Milwaukee Shaw Festival," "Florida Shaw Series," "Shaw on War and Arbitrary Power," "Letter from England, May 1998" by T. F. Evans, "Shaw Collection for Sale," "*Presto Vivace*: Shaw the Music Critic," "Sam Spieg[e]l and Shaw," "Shaw Cornered: Beatrice Webb and GBS," "A Visit with Shaw in His Living-room" by Carlton Miles, "Bernard Shaw's Manuscript" by Mrs. T. P. O'Connor, "Book Review" (of *Bernard Shaw and Gabriel Pascal*, edited by Bernard F. Dukore) by Daniel Leary, "What I Really Wrote About Shaw: Epistle Advisory to Daniel Leary" by Sally Peters, "Obituaries," "Shaw on Video," "News about Our Members," "Society Activities," and "Our Cover." See also entry for Nathan, Rhoda, above.

Shavian 8:3 (Winter 1997–98). The Journal of the Shaw Society. Includes "Editorial," "Ellen Pollock," "Obituary," "To the Editor," "Shaw: Poet or Propagandist?" by Eric Salmon, "Shaw in Synge Street" by Frances McCarthy, "Our Theatres in the Nineteen-Nineties," "Thoughts on *Heartbreak House*," "Plays in Chicago" by Frances Glendenning, "A Real Science Fiction Writer?" (review of *Shaw and Science Fiction* [*SHAW* 17], edited by Milton T. Wolf) by Jo Grant, "Church and Stage" (review of *Church and Stage in Victorian England* by Richard Foulkes) by Alfred Jowett, "Literary Survey," "Scraps and Shavings," and "Notes of Meetings." See also entries for McCarthy, Frances; and Salmon, Eric, above.

Shavian 8:4 (Summer 1998). Journal of the Shaw Society. Includes "Editorial," "To the Editor," "Obituary," "Under the Southern Cross," " 'Not Bloody Likely!' " by Barry Morse, "A Tribute to Stanley Weintraub," "My Years with Shaw" by Peter Cheeseman, "Shaw in Germany" by Heinz Kosok, "Our Theatres in the Nineteen-Nineties," "A Theatrical and Proud of It" (review of *Light Fantastic: Adventures in Theatre* by John Lahr) by Leon Hugo, "Shaw on Film" (review of *Bernard Shaw on Cinema*, edited by Bernard F. Dukore) by Christopher James, "Looking Backward and Forward," "Shakespeare Today" (review of *English Shakespeare* by Peter Holland) by Frances Glendenning, "Literary Survey," "Scraps and Shavings," and "Notes of Meetings." See also entry for Kosok, Heinz, above.

IV. Dissertations

Fletcher, Jennifer Lind. "Interpromotional 'Shaw': The 1996 Shaw Festival Season Discourse and *The Simpleton of the Unexpected Isles.*" University of Guelph, 1997. *Dissertation Abstracts Online* 36–03A: 659. "This thesis is an investigation of the Shaw Festival promotional discourse focusing on the production of meaning in the 1996 season production of *The Simpleton of the Unexpected Isles.* Chapter one introduces the theoretical concepts of the interpromotionality, intertextuality, and cultural materialism; chapter two traces the historical construction of 'Shaw' at the Festival, and chapter three analyzes the ways in which the 1996 promotional material shaped and constructed meaning in that season's production of *The Simpleton of the Unexpected Isles.* The promotional material creates a discourse which naturalizes capitalist principles and class systems, and reaffirms their hegemonic hold on society. A reinforcement of dominant societal values occurs rather than an exploration of the social criticism of Shaw's work."

Granger, Judith. "The Widening Scope of the Shavian Heroine." City University of New York, 1997. *Dissertation Abstracts Online* 58–09A: 3536. "Nineteenth-century constrictions confining Victorian women to a domestic social role were replaced by the Edwardian 'New Woman's' expanded opportunities, presented by Shaw in the evolving roles of the heroines of his plays. Their progressive evolution exemplified the early twentieth-century expansion of Western woman's self-conception and social role." Treats especially *Candida, Man and Superman, Mrs Warren's Profession, Pygmalion, Major Barbara,* and *Saint Joan.*

Muir, Theresa. "Wagner in England: Four Writers before Shaw." City University of New York, 1997. *Dissertation Abstracts Online* 58–05A: 1498. Examines Wagner's reception in nineteenth-century England through a study of four writers. James W. Davison (1813–85), a *Times* music critic, was a Wagner adversary. Joseph Bennett (1831–1911), a *Daily Telegraph* music critic, defended Wagner, but not passionately. Francis Hueffer (1843–88) succeeded Davison at *The Times* and was the first English writer to promote Wagner to the educated public. William Ashton Ellis (1852?-1919) founded and edited *The Meister*, the London Wagner Society's journal, wrote an English-language biography of Wagner, and translated all his prose writings.

O'Hara, Michael Mullen. "Bernard Shaw and the Federal Theatre Project: Plays, Productions, and Politics." University of Maryland, College Park, 1997. *Dissertation Abstracts Online* 58-09A: 3367. From the abstract: "Examines the archival records of nine plays by Bernard Shaw as produced by the Federal Theatre Project (FTP). Using photographs, production reports, technical surveys, costume and set designs, administrative memoranda, newspaper accounts, reviews of the productions, audience surveys, official and personal correspondence of the FTP's personnel, and existing scholarship on the period, this historical study describes the several productions of Shaw's plays by the FTP and suggests their significance."

V. Recordings.

Caesar & Cleopatra. HarperAudio; abridged; #501234; $19.95. Cast includes Dame Judith Anderson, Laurence Hardy, Jack Gwillim, Harold Innocent. Available through BooksAloud, P. O. Box 614, Holmes, PA 19043-0614. Web: http://www.booksaloud.com/about.htm

Candida. Audio Book Contractors; unabridged; #511251; $20.95. Available through BooksAloud, P. O. Box 614, Holmes, PA 19043-0614. Web: http://www.booksaloud.com/about.htm

George Bernard Shaw (30 minutes), #GBSH, $29.95. Also *My Fair Lady* (1964 film starring Rex Harrison and Audrey Hepburn; 171 minutes), #MFLA, $29.95. Also *Pygmalion* (1938, 90 minutes), #PYGM, $29.95. Teacher's Video Company, P.O. Box ENJ-4455, Scottsdale, AZ 85261. Telephone: 1-800-262-8837. Fax: 1-602-860-8650.

Heartbreak House. Audio Book Contractors; abridged; #530893; $24.95. Available through BooksAloud, P. O. Box 614, Holmes, PA 19043-0614. Web: http://www.booksaloud.com/about.htm

Heartbreak House. HarperAudio; abridged; #501235; $27.95. Available through BooksAloud, P. O. Box 614, Holmes, PA 19043-0614. Web: http://www.booksaloud.com/about.htm

Hossick, Malcolm. *Bernard Shaw.* W. Long Branch, N.J.: Kultur Videos, 1998. Not seen. Uses photos and modern film of places associated with Shaw to feature the important events of his life and the historical background that shaped his writings. Order from Kultur, 195 Highway 36,

W. Long Branch, NJ 07764. Phone: 1-800-458-5887; (Canada: 1-908-229-2343). Price: $19.95, plus shipping.

John Bull's Other Island. HarperAudio; abridged; #501236; $35.92. Cast includes Patrick Duggan, Edward Petherbridge, P. G. Stephens. Available through BooksAloud, P. O. Box 614, Holmes, PA 19043-0614. Web: http://www.booksaloud.com/about.htm

Love Among the Artists. Audio Book Contractors; unabridged; #515147; $53.95. Available through BooksAloud, P. O. Box 614, Holmes, PA 19043-0614. Web: http://www.booksaloud.com/about.htm

Major Barbara. Audio Book Contractors; unabridged; #515149; $24.95. Available through BooksAloud, P. O. Box 614, Holmes, PA 19043-0614. Web: http://www.booksaloud.com/about.htm

Man and Superman. B D D Audio Publishing; abridged; #532303; $22.00. Available through BooksAloud, P. O. Box 614, Holmes, PA 19043-0614. Web: http://www.booksaloud.com/about.htm

Man and Superman (with readers Ralph Fiennes, Juliet Stevenson and full cast; "a BBC production"), 4 cassettes, #D4C923, $22.00. Audio Editions: Books on Cassette, P. O. Box 6930, Auburn, CA 95604. Telephone: 1-800-231-4261. Fax: 1-800-882-1840. Web: www.audioeditions.com

Misalliance. Audio Book Contractors; unabridged; #515152; $24.95. Available through BooksAloud, P. O. Box 614, Holmes, PA 19043-0614. Web: http://www.booksaloud.com/about.htm

Mrs Warren's Profession. Audio Book Contractors; unabridged; #515154; $20.95. Available through BooksAloud, P. O. Box 614, Holmes, PA 19043-0614. Web: http://www.booksaloud.com/about.htm

My Fair Lady (1964 film starring Rex Harrison and Audrey Hepburn; 3 hours, 10 minutes; newly remastered in THX), #JOFOX000974 or JQFOX000975 (letterbox), $14.77. Critics' Choice Video, P. O. Box 749, Itasca, IL 60143-0749. Telephone: 1-800-367-7765. Web: www.ccvideo.com. See also *George Bernard Shaw*, above.

My Fair Lady & Guys and Dolls (the stories behind the original Broadway shows as told by the original casts, with Rex Harrison, Julie Andrews, Vivian Blaine, Sam Levene, many others), #CMR-1122, cassette, $4.98. Radio Yesteryear, Box C, Sandy Hook, CT 06482-0847. Telephone: 1-800-243-0987. Fax: 1-203-797-0819. Web: radio@yesteryear.com

Noel Coward Reading His Poems. HarperAudio; abridged; #500303; $12.95. A selection of Coward's verses, plus Coward & Leighton performing Shaw's Interlude from *The Apple Cart.* Available through BooksAloud, P. O. Box 614, Holmes, PA 19043-0614. Web: http://www.booksaloud.com/about.htm

Pygmalion. Audio Book Contractors; unabridged; #500214; $20.95. Available through BooksAloud, P. O. Box 614, Holmes, PA 19043-0614. Web: http://www.booksaloud.com/about.htm

Pygmalion. HarperCollins; abridged; #202818; $18.00. Cast includes Michael Redgrave and daughter Lynn Redgrave. Available from Books Aloud, P. O. Box 614, Holmes, PA 19043-0614. Web: http://www.booksaloud.com/about.htm

Pygmalion. HarperVideo; abridged; #501237; $27.95. Cast includes Michael Horden, Donald Pleasence, Felicity Kendal, Pauline Jameson, Edward Hardwicke. Available through BooksAloud, P. O. Box 614, Holmes, PA 19043-0614. Web: http://www.booksaloud.com/about.htm

Pygmalion. Radiola Company; abridged; #504326l; $4.98. Available through BooksAloud, P. O. Box 614, Holmes, PA 19043-0614. Web: http://www.booksaloud.com/about.htm

Pygmalion. See *George Bernard Shaw,* above.

An Unsocial Socialist. Audio Book Contractors; unabridged; #511279; $41.95. Available through BooksAloud, P. O. Box 614, Holmes, PA 19043-0614. Web: http://www.booksaloud.com/about.htm

VI. Other Media

"**Shaw (G. B.)** Shaw's Clavichord." A fine clavichord made by Arnold Dolmetsch signed by the maker on the soundboard: Arnold Dolmetsch, Haslemere, Nov. 1921, no. 31. The lot includes a letter by Shaw (18 July 1949) giving details of the manner in which he acquired the instrument for £40, written the day the instrument was sold for 110 guineas. A photo illustration is included. *Sotheby's* LN7755 (11 December 1997), item 369. £4,000–6,000.

CONTRIBUTORS

Sidney P. Albert, Professor Emeritus of Philosophy at California State University, Los Angeles, and former member of the *SHAW* editorial board, is the source of the Shaw Collection at Brown University that bears his name. His many articles on Shaw are especially crucial for the study of *Major Barbara.*

John Allett is Associate Professor in the Social Sciences Division at York University, Ontario, Canada, and author of *The New Liberalism: The Political Economy of J. A. Hobson.* He currently teaches a course on Shaw and H. G. Wells.

Charles A. Berst, Professor Emeritus (on recall) at UCLA and member of the *SHAW* editorial board, is author of *Bernard Shaw and the Art of Drama* and editor of *SHAW* 1: *Shaw and Religion.* His newest book is *Pygmalion: Shaw's Spin on Myth and Cinderella.*

Wendi Chen is a doctoral candidate at the University of Minnesota who is completing her dissertation on Shaw's reception in China. Her essay entitled "G. B. Shaw's Plays on the Chinese Stage:—The 1991 Production of *Major Barbara*" appeared in *Comparative Literature Studies* 35:1 (1998).

Fred D. Crawford, General Editor of *SHAW,* is Associate Professor of English at Central Michigan University and author of several books and articles on modern British literature, most recently *Richard Aldington and Lawrence of Arabia: A Cautionary Tale.* He is completing a biography of the American news broadcaster Lowell Thomas and an edition of Thomas's letters.

David Gunby is Professor of English at the University of Canterbury, Christchurch, New Zealand. A specialist in Renaissance drama and joint editor of *The Works of John Webster,* he became interested in the circumstances surrounding the first performance of *O'Flaherty, V.C.* when writing *Sweeping the Skies*, a history of 40 Squadron, Royal Flying Corps.

Gale K. Larson is Professor of English at California State University, Northridge, where he has taught and served in various administrative positions for the past thirty years. He has published on *Caesar and Cleopatra*, has edited that play for Bobbs-Merrill, and has reviewed works on Shaw for various journals.

Michael M. O'Hara, Assistant Professor of Theatre at Ball State University, is currently working on a book about Shaw's relationship with the Federal Theatre Project and has research interests in American, Irish, and British theater of the 1930s.

Sally Peters, Vice President of the Bernard Shaw Society and member of the *SHAW* editorial board, is Visiting Professor of English at Connecticut College and Visiting Lecturer in the Graduate Liberal Studies Program, Wesleyan University. She has published extensively on Shaw, modern drama, and dance, and her biography *Bernard Shaw: The Ascent of the Superman* was a *Choice* Outstanding Academic Book for 1996. She is completing a personal and cultural history of ballroom dance.

John R. Pfeiffer is Professor of English at Central Michigan University and Bibliographer of *SHAW*. His most recent articles are on Richard Burton, John Christopher, Ray Bradbury, Etheridge Knight, and Octavia Butler.

Rodelle Weintraub has edited *Fabian Feminist, Shaw Abroad* (*SHAW* 5), and the Garland *Captain Brassbound's Conversion*. She has also co-edited, with Stanley Weintraub, two Bantam volumes of Shaw's plays: *Arms and the Man & John Bull's Other Island* and *Heartbreak House & Misalliance*.

Stanley Weintraub, Evan Pugh Professor of Arts and Humanities at Penn State, edited the *Shaw Review* and *SHAW* from 1956 through 1990. He has written or edited more than forty books on Shaw and his times, most recently *Shaw's People: Victoria to Churchill* and *Albert: Uncrowned King*.